The Ecclesiology of
St. Basil the Great

The Ecclesiology of
ST. BASIL THE GREAT

A Trinitarian Approach to the Life of the Church

OLGA A. DRUZHININA

Foreword by David Rainey

◆PICKWICK *Publications* · Eugene, Oregon

THE ECCLESIOLOGY OF ST. BASIL THE GREAT
A Trinitarian Approach to the Life of the Church

Copyright © 2016 Olga A. Druzhinina. All rights reserved. Except for brief quotations in critical publications or reviews, no part of this book may be reproduced in any manner without prior written permission from the publisher. Write: Permissions, Wipf and Stock Publishers, 199 W. 8th Ave., Suite 3, Eugene, OR 97401.

Pickwick Publications
An Imprint of Wipf and Stock Publishers
199 W. 8th Ave., Suite 3
Eugene, OR 97401

www.wipfandstock.com

PAPERBACK ISBN 13: 978-1-4982-3566-2
HARDCOVER ISBN 13: 978-1-4982-3568-6
EBOOK ISBN 13: 978-1-4982-3787-1

Cataloguing-in-Publication data:

Names: Druzhinina, Olga.

Title: The ecclesiology of St. Basil the Great : a trinitarian approach to the life of the church / Olga A. Druzhinina.

Description: Eugene, OR: Pickwick Publications, 2016 | Includes bibliographical references and index.

Identifiers: ISBN 978-1-4982-3566-2 (paperback) | ISBN 978-1-4982-3568-6 (hardcover) | ISBN 978-1-4982-3787-1 (ebook)

Subjects: LCSH: Basil, Saint, Bishop of Caesarea, approximately 329–379. | Church—History of doctrines—Early church, ca. 30–600. | Trinity | Title

Classification: BR1720.B3 D89 2016 (print) | BR1720.B3 (ebook)

Manufactured in the U.S.A.   06/22/16

To the most important people in my life:
to my husband, Alexey, whose love and support made it happen,
to my daughters, Elena and Tatiana,
and to my granddaughters, Sofia and Veronica.

Contents

Foreword by David Rainey | ix
Preface | xi
Abbreviations | xiii

CHAPTER 1
Introduction | 1

CHAPTER 2
Trinitarian God and the Human Community | 16

CHAPTER 3
Trinitarian Communion, φιλανθρωπία, and the Concept of the Church | 43

CHAPTER 4
Persons of the Trinity and the Metaphors of the Church | 59

CHAPTER 5
Inward Life of the Church: Education and Transformation through Praises and Prayers to God the Trinity | 82

CHAPTER 6
Unity of the Church and Trinitarian Confession | 121

CHAPTER 7
Trinitarian Philanthropy as a Basis for Ministry of the Church | 147

CHAPTER 8
Monastic Communities as Practical Realization of an Ideal Community | 166

Final Conclusions | 176

Bibliography | 181
Index of Names | 195
Index of Citations to Basil's Works | 199

Foreword

THERE ARE TWO THEOLOGICAL topics that have created interest in recent years. One is the study of the Cappadocian Fathers and the other is ecclesiology. This interest has led Olga Druzhinina to combine both subjects for the first time into a thorough, fully researched theological engagement with St. Basil of Caesarea and ecclesiology. Olga Druzhinina masterfully creates a trinitarian theology for ecclesiology and demonstrates how each Person of the Trinity plays a part in shaping the authentic church.

It appears to me that there is a certain excitement in reading through this research. A reader will be asked to interact with St. Basil's eschatology as well as his mystical reality of the bond with the heavenly and earthly communities. Also, St. Basil developed a metaphorical theology to convey the various ways that we can understand the church's ministry and this is articulated with clarity in Olga's presentation. Importantly, this is not an "otherworldly" concept of the church; instead, this research demonstrates the importance of the church's engagement with the world. This includes the vital link between the church and the monastic communities and their engagement with the world.

Before long, as one digests this book, there will be the discovery of work on Christian leadership, church liturgy and worship, and the emphasis on penitential discipline. All of this combines to identify the unity of the church, which, in many cases today, is not the reality of the church. This book is a welcomed addition to the study of St. Basil of Caesarea, the Trinity, and Ecclesiology. Pastors and priests, as well as theological academics from various disciplines and traditions, will benefit from reading Olga Druzhinina's contribution.

David Rainey
Senior Research Fellow
Nazarene Theological College, Didsbury, UK

Preface

St. Basil the Great left an invaluable legacy for many generations of Christians who lived after him both in the East and in the West. He was a gifted preacher and bishop, a reformer of Eastern monasticism, and a defender of orthodox trinitarian theology. However, what has drawn my attention were his ideas about the church and the relation of his ecclesiology to his understanding of the Triune God. This work began as a doctoral thesis at the University of Manchester and has been slightly revised for publication as a book.

This manuscript would not have seen the light of the day if not for the help of others. I am deeply grateful to my supervisor Dr. David Rainey for his enthusiasm from the moment my proposal was submitted to the university. He assisted and encouraged me during the research and writing of the thesis. His insightfulness and clarity of thought helped me clarify my own ideas. I am thankful for his advice, direction, hospitality, and very thoughtful conversations.

My thanks go as well to a number of my friends from the community at Nazarene Theological College, which always felt like second home. Both faculty and staff have been more than supportive throughout these years: Peter Rea, Don Maciver, Joseph Wood, and Rachel Varughese. They answered many questions, and sent numerous emails as they walked me through the different stages of this journey.

Special thanks must be given to my examiner, Dr. Noble, whose recommendations helped to improve the text of my thesis for publication.

I am also thankful to many people who have helped me with the proofreading: Hazel Maciver, Ruth Copeland-Holtz, Geordan Hammond, Robert Rea, and Paul Green.

The hospitality of my friends meant a lot to me when I had to spend many days far away from my family. My sincere thanks to Don and Hazel

Maciver, Debi and Paul Green, David and Alison Rainey, Kent and Fran Brower, and many others who took care of me during these stressful times and visits.

My deepest appreciation goes to my family and especially to my husband, Alexey, who is always patient and supportive. He and our daughters, Elena and Tatiana, became for me a source of inspiration and joy during the time of my studies.

Finally, I am thankful to God for his guidance. Δόζα τῷ Θεῷ.

Abbreviations

ANF[1]	*Ante-Nicene Fathers*, series 1
CBap	Basil, *De baptismo* (CBap = Concerning Baptism)
CE	Basil, *Contra Eunomium*
De Jud.	Basil, *De judicio Dei*
EHB	Basil, *Homilia exhortatoria ad sanctum baptisma* (EHB = Exhortation to Holy Baptism)
First Clement	*The Letter of the Romans to Corinthians Commonly Known as First Clement*
HE	*Historia ecclesiastica*
Hex.	Basil, *Hexaemeron*
Hom.	Basil, *Homilia(e)*
HS	Basil, *De spiritu sancto* (HS = On the Holy Spirit)
InMJ	Basil, *In martyrem Julittam*
InSQM	Basil, *In sanctos quadraginta martyres*
Letter	Basil, *Epistula(e)*
Life of Macrina	Gregory of Nissa, *De vita sanctae Macrinae* (Life of Saint Macrina)
LR	Basil, *Regulae fusius tractatae* (LR = Long Rules)
NPNF2	*Nicene and Post-Nicene Fathers*, series 2
Oration XLIII	Gregory of Nazianzus, *Oratio XLIII*
PG	Migne, Jacques-Paul, ed., *Patrologia Cursus Completus: Series Graeca*. Paris: J.-P. Migne, 1857.
Prolegomena	Jackson, Blomfield. *Prolegomena: Sketch of the Life and Works of Saint Basil*
Ps.	Basil, *Homiliae in psalmos*

Second Clement	*An Ancient Christian Sermon Commonly Known as Second Clement*
SR	Basil, *Regulae brevious tractatae* (SH = Short Rules)
SPCN	Society for Promoting Christian Knowledge

SHORT TITLES OF THE TRANSLATIONS FREQUENTLY USED

Anderson
St. Basil the Great on the Holy Spirit. Translated by Blomfield Jackson and revised by David Anderson. Crestwood, NY: St. Vladimir's Seminary Press, 1980.

Clarke
The Ascetic Works of Saint Basil. Translated by William Kemp Lowther Clarke. Translations of Christian Literature I. Greek Texts. London: SPCN, 1925.

DelCogliano
St. Basil the Great: On Christian Doctrine and Practice. Translated by Mark DelCogliano. Popular Patristics 47. Crestwood, NY: St. Vladimir's Seminary Press, 2012.

Schroeder
St. Basil the Great: On Social Justice. Translated by C. Paul Schroeder. Popular Patristics 38. Crestwood, NY: St. Vladimir's Seminary Press, 2009.

Wagner
Saint Basil, Ascetical Works. Translated by M. Monica Wagner. Fathers of the Church 9. New York: Catholic University of America Press, 1950.

Way
Saint Basil, Exegetic Homilies. Translated by Agnes Clare Way. Fathers of the Church 46. 2nd ed. New York: Catholic University of America Press, 1981.

CHAPTER 1

Introduction

ST. BASIL THE GREAT, bishop of Caesarea, is recognized by many Christian writers as an outstanding organizer and administrator, although he never wrote any specific document on the church.[1] His writings do not contain discussions on the nature and the structure of the Christian church, but rather show to varying degrees his assumptions about the subject. Even his two sets of rules for monastic communities present only partly his understanding of life in the Christian community. Therefore, to write about the ecclesiology of St. Basil is to attempt to draw out from his multitudinous writings something that he only discusses quite allusively or in connection with other matters. This is probably one of the reasons his ecclesiology has not received much scholarly attention to date. Although there are important scholarly studies of St. Basil's trinitarian thought, and researches concerning his ideas of monasticism, as well as excellent biographical studies, there is a significant lack of secondary source material on St. Basil's view of the church. The fact that only one book concerning St. Basil's ecclesiology was published in English[2] shows that a fuller and more nuanced research in this area of his thought is necessary.

The objective of this book is to produce an account of the teaching of St. Basil on the church, and to consider the relation of his ecclesiology to his

1. As Vischer states, "Basilius ist nicht durch seine Lehre von der Kirche bedeutsam, sondern durch sein tatsächliches kirchliches Handeln" (Basil is famous not for his church teaching but for his church actions). Vischer, *Basilius der Große*, 52; translation is mine.

2. Fedwick, *The Church and the Charisma of Leadership in Basil of Caesarea*.

understanding of the Triune God, including divine plans for humanity and God's actions in the history of the world.

St. Basil's written material consists of many letters addressed to different types of people, homilies composed to deal with many situations, and treatises that introduce us to his point of view on several important spiritual issues. Many of these works are devoted to exploring trinitarian doctrine and the role of the Holy Spirit in particular. Consequently, traces of thoughts relevant to his understanding of the church can be found among his works initially written in connection with trinitarian discussions. Collecting the ideas from St. Basil's separate sayings about the church, the author of this book attempts to accomplish two things: (1) to show that St. Basil's approach to the church is indeed trinitarian, and (2) to explore how he perceives the relation of this special community to the Trinity.

ST. BASIL'S THEOLOGY IN RECENT SCHOLARSHIP

As mentioned above, in recent scholarship rather insufficient attention has been paid to the ecclesiology of St. Basil the Great. Published in 1979, the book *The Church and the Charisma of Leadership in Basil of Caesarea* by Fedwick remains the only book in English, which discusses his ecclesiology. Using mostly a pneumatological approach, the author produces an account of St. Basil's understanding of leadership in the church, which is empowered and guided by the Holy Spirit. However, the relationship of the other two Persons of the Trinity to the life of the church were not treated in detail.

Two more books concerning St. Basil's understanding of the church were published in German. The first book, written by Lukas Vischer, *Basilius der Große: Untersuchungen zu einem Kirchenvater des vierten Jahrhunderts*, briefly discusses different themes. It includes his views on the unity of the church (chapters 3–5), which the author presents as constituted by the agreements of the bishops united by the confession of the same faith, the relation of the church and the state (chapter 7), and an overview of St. Basil's social work (chapter 8). The second and more recent book, *Spuren der Alten Liebe: Studien zum Kirchenbergriff des Basilius von Caesarea*, which was published in 1991 by Klaus Koschorke, introduces St. Basil's vision of the church as the body of Christ, which is in the process of declining from its previous state of "old love" and peace. Koschorke's study also covers various aspects of St. Basil's ecclesiology: the life of his monastic communities, the sacraments, the relation of the church and the state, the unity of the church, St. Basil's attitude toward the church of Rome, and the role of councils.

What has not yet received sufficient investigation and critique in research³ is the role of God the Trinity in the life of the church, which occupies a considerable place in St. Basil's thought. The authors of these books provide a great deal of insight into St. Basil's understanding of the present situation in the church, but they do not discuss the eschatological perspective, which reflects the involvement of all Persons of God in creation of this special community and in the maintaining of its life while leading all believers to the ultimate goal. Scholars also do not take into account St. Basil's view of the church as a two-dimensional mystical reality that exists in heaven and on earth at the same time with the strong bond between these two parts.

Although there are outstanding studies that discuss St. Basil's trinitarian ideas, they do not consider his ecclesiology.⁴ For example, in 1996, Volker Henning Drecoll published in German a chronological study, which presents the development of St. Basil's trinitarian theology from his earliest through his latest writings.⁵ In 2007, Stephen M. Hildebrand produced a book that became the first English monograph to describe St. Basil's trinitarian thought.⁶ However, no one has yet addressed St. Basil's ecclesiology in relation to his trinitarian theology.

DEFINING THE ESSENTIAL ASPECTS OF ST. BASIL'S ECCLESIOLOGY

Ecclesiology is the area of Christian theology, which deals with the doctrine of the church. Usually the following aspects are discussed: origins of the church, its biblical images, its relationship with God, its destiny, its role in salvation, its membership, its leadership and governance, hierarchy, its

---

3. There were also a couple of relatively small articles devoted to the ecclesiology of St. Basil, which discussed similar ideas. The recent one was published in 1969 by B. Krivocheine. It is available in Russian: Василий Кривошеин, «Экклезиология Святого Василия Великого.» The previous article was published in 1922: Batiffol, "L'ecclésiologie de s. Basile."

4. The development of scholarship on St. Basil's trinitarian thought can be found in Hildebrand who asserts that scholars approached St. Basil's teaching on the Trinity from a "predominantly philological and philosophical point of view." See Hildebrand, *The Trinitarian Theology of Basil of Caesarea*, 198–206.

5. Drecoll, *Die Entwicklung der Trinitätslehre des Basilius von Cäsarea*.

6. Hildebrand, *The Trinitarian Theology of Basil of Caesarea*. Among the recent scholarship on the fourth century there can also be mentioned books written by Behr and Ayres who devoted several chapters to the discussion of Basil's teaching on the Trinity. See Behr, *The Nicene Faith*, 263–324; and Ayres, *Nicaea and its Legacy*, 187–243.

structure, authority,[7] its sacraments and discipline, its ministry, and its role in the world.[8]

Although St. Basil does not provide any systematic explanation or definition of the church, these elements of ecclesiology are present in his writings to some extent.[9] Usually, the most important themes from his point of view are discussed explicitly and on several occasions.[10] Therefore, these texts provide a resource for acquiring a proper understanding of St. Basil's doctrine of the church. Accordingly, a two-fold methodology will be used. On the one hand, we will follow an outline, which reflects the main themes of St. Basil's ecclesiology; on the other hand, we will investigate his texts in order to find a relation between his ideas of the church and his ideas of the Triune God.

Owing to St. Basil's way of thinking, many aspects of his ecclesiology are interrelated and they should be discussed together. This suggests that the best way to treat the material is thematically rather than to discuss different elements on separate basis. In St. Basil's writings, there are at least three significant themes that unite all elements. The first theme, the relationship between the church and the Triune God, as one of the most important aspects of St. Basil's ecclesiology, will create a framework for our research. The second theme, which influences all other aspects and provides the perspective, is the ultimate destiny of the church and the eschatological future of humanity. The third one is a theme of love: love of God to humanity, love of humans toward the Triune God and relationships of love among believers. All these three themes form the basis for St. Basil's teaching and practice.

There are several other aspects of ecclesiology that take a prominent place in his writings and should be considered in this book. The biblical images of the church are an obvious part of St. Basil's teaching. The body of Christ, the people of God, the house of God, the heavenly kingdom are mentioned a number of times in his letters, homilies and treatises. These and many other images serve as an additional source of information and reveal essential characteristics of the church.

---

7. Although St. Basil did not say much about authority, he does mention in the fifth chapter of this book that for him both "written and unwritten" traditions had equal authority.

8. See Kärkkäinen, "Ecclesiology," 251–62. See more details in McGrath, *Christian Theology*, 375. See also a list of aspects of ecclesiology in Haight, *Christian Community in History*, viii.

9. We have to mention that St. Basil does not discuss the structure of the church.

10. For example, baptism is one of the themes, which St. Basil discussed in several of his works. Also we can notice that throughout his writing St. Basil extensively uses biblical images of the church.

Sacraments or "mysteries" of the church occupy a significant place in St. Basil's conceptual framework. In his thinking, this is related to the role of the church in salvation and involves the idea that salvation cannot be found outside the church and without her mysteries. Although St. Basil does not discuss the membership of the church explicitly, he provides an answer to a question, "Who constitutes the church?" This aspect of ecclesiology is treated by St. Basil in connection with many other themes: a proper confession of faith, the legitimacy of the mystery of baptism, and an involvement of already departed believers in the life of the church on earth.

A discussion of the unity of the church is another leading theme in St. Basil's writings, which runs through many of his letters and other works. It encompasses several aspects of ecclesiology: involvement of God in the life of the church, governance of the church, the role of bishops and leaders, hierarchy and ministry of bishops as "eyes of the body," discipline and obedience of bishops to the conciliar decisions.

Finally, we can observe that St. Basil was profoundly concerned with both the trinitarian teaching of the church and the ministry of the church. In this sense, his ecclesiology was always informed by and expressed through his practice. Therefore, an account of the ministry of the church and her role in the world should be included in this book. This implies that the life of his monastic communities as a practical application of his teaching should be considered as well.

We have to mention that so called "marks" of the church (One, Holy, Catholic, and Apostolic), which were officially voiced at the Council in Constantinople soon after St. Basil's death, are not discussed in this book separately. However, the traces of thoughts that are connected with these "marks" are present in St. Basil's understanding of the church and can be found throughout this book.[11]

---

11. The oneness of the church is discussed in chapters 4 and 6 of this book and it is explicitly shown through St. Basil's use of metaphors. The catholicity of the church is mentioned in chapter 6 where the unity of the church is discussed. The apostolicity is linked (1) with the teaching of the church that in St. Basil's thinking was received from the apostles and the Fathers and (2) with apostolic succession. Although St. Basil does not use this term, he believes that the bishops have "the thrones of the Apostles" (chapter 6, n55). The holiness of the church in St. Basil's understanding is connected with the presence of the Holy Spirit and it is also discussed through the metaphors related to Christ (for example, "the perfect dove of Christ").

CHAPTERS OUTLINE

The book consists of eight chapters including the introduction and focuses on the analysis of a trinitarian approach to the life of the church. It covers a wide range of themes, which uncover St. Basil's teaching on the church and its interrelation with his trinitarian ideas. Following the introduction, the second chapter reveals the connections in St. Basil's thought between God's plan at the creation of the world, the existence of the church and the destiny of humanity, which is Christlikeness and life eternal in the heavenly *ekklesia* with the Father, Son and Holy Spirit. The chapter also focuses on God's plan for humans, which includes the original idea of corporate living and the divine activity of all Persons of the Trinity in the establishing of the church as a special community after the Fall.

Consequently, the third chapter elaborates on a more detailed description of St. Basil's understanding of the church as the unique two-dimensional reality, where the Triune God assembles his children because of his love of humanity, providing for them the proper environment for their growth and development. It argues that God's philanthropy serves as a means and as an example for Christians, which they are supposed to follow, serving their fellow believers from this special community. Supporting each other, they are encouraged to grow together in love through changes and transformation toward Christlikeness and life in the eschatological community, which awaits them.

The challenge for the research is to formulate St. Basil's ecclesiology in a manner that he himself would most likely have done using his large written corpus. By considering St. Basil's own way of describing the role and characteristics of the church, in chapter 4, this book analyses his use of metaphors in order to gain a better understanding of his point of view. First, this approach does justice to St. Basil's mystical thinking. Secondly, it provides us with the material, which helps to see, through his imagery and illustrations, the overall picture of the relations of the trinitarian Persons and the church.

Chapter 5 continues to disclose St. Basil's concept of the church and introduces us to the inner life of the Christian community presenting his ideas about liturgy, mysteries and disciplinary methods. It attempts to show the underlying concern for proper trinitarian teaching and the orthodox theology, which is recited during liturgy, and used in the mysteries of the church.

Chapter 6 of this book demonstrates that trinitarian confession becomes for St. Basil the criterion for deciding who belongs to fellowship of the church and who can be considered lost because of their rejection of this "saving confession." This chapter highlights St. Basil's idea that proper trinitarian theology should become the foundation for the unity of the church. It proceeds with the analysis of the role of Christian leaders and councils, which should serve as a means of keeping unity and peace inside the local congregations as well as between them.

Another aspect of Basil's ecclesiology, namely, the church's ministry, is also examined on the basis of trinitarian philanthropy and God's plans for humanity. Special attention in chapter 7 is paid to the criteria of human worthiness in the eyes of God the Trinity in spite of social differences and ranks in society. This chapter investigates St. Basil's perception of Creator's dealing with this world, and provides answers to the questions why and how love of the Triune God should be visible through acts of Christians in the church.

Chapter 8 draws the book to its conclusion by discussing the practical realization of St. Basil's understanding of the church in the life of his monastic communities. It shows to what extent St. Basil was able to apply his principles and ideas based on "the law of love," which reflects trinitarian communion and philanthropy.

HISTORICAL SETTING AND FORMATIVE EVENTS IN ST. BASIL'S LIFE

Theological views of St. Basil and his vision of the church in particular were influenced and conditioned by the significant events and developments of his time. Therefore, it will be helpful to preface the analysis of his writings[12] with a very short biographical sketch in order to introduce the immediate context in which he developed his understanding of the church.[13]

St. Basil of Caesarea was born around 330 AD in a rich family of landowners whose holdings were scattered over Cappadocia, Armenia Minor, two provinces of Pontus, and perhaps Galatia.[14] He was the first son and

---

12. The conclusions in this book are based largely on the analysis of primary texts. However, whenever it is possible the opinions of other scholars are taken into consideration.

13. Obviously, a primary source of information is the writings of St. Basil and his friends. The very detailed biography of St. Basil can be found in Rousseau, *Basil of Caesarea*. See also a more recent publication by Radde-Gallwitz, *Basil of Caesarea: A Guide to His Life and Doctrine*. Several short articles provide the background information, which can be very helpful. Young, "The Cappadocians," 135–72; Louth, "The Cappadocians," 289–95. See Георгий Флоровский, Восточные Отцы IV века, 68–111 (Florovsky, *Eastern Fathers of IV century*).

14. See Kopecek, "The Social Class of the Cappadocian Fathers," 453–66.

the second surviving child in the family with ten children. As the oldest son, he had the privilege of spending more time with his father, also named Basil, a famous rhetorician at Neo-Caesarea in Pontus, who died prematurely around 345.[15] From his childhood, he was introduced to the church of Christian martyrs because his ancestors were among those heroes of faith who survived the great persecutions. In this Christian family among his relatives and friends, St. Basil first experienced the church, which was "founded on the blood of Christ and that of many of his followers."[16] His ideal of the church and his ideas of Christian lifestyle were formed or influenced by his family members: by his grandmother St. Macrina the elder,[17] by his faithful Christian father, by his mother Emmelia,[18] the daughter of a martyr, by his older sister St. Macrina the younger,[19] and her model of the ascetic life, and even by his younger brothers, two of whom became bishops (St. Gregory of Nyssa and St. Peter of Sebaste).

We should mention that his first experience of the church outside the family had not met his high expectations. When he discovered divisions among the Christians, it grieved him deeply. He wrote in his first preface to the *Moralia* that he had seen "a great and exceeding distort on the part of many men both in their relations with one another and their views about the divine Scripture."[20] This disappointment most likely played a crucial role in his life and later on made him pursue his ideal of the church. Until the end of his life, he worked to foster unity in the church.[21]

St. Basil received a good classical Greek education. He went to study in Caesarea, continued his studies in Constantinople, and finished his education in Athens. Although this education consisted of Greek literature, philosophy, and oratory, it provided a foundation for the later theological discussions. Therefore, this education helped St. Basil to develop his oratory skills and to take part in discussions concerning the Trinity. It should not go

---

15. See Fedwick's chronology of Basil's life in his *The Church and the Charisma of Leadership in Basil of Caesarea*, 134.

16. Fedwick, *The Church*, 4.

17. *Letter* 204.6. As St. Basil states in this epistle, "What clearer evidence can there be of my faith, than that I was brought up by my grandmother, blessed woman, who came from you? I mean the celebrated Macrina who taught me the words of the blessed Gregory." See also *Letter* 223.2. All quotations from *Letters, De Spiritu Sancto,* and *Hexaemeron* are taken from *NPNF2* (trans. Jackson), except as quoted from different sources.

18. See St. Basil's opinion of his mother in *Letters* 30.

19. *Life of Macrina*, PG 46:966CD. See translation by Clarke, *The Life of St. Macrina*, 28.

20. *De Jud.* (Clarke, 77). PG 31:653B.

21.. See similar notion in Behr, *The Nicene Faith*, 106.

unnoticed that he was born only five years after the first Council in Nicaea where Christians were able to formulate and voice their theological statements. St. Basil belonged to a generation that was "at hand with the spiritual capacity for a further development of theology, a development which was needed if a clear and self-consistent solution was to be found to the problem of the Trinity, after all the confusion of the past."[22] In this sense, his education played its role in his preparation for the ministry, which influenced the life of the church in the fourth century.[23]

St. Basil returned home in 355 and began his career as a rhetorician. He taught for a year, but a sudden "spiritual awakening"[24] occurred in his life[25] after which St. Basil gave up his position as rhetor in Caesarea and totally committed himself to Christian asceticism. This "spiritual awakening" made him search for a spiritual guide in his life. With this aim in mind, St. Basil journeyed through Egypt, Palestine, Syria, and Mesopotamia visiting the famous ascetics. Their distinct way of Christian life and Christian practices influenced St. Basil's understanding of Christianity and the role of the church in the lives of believers.[26] Early Christian monasticism was a popular movement, which allowed monks to assume a special spiritual role, particularly in the East. Some monastic groups set up their own organizations parallel to the existing ecclesial community. This inevitably raised questions of Christian institutional structure and church unity itself.[27] According to Meyendorff, "No one better than St. Basil of Caesarea understood the challenge of monasticism to the Church as a whole and attempted

---

22. Lietzmann, *The Era of the Church Fathers*, 21.

23. During his studies, he met his friend St. Gregory of Nazianzus whose friendship also exercised a significant influence on the life of St. Basil.

Very often St. Basil's theology was studied by scholars as a part of Cappadocian thought. In order to emphasize St. Basil's originality in this book the references to other Cappadocians are reduced to a minimum because their particular understanding of the church has not yet been thoroughly studied. Therefore, it seems too early to draw a comparison between these famous theologians.

24. St. Basil wrote about this experience in his *Letter* 223.2. More details in Quasten, *Patrology*, 204.

25. Gregory of Nyssa insists that their sister Macrina "took him in hand" and converted him to the ascetic life. See *Life of Macrina*. PG 46:966BC. Clarke also suggests that the tragic death of Basil's brother Naucratius is connected to this conversion. See Clarke, *St. Basil the Great: A Study in Monasticism*, 23.

26. As St. Basil shared this experience, he stated, "whomsoever I found walking in the rule of godliness delivered, those I set down as fathers, and made them my soul's guides in my journey to God." See *Letter* 204 6.

27. See Meyendorff, *The Byzantine Legacy*, 197–98.

to understand the phenomenon in the framework of Christian theology and ecclesiology."[28]

After his monastic journey, St. Basil returned home, sold his property and distributed the proceeds among the poor. Under the influence of his sister Macrina, he settled at Annesi in Pontus where he devoted himself to the life of asceticism. St. Basil lived with his family members on the family property.[29] His desire to keep simplicity in every aspect of his life and his perception of the primitive church, described in Acts, was reflected in his teaching about the Christian communities. During this time, St. Basil started to write his *Moralia*[30]—a manual for the Christians who were seeking spiritual perfection. These rules with the accompanying biblical proof texts show his ecclesiological ideas related to duties and practices of believers that he believed should be integrated into the life of the church.

In 359, Basil attended the Council of Seleucia and after that time, he became more actively involved in the life of the church. After his ordination as presbyter by Eusebius, he stayed for a while in Pontus,[31] but in 365, St. Basil came back to the church in Caesarea. According to St. Basil, it was a critical period in the life of the church in the East and the crisis was not only external but also internal, as Christians became involved in a domestic war against Christians.[32] From now on and especially after Eusebius's death, when Basil was elected as his successor, he worked hard in order to defend orthodoxy and bring unity in the church.

As bishop of Caesarea, St. Basil also devoted himself to social and charitable work and was able to apply his theological ideas and principles about the ministry of the church in practice. He built the "new city" of the "Basilieas" with a hospital for the sick, a hospice for the elderly, and with places for workers. For these social actions and achievements, Adalbert Hamman calls St. Basil "one of the first social apostles raised by the church."[33] St. Basil died on 1 January 379,[34] after nine years of his episcopate

---

28. Ibid., 198.

29. Here his friend Gregory of Nazianzus visited him several times and took part in a composition of an anthology of texts that were drawn from Origen's work and called the *Philocalia*.

30. Some scholars suggest that only the first draft of *Moralia* was composed at that time. See Fedwick, *The Church*, 139.

31. There was an apparent misunderstanding between Eusebius and Basil at that time. See *Oration* 43. 28. See details in Fedwick, *The Church*, 140.

32. *Letter* 258. See also Meredith, *The Cappadocians*, 23.

33. Hamman, *How to Read the Church Fathers*, 79.

34. There are suggestions among scholars that St. Basil may have died as early as September 377. This debate is examined in more detail in Appendix III of Rousseau,

where he served with all his strength as pastor, statesman, theologian, and defender of the faith. This service and all his achievements made him a Church Father and famous leader of the church.

THEOLOGICAL SETTING

The doctrine of the church in its full theological sense was not yet developed at the time of St. Basil.[35] Those who wrote on this issue before him had not formulated their understanding of the church in precise terms. The writings of the Apostolic Fathers mostly consist of responses to internal and external pressures and conflicts connected with Jewish and pagan influence. These were attempts to explain the essential characteristics or defining marks of the Christian life.[36] The only work on the church before the fourth century was written by Cyprian, bishop of Carthage.[37] However, even this book—*On the Unity of the Church*—was a response to schisms in the church.[38]

The years of St. Basil's life were the years of theological controversy and divisions in the church and, consequently, ecclesiology was not a dominant theme at that time.[39] The Arian crisis made the church articulate trinitarian ideas with greater clarity: the existence of the three in one Godhead and the equality of the Son and the Spirit were crucial. Consequently, at that period, theologians were not interested in creating a doctrine of the church in a strict sense. St. Basil of Caesarea was not an exception. Therefore, the question of church existence and organization was often mentioned in his writings in connection to trinitarian teaching.

Although there is no evidence that St. Basil was directly influenced by earlier theologians, it is necessary to mention that he was not the first one in whose writings we can find a notion of a trinitarian approach to ecclesial

---

Basil of Caesarea, 360–63.

35. See Gunton, *The Promise of Trinitarian Theology*, 60. See also a very helpful summary about the development of ecclesiology in chapter 8 and chapter 15 in Kelly, *Early Christian Doctrines*, 189–220, 401–8. He writes, "Eastern teaching about the Church remained immature, not to say archaic, in the post-Nicene period." Kelly, *Early Christian Doctrines*, 401.

36. Paget, "The Vision of the Church in the Apostolic Fathers," 194.

37. Cyprian, *On the Unity of the Church*.

38. According to Torrance, "There was indeed no significant monograph on the subject between Cyprian's *De Unitate* and Wycliffe's *De Ecclesia*." See Torrance, *Theology in Reconstruction*, 266.

39. Giles asserts that during the fourth century theologians were engaged in debates about the person of Christ and the Trinity and "no attention was given to the doctrine of the church." See Giles, *What on Earth is the Church*, 214. See also *Letter* 144.

life. In the early Christian texts, there is "an emerging consciousness that the God who is Three is the origin of the church and source of its unity."[40]

Several examples can be given concerning this issue. Clement of Rome, in his letter to the Corinthian church, called on the believers to live in peace based on the life of the Trinity. He explains, "For as God lives, and as the Lord Jesus Christ lives and the Holy Spirit (on whom the elect believe and hope), the man who with humility and eager considerateness and with no regrets does what God has decreed and ordered will be enlisted and enrolled in the ranks of those who are saved through Jesus Christ."[41]

There were similar trinitarian ideas connected with the ethical norms of the church in the writings of Ignatius of Antioch.[42] Also Cyprian, bishop of Carthage, in his treatise *On the Lord's Prayer*, described the church using the trinitarian formula. He believed that the church is "the people united in one in the unity of the Father, and of the Son, and of the Holy Spirit."[43] Tertullian wrote as well about the connections between the church and the divine three: "For the very Church itself is, properly and principally, the Spirit Himself, in whom is the Trinity of the One Divinity—Father, Son and Holy Spirit. (The Spirit) combines that Church which the Lord has made to consist in 'three.'"[44]

However, St. Basil was a theologian who not only shared a similar notion of the role of the Trinity in the life of the church but also elaborated a new theological language and a new terminology. He came to a relational understanding of Godhead and tried to explain in more detail the relation of each Person of the Trinity to the church.[45]

St. Basil's approach to God, which underlines his whole theology and the doctrine of the church in particular,[46] is the apophatic approach. It is often called negative theology because it rejects that the human mind can reach the very essence of God. St. Basil is known as one who together with Gregory of Nazianzus and Gregory of Nyssa, developed this way of thinking

---

40. Hunt, "The Trinity and the Church," 217.

41. *First Clement* 58.

42. Ignatius of Antioch, *To the Ephesians* 9.1. See also Ignatius of Antioch, *To the Magnesians* 13.1.

43. Cyprian, *On the Lord's Prayer* 4.23.

44. Tertullian, *On the Modesty* 21.

45. See chapter 4 of this book. St. Basil used metaphors to explain the relationship between God the Trinity and the church.

46. The apophatic approach to the church will be mentioned in chapter 3 of this book.

and affirmed "the absolute transcendence of God and excluded any possibility of identifying Him with any human concept."[47]

This theological approach primarily developed out of discussions about God's essence and the Sonship of Christ raised by heretics. In his answer to the different heretical statements, St. Basil provided necessarily limited language about God when he sought to express the incomprehensibility of the mystery of the Trinity and its ineffable essence. Trying to explain the unity of God and the harmony of inner relationships with the threeness of Persons, St. Basil said that he used "terms not found in Scripture, yet all the same not alien from the godly sense of Scripture."[48]

The great contribution made by St. Basil to the doctrine of Trinity was his ability to redefine the words *"hypostasis"* and *"ousia"* in order to provide the correct language necessary to describe the distinct nature of the Father, Son and Holy Spirit.[49] As Boris Bobrinskoy put it, "St. Basil was the first to clear the term *hypostasis* of its ambiguities."[50]

The first time the Persons of the Trinity were described by the word *hypostasis* in Origen.[51] However, the words, *ousia* and *hypostasis*, were used as synonyms with one meaning "being." Later on, St. Basil uses *hypostasis* in his writings to emphasize the distinction between the Persons. At the same time, St. Basil builds on Athanasius's ideas and underlines the unity of God through the term *ousia*. As writings of Athanasius show, these terms meant for him exactly the same thing.[52] Defending divinity of the Son and substantial unity in the Holy Trinity,[53] Athanasius did not explain clearly "the otherness" within the very substance of God. It was only implied by him through

47. Meyendorff, *Byzantine Theology*, 11. Later on, this idea that God's essence is incomprehensible became "the major axiom for Eastern Christian thought." See Olson, *The Story of Christian Theology*, 181. This approach was later developed by other theologians and became "the fundamental characteristic of the whole theological tradition of the Eastern Church." See Lossky, *The Mystical Theology of the Eastern Church*, 26.

48. He was talking about *ousia* and *hypostasis*. See *De Fide* (Clarke, 91).

49. See Hildebrand, *The Trinitarian Theology of Basil of Caesarea*, 58.

50. Bobrinskoy, *The Mystery of the Trinity*, 234. The Latin equivalent of the Greek term *hypostasis* was *substantia* and these words correspond to some degree etymologically (*hypo-stasis—substantia*). But the meaning of the content was different with the translation into Latin: "If Eastern theology spoke of two hypostases, in Latin that amounted to a difference in substance between Father and Son." See Dunzl, *A Brief History of the Doctrine of the Trinity in the Early Church*, 72. See also a very good summary about the meaning and use of the word *hypostasis* by classical Greek writers in Stead, *Philosophy in Christian Antiquity*, 174–77.

51. See Prestige, *God in Patristic Thought*, 179.

52. See Zizioulas, *Being as Communion*, 87. He refers to Athanasius words in PG 26:1036.

53. See details in Jevtich, "Between the 'Niceaens' and the 'Easterners,'" 242.

the argument that the Son has always belonged to God's *ousia*.[54] Developing the meaning of the terms, which were used by earlier theologians, such as Origen and Athanasius, St. Basil was able to increase the capacity of the language and to show different shades of meaning, which enabled these words to perform different functions.

St. Basil also differs from Athanasius in speaking of the Father as the origin of the Son and the Spirit. As Noble explains, "The significant point of the doctrine of the Trinity held by Cappadocians was that they did not see the *ousia* or 'being' of God as the guarantee of unity, as if the *ousia* were some fourth entity ontologically superior to the three Persons (*hypostases*) . . . for Cappadocians, the guarantee of the Trinity was the Father, who was the *arche*, the "origin" or "source," of the Son and the Spirit."[55] The theme of the Father as the source of the Son's existence was used "as a prophylactic against charges that pro-Nicenes teach a plurality of Gods or that the Godhead is divided."[56] Therefore, the Monarchy of the Father was pointing to communion within the Trinity. St. Basil's achievement of the "desynonymising" of *ousia* and *hypostasis* made possible the distinction between the Persons.[57] At the same time, the idea of Monarchy of the Father allowed holding together the unity and plurality of God. St. Basil's model of Godhead presented a view of the divine being as a being, which is a communion of Persons (*koinonia*).[58] For St. Basil "one *ousia*, three *hypostaseis*"[59] meant that there were relations within one Godhead and the Persons of God were inseparable and indivisible and yet not identical in every way.[60] St. Basil was able to reconsider the word *hypostasis*[61] and create the relational approach to God.

---

54. See this idea in Zizioulas, *Being as Communion*, 86–87.

55. Noble, *Holy Trinity: Holy People*, 214.

56. Ayres, *Nicaea and its Legacy*, 206.

57. Gunton, *The Promise of Trinitarian Theology*, 9.

58. Collins, *Trinitarian Theology West and East*, 151.

59. We have to mention that the whole formula *one ousia, three hypostaseis* does not appear in St. Basil's works. See the history of the formula in Lienhard, "Ousia and Hypostasis," 99–121. See also Hildebrand, *The Trinitarian Theology of Basil of Caesarea*, 58.

60. Olson, *The Story of Christian Theology*, 185.

61. In the beginning, St. Basil was also using the word *prosopon* (with the meaning "person") in trinitarian disputes, but later he dismissed this term. A very detailed analysis of both terms and their use in St. Basil's writings can be found in Turcescu, "Prosōpon and Hypostasis in Basil of Caesarea's 'Against Eunomius' and the Epistles," 374–95. See also Hildebrand, *The Trinitarian Theology of Basil of Caesarea*, 76–101.

Contrary to the philosophical suggestions that God was an unchanging being, eternal, and completely outside space and time,[62] St. Basil's concept of God as an inseparable communion of Persons was related to creation and to the church in particular. The trinitarian disputes and debates, which occupied the minds of many people of that time including St. Basil and his friends, influenced the development of St. Basil's ecclesiology. Consequently, his views of the church became intrinsically woven with his understanding of the trinitarian God and his actions in this world.

---

62. See Stead, *Philosophy in Christian Antiquity*, 58.

CHAPTER 2

Trinitarian God and the Human Community

FOR ACQUIRING A PROPER understanding of St. Basil's ecclesiology, a good point to start is his view on the beginning of the human race and the very foundation of the world, which was created through the initiative of God the Trinity. This will show us the perspective from which St. Basil sees the church, her relation to God and to his plan for humanity, which includes perfection in godliness and the eschatological future.[1]

In St. Basil's thought, God exists in divine fellowship or *koinonia*, but he has a relationship with the outside world, which is his creation. The church, as a human community, belongs to this world. Consequently, we will consider the economy of all Persons of the Trinity in relation to the life of the church as a part of his created order.

---

1. Baghos states in his article that St. Basil in his writings "puts forward a holistic eschatological vision whereby the glorious transfiguration of the world at the end of time was already precipitated on the very first day of the creation." The proper domain of this existential dimension of the eschatological state is "the life of the Church." See Baghos, "St. Basil's Eschatological Vision," 85.

GOD'S PLAN FOR HUMANS: CREATED FOR LIFE IN COMMUNITY

St. Basil's understanding of creation has to do with dogma and with the practical application to the lives of believers.[2] It is about life in a community as God has prepared for us. In his *Hexaemeron*, which are homilies about the creation of the world, St. Basil shows this as the intent of God's work: human persons are created not to be solitary, but to live and to grow together in love.

> [T]he Lord calls Himself a vine and His Father the husbandman, and every one of us who are grafted by faith into the Church the branches . . . He wishes that the claspings of love, like the tendrils of the vine, should attach us to our neighbours and make us rest on them, so that, in our continual aspirations towards heaven, we may imitate these vines, which raise themselves to the tops of the tallest trees.[3]

Throughout his works, St. Basil shows and defends the trinitarian way of creation.[4] He teaches that the whole Trinity was involved into this process. St. Basil perceives God the Father as "the original cause of all things that are made."[5] He also asserts that "the Holy Spirit took an active part in the creation of the world"[6] and that through Christ everything was created: "You are therefore to perceive three, the Lord who gives the order, the Word who creates, and the Spirit who confirms."[7]

According to St. Basil, this created world "drew its origin from God"[8] who is "beneficent Nature, Goodness without measure."[9] Consequently, creation itself is good. "Being good, He made it an useful work," Basil says, "Being wise, He made it everything that was most beautiful. Being powerful

---

2. See Флоровский, *Восточные Отцы IV века*, 8. The question of creation was a very important one in St. Basil's theology. In order to prevent heretical teaching about creation being introduced into the church, St. Basil explained his understanding of creation in his homilies *Hexaemeron*.

3. *Hex.* 5.6.

4. St. Basil wanted to prove to heretics of his time that the Holy Spirit was actively involved in creation. He argued that it was the Spirit of God who "prepared the nature of water to produce living beings" and it is the same Spirit "which completes the divine and blessed Trinity." See *Hex.* 2.5.

5. *HS* 16.38.

6. *Hex.* 2.5.

7. *HS* 16.38.

8. *Hex.* 1.1.

9. Ibid., 1.2.

He made it very great."[10] Although St. Basil keeps the idea of otherness and radical difference between God and the world, he believes that God is involved in it and cares for his creation: "God has foreseen all, He has neglected nothing. His eye, which never sleeps, watches over all. He is present everywhere and gives to each being the means of preservation."[11]

God created the world according to his will[12] and to his plan. He created it out of nothing. Everything that came into existence was created by God and did not have any preexistent form. St. Basil concludes that nothing has the same honors as God who is "the Creator and the Demiurge of the world."[13] Only his wisdom and power linked all the diverse parts of the universe with "indissoluble attachment and established between them so perfect a fellowship and harmony that the most distant, in spite of their distance, appeared united in one universal sympathy."[14]

Following St. Basil's flow of thought, this "perfect fellowship" and "harmony" must include the creation of humans. Unfortunately, St. Basil finished his account of creation in the nine discourses of *Hexaemeron* without discussing in detail the creation of humans. He only briefly mentions man's creation in the last paragraph of the ninth homily, expounding the verse from Genesis 1:26.[15] However, the creation of the first man and woman is discussed in his homily *On Psalm 1*. St. Basil's exegesis of the text of this psalm implies that they were created as the first human community whose

---

10. Ibid., 1.7. In the next chapters of *Hexaemeron* Basil argued that evil did not have its origin in God. He considered "rightly so called" evil as "the condition of the soul opposed to virtue, developed in the careless on account of their falling away from good." See *Hex.* 2.4–5. See also *Hom.* 9 in PG 31:329A–53A

11. Ibid., 7.5.

12. Ibid., 1.6–7.

13. Ibid., 2.2. On the significance of the idea of creation "out of nothing" (*ex nihilo*) in the Eastern Church, see Zizioulas, *Lectures in Christian Dogmatics*, 88–98.

14. Ibid. One more time in this homily St. Basil confirms the idea that before the world was created matter did not exist: "But God, before all those things which now attract our notice existed... created matter in harmony with the form which He wished to give it."

15. In this ninth homily, St. Basil promised to return to the subject, but it seems that he was not able to fulfill his promise. There are two homilies, which are published among St. Basil's works, *De hominis structura*, Oratio I and II, but their authenticity was rejected by many scholars. See a good explanation in Orphanos, *Salvation and Creation*, 70–71. He declares that the reasons for the rejection are serious ones: "a) These homilies are not mentioned by ancient authors such as Jerome, Cassiodorus, who knew only nine homilies on the *Hexaemeron*. b) The same homilies, in a slightly different form, are to be found among the works of Gregory of Nyssa, and c) From the point of view of style and content, there is a considerable difference between them and the authentic works of Basil."

members were equal in honor: "[There was] one gracious act of God for man and woman when there was one creation of equal dignity for both of them,"[16] and each of them is "a part of a whole."[17] In this sense, the man from the text is not just one particular person, but also the representative of the family or community, which is righteous before God. St. Basil communicates the idea that woman is included in the community as well. Although he writes in this passage that man is "a principal part of a whole, which was manifested,"[18] he does not mean a major subordination. On the contrary, he posits that husband and wife have the same nature (φύσις μία) and that their actions or operations (ἐνέργειαι) are the same.[19] Probably, the only reason for man to be a leading part is the sequence of creation: a man was created first, and a woman was created after him. Hence, in the beginning of the world God created not a solitary person but the community where persons were equal. Interestingly enough, this relationship between a man and a woman in the first human community reminds us of St. Basil's thought on the relationships inside the Trinitarian community: Monarchy of the Father with the equality of Persons.[20]

This man and woman were distinguished from the animals and from the rest of creation because, Basil concludes, God "deemed *them* worthy of knowledge of Himself, equipped *them* with reason beyond all other creatures, allowed *them* to luxuriate in the inconceivable beauties of Paradise, made *them rulers* of all earthly things."[21] They had a privilege and an ability to know God and they were created in the image of their Creator.[22] Although St. Basil does not explain what the image of God meant, throughout

---

16. *Ps.* 1, PG 29:216D; translation is mine.

17. Ibid., PG 29:217A. A similar idea can be found in the *Homily on the Martyr Julitta*. "I am from the same lump as men. We have been made according to the image of God, as they also are. By creation, the female, with the same honor as the male, has become capable of virtue." PG 31:240D–241A.

18. Ibid., PG 29:217A; translation is mine.

19. Ibid., PG 29:217A.

20. In St. Basil's trinitarian theology the unity of the Triune God is attributed not so much to the common substance shared by the Godhead as to the person of the Father. This idea of unity is grounded in the concept of the Father's "Monarchy." See *HS* 18.47. The three divine hypostases are equal in divinity, but the Father is not "caused" by any other person. See *HS* 5.9, and *HS* 16.37.

21. In the original text it is singular *he* and *him* instead of plural *them*, but St. Basil speaks of ανθρωπος, which in this context means humanity and not the individual man. See *LR* (Clarke, 156). PG 31:913B.

22. *Ps.* 1, PG 29, 217A. See also *Ps.* 48, PG 29:437D and *LR*, PG 31:913B. See also *Hom.* 4, PG 31:222CD. See also *Hom.* 3 (Wagner, 441).

his writings we can find several phrases that imply that as humans we are created for a fellowship with our God and with each other.[23]

One of the divine attributes, which reflects the image of God in human beings, is the main faculty of the soul—a human mind (νουν) or intellect (λόγος)[24] that can acquire knowledge of God.[25] According to St. Basil, people without reason do not have "the distinguishing mark" of a human. This special mark includes "the understanding of God the Father, and the reception of the Word, which from the beginning existed with God, and the enlightenment (or illumination) that is given through the Spirit."[26] All these actions characterize humanity's ability to have a relationship with God the Trinity. From the beginning, St. Basil says, there was an opportunity for humans to have "close communion" (οἰκείωσις) with God that could lead to "the imitation of Christ" and to perfection of life.[27] Now this perfection is supposed to happen in the community of believers after "a cleansing of the soul from the filth that has grown on it from the carnal mind" (τὸ σαρκικὸν φρόνημα).[28]

This human faculty, intellect (λόγος) or mind (νουν), was created in man not only to communicate with God, but with other people as well. For this reason, God gave them a special skill that allows people to use words and to share the deep "thoughts of their hearts."[29] St. Basil believes that there is an innate inclination in human beings to have fellowship with each other. Their nature is created in such a way that they are supposed to live in society and to love their neighbors.[30] This kind of fellowship suggests "the spirit of sharing, mutual love and what is proper to their nature."[31] God blesses people with a nature that makes them live together and depend on one another. People possess "the power to love" that was "implanted" in them

---

23. See, for example, homily on *Ps.* 14.1.6, PG 29:261D; *Hom. 3*, PG 31:197D; *Letter* 97, PG 32:493; *LR*, PG 31:917A.

24. *Letter* 233.1. For the purpose of this study, we will discuss in detail only one of the divine attributes, "reason," which reflects the image of God in man. However, we have to mention that in St. Basil's thinking the image of God in man includes the reflection of some other divine attributes, such as "immortality, freedom, will, love, perfection, and holiness," which are common to the three persons of the Holy Trinity. See Aghiorgoussis, "Application of the Theme 'Eikon Theou' (Image of God) according to Saint Basil the Great," 270.

25. *Ps.* 48, PG 29:433B. See also *Hom. 4*, PG 31:222CD.

26. *Ps.* 48, PG 29:445B.

27. *HS* 15.35.

28. Ibid.

29. *Hom. 3*, PG 31:197D (Wagner, 431).

30. Ibid.

31. *Ps.* 14, PG 29:261.

in the moment they were created.³² In this sense, there is "the necessity of fellowship" in "our bodily constitution."³³ As St. Basil puts it,

> Who does not know that man is a tame and sociable (κοινονικὸν) animal, and not a solitary and fierce one? For nothing is so characteristic of our nature as to associate with one another, to need one another, and to love our kind. So the Lord Himself first gave us the seed of these things, and accordingly demands their fruits, saying: "A new commandment I give unto you, that ye love one another.³⁴

This commandment people have to practice in the community of believers, and they have to promote this kind of living in the world around them.³⁵ God expects human beings to use their natural inclinations in order to live properly according to his plan, which he prepared for them from the beginning of creation: "God the Creator ordered that we may need one another . . . in order that we may be linked with one another."³⁶

St. Basil believes that there is a purpose in everything that God made to exist, and that this visible world is created as a place of wonderful order. It has a value in and of itself, but it is also a place of education, a school, where these human souls had the opportunity to learn and to develop.

> You will finally discover that the world was not conceived by chance and without reason, but for an useful end and for the great advantage of all beings, since it is really the school where reasonable souls exercise themselves, the training ground where they learn to know God; since by the sight of visible and sensible things the mind is led, as by a hand, to the contemplation of invisible things.³⁷

---

32. *LR* (Clarke, 154).

33. *Letter* 97, PG 32:493.

34. *LR* (Clarke, 157). St. Basil also uses phrase "social animal" in his homily on *Ps.* 14.6 (DelCogliano, 100).

35. In spite of the fact that some passages of St. Basil's ascetic works can be interpreted as favoring the constitution of particular communities, his *Ascetica* (both Long and Small) offer the understanding of the church as a community that is trying to live a perfect life in the middle of the world. It is obvious that St. Basil described mostly spiritual withdrawal from sinners and not a "bodily (σοματικως) withdrawal" from the world. *Letter* 2.2. See also more details on this topic in Fedwick, *Church*, 18–19.

36. *LR* 7 (Clarke, 163).

37. *Hex.* 1.6.

The ultimate goal of these human creatures was to achieve the "mind of Christ,"[38] to enter into personal relationships with God, to be in communion with him,[39] and to become like God.[40] In St. Basil's works, the realization of this "likeness" to God is perceived as humanity's dignity and the purpose of his creation.[41] Unfortunately, the first humans, Adam and Eve, failed this enterprise and did not follow humanity's destiny. Consequently, this image of God in them was corrupted and they lost the life according to their nature.[42] This brought people to a position where instead of reflecting the image of their Creator they began to resemble senseless animals.[43] Their sin led to "the alienation" from God and to the break of "close communion with God."[44] This was equal to death because "God is Life, and the loss of life is death."[45] "Death and its concomitants"[46] became the reality of the result of disobedience. The fall of humankind marked the immediate marring of the divine image in them and the primordial experience of community was destroyed.[47]

In St. Basil's thought, as in many of the Eastern Fathers, there is a way of distinguishing between "image" (κατ' εἰκόνα) of God and "likeness" (καθ' ὁμοίωσιν) of God.[48] According to this thinking, the ultimate destiny of people was to achieve the likeness of God. Already in the beginning, they had this divine "image," but the "likeness" should be fully realized only at the end. What is present in the "image" is the potential likeness with God.

38. *Ps.* 48, PG 29: 445B.
39. *HS* 15.35.
40. *HS* 1.2.
41. *Ps.* 48.8, PG 29:449BD.

42. Orthodox thought tends to speak of the image of God as being distorted or diminished but never destroyed by human sin. See, for example, Lossky, *The Mystical Theology*, 124. See *Ps.* 61 where St. Basil compares the state of humans with the building that was shaken but not completely destroyed. PG 29:473C.

43. *Ps.* 48.8, PG 29:449BD.
44. *HS* 15.35.
45. *Hom.* 9.7, PG 31:345A; translation is mine.
46. *LR* (Clarke, 156).

47. See Grenz, *Theology for the Community of God*, 192. St. Basil believes that though both body and soul were corrupted by sin, human nature did not become totally depraved. See *Ps.* 61.3. PG29:473CD. See the discussion of original sin and its effects on human nature in Orphanos, *Creation and Salvation according to St. Basil of Caesarea*, 90–91.

48. See more information about other Eastern Fathers in Aghiorgoussis, "Application of the Theme 'Eikon Theou' (Image of God) according to Saint Basil the Great," 275. St. Basil followed the tradition that was already developed by previous Church Fathers, such as Irenaeus and Athanasius.

Through the "soul's operations" of "man," it is possible to deploy this potential and to develop it into likeness of God when "man"[49] becomes what he/she was supposed to be from the beginning of the world.[50] In order to reach this purpose, the divine image should be restored in people in a way that they would be able to use the faculties of their soul—knowledge and love. Fallen creatures were not able to do this with their own strength, so God acted in this world on "their behalf" and for their glorious future.

> We were called back from death and made alive again by our Lord Jesus Christ Himself... He redeemed us from the curse... that He might bring us to the life of glory. And He was not content merely to quicken us when we were dead, but He bestowed the dignity of divinity, and prepared eternal resting places, surpassing all human thought in the greatness of their delight.[51]

Even after the first humans had fallen into sin, "God did not neglect *them*."[52] St. Basil believes that God did not abandon his plan for his creation but corrected it with due regard to what had happened in the past. Through his Son and the Holy Spirit, God continued to lead this created world and people to their ultimate end to become perfect and to live in eternal glory. Through the Holy Spirit, he continues to enlighten people in order to make their souls able to be qualified for the contemplation of God.[53] All these happen to people in the community of God, his church, during and after their baptism. At that moment, "the Spirit pours in the quickening power, renewing our souls from the deadness of sin unto their original life."[54] Through the same Spirit in the church

> comes our restoration to paradise, our ascension into the kingdom of heaven, our return to the adoption of sons, our liberty to call God our Father, our being made partakers of the grace of Christ, our being called children of light, our sharing in eternal glory, and, in a word, our being brought into a state of all "fullness of blessing," both in this world and in the world to come.[55]

---

49. The word "man" is not related to gender; the meaning is a human being or humankind and includes both man and woman.

50. See *Letter* 233. 1.

51. *LR* (Clarke, 156).

52. Ibid.

53. *EHB* 1; PG 31:424C. The literal phrase in St. Basil: "He who is not baptized is not enlightened."

54. *HS* 15.35.

55. *HS* 15.36.

In St. Basil's thought, the phrase "the world to come" means that this world, "which was begun in time, is condemned to come to an end in time."[56] The existed "world must change" and all the changes will lead to "the end of all things and the regeneration of the age."[57] This implies "the renewing of the world,"[58] or eschatological new creation. The re-creation of the world will result in the banishment of death and "the full enjoyment"[59] when "God, the Creator of the universe and the just Judge . . . rewards all the actions of life according to their merit."[60] The "end of humans" will come with "the rule of God" and "the blessed life in the world to come," which is the best possible future that God can provide for "the rational nature" of people.[61] The picture of the eschatological community in heaven, which St. Basil also calls "the church" (*ekklesia*), can be found in his exegetical work *On Psalm 45*.[62] He describes this eschatological reality as a great and beautiful city, the new heavenly Jerusalem. In this city, people will live together in peace and harmony, not only human souls but also all intelligent creatures and some pre-cosmic powers. Consequently, this vision of a future conveys Basil's idea of God's purpose for his people. They should be brought together in a corporate community and do not live as isolated individuals.

On one hand, St. Basil conceives the continuous restoration of the image of God in people as the different stages of individual Christian perfection, which included purification and *askesis*. He believes that this can help to "clean the Royal Image and restore its ancient form" through "the withdrawal of the passions which, coming afterwards gradually on the soul from its friendship to the flesh, have alienated it from its close relationship with God."[63] On the other hand, he keeps reminding his listeners and readers that it is impossible to achieve the likeness of God without life in the community. This perfection should be performed through our experience of the community, otherwise "the greatest commandment of all and that

---

56. *Hex.* 1.3.

57. Ibid., 1.4.

58. Ibid., 1.3.

59. *HS* 15.36.

60. *Hex.* 1.4. In St. Basil's thought, not only humans but the entire creation will be transformed into something divine and sinless. See this idea in Orphanos, *Creation and Salvation*, 155.

61. *Ps.* 48.8, PG 29:432A–B.

62. *Ps.* 45, PG 29:421CD, 424A. This is the church of people, who have "heavenly citizenship" and whose names are "written in heaven."

63. *HS* 9.23.

which conduces to salvation is neglected, and neither is the hungry fed nor the naked clothed."[64]

This statement implies that person's salvation in some sense depends on their life in the community. The eternal life in the "world to come" includes existing forever in fellowship with God and with other people when human nature will be present in its "fullness of blessing."[65] Perfected and redeemed people will live within a renewed creation, and enjoy the presence of their Creator, but this perfection of human nature should start in this world and in the community of believers. St. Basil sees the church as the place where God is present and where he works with his people.[66] In this sense, the church is an agent of this new creation where the Holy Spirit transforms and regenerates those who are willing to become like God.

> Through His aid [the Holy Spirit] hearts are lifted up, the weak are held by the hand, and they who are advancing are brought to perfection . . . souls wherein the Spirit dwells, illuminated by the Spirit, themselves become spiritual, and send forth their grace to others. Hence comes foreknowledge of the future, understanding of mysteries, apprehension of what is hidden, distribution of good gifts, the heavenly citizenship, a place in the chorus of angels, joy without end, abiding in God, the being made like to God, and, highest of all, the being made God.[67]

"The being made God" can be interpreted as being made persons in special relations, being made a community, which has a communion with God. People will receive "the heavenly citizenship" where their communication with God will be restored completely and where reconciliation with God will be reflected in their relations with other people. Therefore, God's intention for his creation is eschatological new creation and the establishment of community where people will be regenerated and transformed into the likeness of God.

---

64. *LR* (Clarke, 164). PG 31:929B.

65. *HS* 15.36.

66. *Letter* 97; PG 32:493. "The Lord has told us that he will be in the midst where two or three call on him in concord." See also *Hom.* 3, PG 31:213A, "[F]or you God among people."

67. *HS* 9.23.

DIVINE ECONOMY AND THE LIFE OF THE CHURCH[68]

St. Basil's view of the Christian community is intimately linked with his understanding of the Trinity and the economy of every divine Person.[69] This economic activity means that they have varying functions, but they are still involved in the same divine plan concerning God's working in the world and with his people. As we have seen in the account of creation, the church is the outcome of the Father's will, which he shares with the Son and with the Holy Spirit when all of them are engaged in the economy, which helps the realization of this special community. St. Basil states that for "the Church of God" (the Father) alone "Christ died" and on this church "He poured out the Holy Spirit richly."[70] There are distinct contributions of each Person of divine Godhead. In our examination of the elements of the divine economy that forms the basis for Basil's understanding of the church, we will indicate the main characteristics of work done by each divine Person and connect this with his idea of such community as the church.

For the purpose of this study, we will discuss different aspects of economies of each Person of the Trinity on their own. However, we have to mention that in St. Basil's thought there is unity of God at the level of *ousia* and plurality of God as distinct *hypostaseis*. Already in his early theological discussion with Eunomius St. Basil argues that there is "a unity of *ousia* between Father and Son, although what that essence is remains unknown."[71] Ten years later, in his letter *To the notables of Neocaesarea*, he explains in more details the same idea of unity including the Holy Spirit:

> For of Father, Son, and Holy Ghost there is the same nature and one Godhead; but these are different names, setting forth to us the circumscription and exactitude of the meanings. For unless the meaning of the distinctive qualities of each be unconfounded, it is impossible for the doxology to be adequately offered to Father, Son, and Holy Ghost.

---

68. We will not discuss here St. Basil's understanding of the divine economy in general (it could be a good topic for a separate book), but we will look at the theological ideas, which are connected with the life of the church.

69. As Rousseau noted, there are three main parts in St. Basil's theological thought: theology of the Trinity, theology of human nature, and the community "within which that nature had to operate." See Rousseau, *Basil of Caesarea*, 271.

70. *De Jud.* (Clarke, 77). PG 31:653AB.

71. Ayres, *Nicaea and its Legacy*, 194. Ayres refers to *Contra Eunomium* 1.19.

> ... he who fails to confess the community of the essence or substance falls into polytheism, so he who refuses to grant the distinction of the hypostases is carried away into Judaism.[72]

Feeling the need to share again about the idea of unity of *ousia* and the distinction between *hypostaseis*, two years later in a letter addressed to his friend Amphilochius, St. Basil writes:

> The distinction between *ousia* and *hypostasis* is the same as that between the general and the particular; ... Wherefore, in the case of the Godhead, we confess one essence or substance so as not to give a variant definition of existence but we confess a particular hypostasis, in order that our conception of Father, Son and Holy Spirit may be without confusion and clear.[73]

The unity of God is also emphasized in St. Basil's writings through the idea of the Father as the source of the Trinity, which will be discussed below as part of the Father's economy.

Economy of the Father in Basil's understanding of the church

We mentioned earlier in this chapter that St. Basil believes in the Monarchy of the Father,[74] which means that everything in the economy begins with the Father, and united by him. Every initiative of the Father is executed by the Son and by the Spirit in their conjoint action. The work that is related to the church is conceived by the Father. He wills "that all men be saved and come to the knowledge of truth,"[75] and he accomplishes it through the Son and the Spirit. In his treatise, *On the Holy Spirit*, defending the unity of God, St. Basil writes, "Let no one accuse me of saying that there are three unoriginate persons ... The Originator of all things is One: He creates through the Son and perfects through the Spirit."[76] Later in chapter 18 of the same treatise, St. Basil explains, "Divine knowledge ascends from one Spirit through the one Son to the one Father. Likewise, natural goodness, inherent holiness and royal dignity reaches from the Father through the Only-Begotten to

---

72. *Letter* 210.4–5.
73. *Letter* 236.6.
74. We mentioned "Monarchy" when we discussed the creation of the first humans. See also *HS* 43.47. According to St. Basil, as "the source of all gifts," the Father has a different "rank" among the Persons of the Godhead—he is always supposed to be the first. See *HS* 16.37–38.
75. *SR* (Clarke, 320). PG 31:1248C
76. *HS* 16.38.

the Spirit. Thus, we do not lose the true doctrine of one God by confessing the persons."[77] Although St. Basil believes that God the Father is the source of everything, he keeps reminding his readers that there is not any subordination: "Those who teach subordination, and talk about first, second and third, ought to realize that they are introducing erroneous Greek polytheism into pure Christian theology."[78] In St. Basil's opinion, there is "a communion" among the three Persons of the Trinity, but the Father is "the first principle of existing things," and the Godhead is caused by him.[79] Therefore, we come to a conclusion that in St. Basil's thought God the Father creates the church through the Son, and he perfects her through the Spirit, and all this is done in unity.

The term *hypostasis* helps St. Basil to define the role of each divine Person and the eternal relations of the trinitarian Persons. There are unique hypostatic properties and attributes inherent in each divine *hypostasis*. As St. Basil phrases it, "Hypostasis is contemplated in the special property of Fatherhood, Sonship, or the power to sanctify."[80] God reveals himself as the Father of the only-begotten Son, and he is the one from whom the Spirit proceeds. The *hypostasis* of the Father is the source and cause of the Son and of the Spirit. Consequently, in St. Basil's thought, the personal relations inside the Trinity originate from the Father and "knowledge of His own nature naturally belongs to the Father first."[81] The Father is "the Source of the relations whence the *hypostaseis* receive their distinctive characteristics."[82] This relationship between the Father and the Son, between the Father and the Spirit, and between the Son and the Spirit is unique and mystical.[83] The revelation of God as Fatherhood, Sonship and Sanctification[84] introduces us into the eternal being of God. However, this divine paternity is not an anthropomorphism drawn from a human experience.[85] St. Basil's apophatic approach guards against such interpretation. On the contrary, this paternity is the foundation of human relationship and it could be reflected analogically in the relations between people in his church.

---

77. Ibid., 18.47 (Anderson, 74–75).
78. Ibid. (Anderson, 75).
79. Ibid., 16.38 (Anderson, 61–62).
80. Letter 214. 4.
81. Letter 236.1.
82. Lossky, *Mystical Theology*, 58–60.
83. HS 17.43.
84. Letter 236.6.
85. The idea is taken from Bobrinskoy, *The Mystery of the Trinity*, 268.

The economy of the Father is connected with his Monarchy and the divine initiative. He is the one who sends the Son, into whose likeness Christians are supposed to be transformed. He also sends the Spirit who organizes the church where the conditions are provided for such a transformation. All trinitarian Persons work in unison, but in St. Basil's thinking the Father plays the role of original Source of everything and every action done by the Trinity, including creation of the church and its development.

Economy of the Son and the life of the church

The economies of Christ and the Spirit in St. Basil's thought belong together, and they are hardly separated.[86] He states that the Holy Spirit "being inseparably present was with the very flesh of the Lord," and the Son's "every operation was wrought with the co-operation of the Spirit."[87] St. Basil insists that all "things done in the dispensation of the coming of our Lord in the flesh;—all is through the Spirit."[88] This leads us to a conclusion that when we discuss the economy of the Son we have to remember the role of the Spirit in it. At the same time, the economy of the Spirit is strongly related to the economy of Christ. However, for the purpose of this study we will try to discuss some aspects of both economies, of the Son and of the Spirit, on their own.

In St. Basil's thought, the existence of the community of believers, the church, is connected with the coming to earth of the Son of God who became the *"in-humanated* God" (τὸν ἐνανθρωπήσαντα Θεὸν).[89] In him the union of created and uncreated was realized because he was not "soulless flesh, but Godhead using flesh endued with soul."[90] He was "God in human nature" (Θεὸν ἐν ἀνθρώπου φύσει) who through the "economy of incarnation" descended to "mean and weak" humanity.[91] He came to "destroy death"

---

86. In Eastern Orthodoxy this tendency has been kept and their understanding of the church is founded on a "twofold divine economy": the work of Christ and the work of the Holy Spirit. See Lossky, *The Mystical Theology*, 156. See also Kärkkäinen, *An Introduction to Ecclesiology*, 23.

87. *HS* 16.39.

88. Ibid., see also 19.49.

89. *Ps.* 45, PG 29:425C; translation is mine. This word *"in-humanated"* was invented in order to communicate the real meaning of the Greek text. It is possible to use the English word "incarnated," which is a literal translation of another Greek word σαρκώσεως. St. Basil used this word in his *Letter* 265.2 and the meaning is slightly different.

90. *Letter* 236.1.

91. *Ps.* 45.5, PG 29:400AB. See similar idea in *Hom.* 27, *On the Holy Birth of Christ*, PG 31:1460BC.

and to give "a hope of resurrection."[92] St. Basil believes that now Christ can reside in believers through the Holy Spirit.[93] Also he dwells "in the midst of the city," and "the name of this city is the Church."[94] There is always a corporate aspect in St. Basil's thinking concerning the divine economy. It is not about individuals, but about salvation for the whole of fallen humanity because "the holy and precious blood of Jesus Christ our Lord" was "shed for us all."[95]

The role of Christ in the divine economy is especially important because he is "the Mediator" between God and people.[96] St. Basil compares his mediatory function in salvation with that of Moses, through whose help people were able to know truth and to receive the words of God. Christ, our "God and Savior," can regenerate and renew us in order that we can see "the great light of truth" ourselves.[97] He is also "the Peacemaker who makes peace and reconciles completely two in one new human." This reconciliation happens "in the heaven and on the earth" and all this through Christ's "blood on the cross."[98] In this sense, salvation starts with the union of these two separated natures in Christ, and it finishes with the union of God and humanity.[99]

Throughout his writings, St. Basil uses different titles for Jesus, which "Scripture designates Him," in order to explain his role and activity: Shepherd, King, Physician, Bridegroom, Way, Door, Fountain, Bread, Axe, Rock, true Light, righteous Judge, and Resurrection. According to St. Basil, these titles set forth "the variety of the effectual working which, out of His tenderheartedness to His own creation, according to the peculiar necessity of each,

---

92. *Hom.* 3, PG 31:213A.

93. *Ps.* 15, PG 29:429B. See another example, where St. Basil says that apostle "Paul had Christ speaking in him," *Ps.* 44.5, PG 29:397CD.

94. Ibid., PG 29:424B.

95. *Ps.* 48.4, PG 29:441A. This corporate way of thinking can also be noticed when St. Basil refers to the fall. He employs the first personal *plural* pronouns in his expressions connected to this event. He thinks of the whole of mankind when he uses sentences that say the fall happened to "us" and it is the result of "our" insult (PG 31:349C) and "we" have drawn death upon "ourselves" (PG 345AB). See this idea in Orphanos, *Creation and Salvation*, 92.

96. HS 14.32.

97. Ibid.

98. *Ps.* 33.5, PG 29:361C. See this idea also in *Ps.* 45: "He himself is our peace, he it is who has made both one, that of the two he might create one new man." The translation is from Way, *Exegetical Homilies*, 309.

99. The notion of this idea can be found in *Letter* 97: "The Lord Himself undertook the economy, that by the blood of His cross He might make peace between things in earth and things in heaven."

He bestows upon them that need."[100] Each title refers to the particular action of Jesus that he has undertaken to help people to reach "the blessed end" that "through Him" we may know the Father.[101] Therefore, people have had their "approach to the Father through Him, being translated from 'the power of darkness to be partakers of the inheritance of the saints in light.'"[102]

The divine economy is revealed as love poured out for humans and for a suffering world. This "Savior's love for mankind (φιλανθρωπία)"[103] is so great that he "patiently endured to suffer our infirmities with us, and condescended to our weakness."[104] All these things he does voluntarily "working effectually for His own creation in goodness and in pity, according to the will of God the Father."[105] For this purpose, St. Basil writes,

> Those that have lapsed from the lofty height of life into sin He raises from their fall: for this reason He is Resurrection. Effectually working by the touch of His power and the will of His goodness He does all things. He shepherds; He enlightens; He nourishes; He heals; He guides; He raises up; He calls into being things that were not; He upholds what has been created. Thus the good things that come from God reach us "through the Son," who works in each case with greater speed than speech can utter.[106]

St. Basil believes that through the work, which Christ had accomplished, people were "called back from death and made alive again."[107] They were "redeemed from the curse" and released from their "weaknesses" because he bore their "diseases" in order that they might be "healed."[108] Commenting on Psalm 48, St. Basil develops this metaphor and expresses the idea that Christ is "the Physician of our souls" that provides help to all in need because of his love.[109]

---

100. *HS* 8.17. The whole eighth chapter of *On the Holy Spirit* describes the economy of Christ in a great detail.

101. Ibid., 18, 19.

102. Ibid., 18.

103. This idea of φιλανθρωπία was developed later in Eastern Orthodoxy and was connected with idea of "providence." See Lossky, *Mystical Theology*, 139.

104. *HS* 8.18 (Anderson, 36).

105. Ibid.

106. Ibid., 19.

107. *LR* (Clarke, 156). See also *HS* 15.35.

108. Ibid.

109. *Ps.* 48, PG 29:433C.

As the result of their sin, people were separated from God, but he "assumed human flesh" in order to make them "once more His own" and to have fellowship with him.[110] Through "the blood of the Only-begotten," people were "set free from the dishonoring slavery."[111] Christ alone, St. Basil writes, "can offer a propitiation to God for us all."[112] In order to enrich us, he "emptied Himself" (κενώσας ἑαυτὸν) taking up the condition of "a slave," which in this context implies human nature.[113] According to St. Basil, this unity of divine and human natures in Christ allows him to "destroy death's reign" and to "kill sin in the flesh."[114] "The Redeemer" pays "the fine to death on our behalf"[115] and reconciles people to God. For St. Basil, this means that the immediate aim of humanity's redemption is salvation from sin. At the same time, their salvation will be fully realized only in the age to come in their union with God. There is a "great mystery of salvation," St. Basil writes, which includes "the gradual progress of our education, while being brought to perfection in our training for godliness."[116] We have to mention that when St. Basil uses a word "godliness," he implies, first of all, Christ-likeness. Christ's ability to unite human and divine natures provides for humans the opportunity to become like him after they obtain the citizenship in heaven.

> Renunciation, then, so we have seen, is a loosing of the chains which bind us to the present material and transitory life, a freeing from human obligations, making us more ready to start in the God-ward way ... And greatest of all, it is beginning of our being made like unto Christ ... which likeness unless we have first attained, it is impossible to reach the manner of living prescribed by the Gospel of Christ.[117]

From the previous passages, we can conclude that human sin and the Fall led to an alienation from God and to a deadly "disease"[118] that the hu-

---

110. *Letter* 261.2.

111. *Hom.* 4, PG 31: 224A

112. *Ps.* 48.4, PG 29:441A.

113. *Ps.* 33.5, PG 29:361D. This idea of κενώσις is important for the understanding of Christ's economy and was developed further by other theologians. See Lossky, *Orthodox Theology: Introduction*, 100–102.

114. *Letter* 261.2.

115. Ibid.

116. *HS* 14.32.

117. *LR* (Clarke, 169). PG 31:940C.

118. See also *Hexaemeron* 9.4, where St. Basil says that "a disease of the soul" is all vices.

man race had to suffer. The only medicine or solution to this problem was the incarnation of the Son and his blood on the cross, which provided the way to a communion with God and to life in "the Heavenly Kingdom."[119] In this case, St. Basil's thinking demonstrates the important Eastern view of Christ's economy. Although the whole economy passes through the cross, the main goal of this pass remains as it had been from the moment of creation: the union of created humanity with God.[120] St. Basil does not stop at the cross and suffering, but he moves on to the heavenly kingdom and the new community. He looks at redemption from an eschatological perspective.[121] St. Basil leads us through the cross, but then goes beyond to the church of the "firstborns" whose names are "written in the heaven" and to "the rejoicing assembly of saints."[122] He believes that "through flesh" and "by his own suffering" Christ "might grant us freedom from suffering."[123] The Lord Jesus Christ himself, St. Basil says, became "a curse on our behalf and underwent the most dishonorable death, that He might bring us to the life of glory," and for this life he "prepared eternal resting places."[124]

As we mentioned earlier, the understanding of salvation in St. Basil has a corporate aspect, which is reflected in the economy of Christ. St. Basil conveys this idea through one of the great biblical images—the image of the church as body of Christ.[125] St. Basil states that Christ died for the church,[126] and all who believe in him are "the members of Christ."[127] He is the Savior, and he does not save people in order to let them live in isolation, but to join his body, the church.[128] This image implies that ultimate salvation cannot

---

119. *LR* (Clarke, 169).

120. See more on this topic about the ecclesiological differences based on the economy of Christ in the Eastern and Western theologies in Zizioulas, *Lectures in Christian Dogmatics*, 133–34.

121. The eschatological perspective, which we see in St. Basil, became one of the distinctive features of the Eastern theology. According to Florovsky, "Eschatology is not just one particular section of the Christian theological system, but rather its basis and foundation, its guiding and inspiring principle, or as it were, the climate of the whole of Christian thinking. Christianity is essentially eschatological, and the Church is an 'eschatological community,' since she is the New Testament, the ultimate and the final, and, consequently, 'the last.'" Florovsky, "The Patristic Age and Eschatology: Introduction," 63.

122. *Ps*. 45.4, PG 29:424A.

123. *HS* 8.18.

124. *LR* (Clarke, 156).

125. *Letter* 253.1; *Ps*. 44.5, PG 29:397CD; *De Jud.*, PG 31:660A; *HS* 5.9.

126. *De Jud.*, PG 31:653AB.

127. *Ps*. 44.5, PG 29:397CD.

128. Ibid.

be achieved individually because it is a process of restoration,[129] which includes co-operation with the other members of the body. In this sense, the economy of Christ results in the incorporation of redeemed people into the new community, his body, which has the ability to have fellowship with God.

Economy of the Spirit and the life of the church

In St. Basil's theology, the Spirit is indivisibly united with the Father and the Son.[130] St. Basil's thought moves from the economic to the immanent Trinity, "from the Spirit's activity in salvation and baptism to the nature of his being and his relationship with the Father and the Son."[131] The Holy Spirit is the facilitator of "the close relationship with God" through which believers can cry in their hearts "Abba, Father," and as such, he is called "the Holy Spirit of our God" and "the Spirit of His Son."[132]

As was previously noted, St. Basil's understanding of the economy of the Spirit is strongly linked with his view of the economy of the Son. "Is it Christ's advent? The Spirit is forerunner," Basil says, "Is there the incarnate presence? The Spirit is inseparable."[133] At the same time, the Spirit executes his own functions, and he has his own role. The Holy Spirit works here on earth in order to fulfill the divine plan of salvation and help people to recognize God's presence through different actions.

---

129. *Hom.* 20.1, PG 31:525AB. St. Basil believes that the part of the process of restoration is the restoration of the original state of humans, which they had at the moment of creation, and which they lost after the Fall. See also this idea in his homily *On Psalm 61* where St. Basil compares the state of a human with a building that God can restore after the reconstruction. PG 29:473C. See Way, *Exegetical Homilies*, 344.

130. *HS* 16.37. Basil believes that "in every operation the Spirit is closely conjoined with, and inseparable from, the Father and the Son." See also ibid., 13.30, "the Spirit is ranked together with God . . . on account of the natural fellowship" and "invited by the Lord." Ibid., 16.38, 18.45, 19.49, 26.63, 27.68.

131. See Hildebrand, *The Trinitarian Theology of Basil of Caesarea*, 174. See the same idea in Bobrinskoy, *The Mystery of the Trinity*, 233. At that time, some theologians ignored the Holy Spirit and the others adopted the teaching known as Pneumatomachianism, which denied the equality of the Holy Spirit with Father and Son. They believed that the Holy Spirit was a creature, or a force, or a power of God the Father. St. Basil was concerned that this wrong teaching about the Holy Spirit entered the church and he wrote one of his main treatises on behalf of the Holy Spirit. See more information in Olson, *The Story of Christian Theology*, 177. For better understanding of the context, see also Ayres, *Nicaea and its Legacy*, 211–17.

132. *HS* 19.49. See also *De Fide* (Clarke, 96).

133. Ibid.

Working of miracles and gifts of healing are through the Holy Spirit. Demons were driven out by the Spirit of God. The devil was brought to naught by the presence of the Spirit. Remission of sins was by the gift of the Spirit, for "ye were washed, ye were sanctified . . . in the name of the Lord Jesus Christ, and in the Holy Spirit of our God."[134]

In the same way, as St. Basil describes the work of the Son through his titles, so he explains the operations of the Spirit through the titles designated to the Spirit: Supplier of life[135] or the Lord of life,[136] the Spirit of adoption,[137] origin of sanctification,[138] the *Paraclete* or the Comforter,[139] and the Spirit who loves people (φιλανθρώπου Πωεύματος).[140] Explaining these titles, St. Basil implies that the life of a believer should be transformed by the Spirit in the community through adoption, sanctification, and love. At the end of his treatise *On the Holy Spirit*, he adds a remarkable statement about the role of the Spirit as a trinitarian Person:

> [I]t is impossible to see the image of the invisible God, except by the illumination of the Spirit . . . through the illumination of the Spirit we behold the effulgence of the glory of God; and through the impress we are led up to Him [Father] of whom He [Christ] is the impress and exact representation.[141]

St. Basil believes that this is the Spirit who "confirms"[142] the work in the divine economy, and he is the "perfecting cause"[143] through which "all things" are done in the economy of Christ.[144] In this sense, the Holy Spirit fulfils the economy of Christ, which leads to the creation of eschatological community. The Holy Spirit as "the Comforter and the Spirit of truth" brings together a corporate body of people who have been saved.[145] Through prophets and apostles, the Spirit gathers them from different nations, with

---

134. *HS* 19.49.
135. Ibid., 9.22.
136. Ibid., 13.29.
137. Ibid., 11.27–28.
138. Ibid., 9.22.
139. Ibid., 9.23; 19.48.
140. *Ps.* 33.5, PG 29:361D.
141. *HS* 26.64–65 (Lewis, 123). St. Basil refers to Heb 1:3.
142. Ibid., 16.38.
143. Ibid.
144. Ibid., 16.39, see also 19.49.
145. *Ps.* 48, PG 29:433A.

different socio-economic status, and both male and female.[146] He breaks down all the existing borders, which divide society. Using the words from Psalm 19:4, St. Basil shows that the Spirit of God is able to reach any person who lives on the earth, including any geographical location, and help him or her join the community. People from different cultural settings and from different languages can be assembled together.[147] This means that the work of the Spirit in the process of salvation is connected with the establishment of a different social reality. According to St. Basil, this work is directed toward the formation of the body of Christ, which is consists of restored people who were reconciled to God and with each other.[148] The Holy Spirit is the Person of the Trinity who brings order in the church and equips believers with the gifts for their ministry. As St. Basil phrased it,

> And is it not plain and incontestable that the ordering of the Church is effected through the Spirit? For He gave, it is said, "in the church, first Apostles, secondarily prophets, thirdly teachers, after that miracles, then gifts of healing, helps, governments, diversities of tongues," for this order is ordained in accordance with the division of the gifts that are of the Spirit.[149]

The diversity of gifts exists because God "put the members in the body, everyone of them as He willed,"[150] and these gifts are given for the purpose of serving one's neighbors. Through all of them, the Spirit constitutes the church and makes it one living organism. St. Basil discusses this topic in several of his works,[151] and in each, he emphasizes the interdependence of believers. As the members of the body of Christ, they should have "the same care for one another, according to the inborn spiritual communion of their sympathy."[152] "As parts in the whole, St. Basil continues, so are we individually in one Spirit, because we all 'were baptized in one body into one spirit.'"[153]

---

146. Ibid., PG 29:433B.

147. Ibid., PG 29:433A. Although everything is done through the apostles and prophets, the main idea behind the text is that the Holy Spirit is the one who makes it happen.

148. Ibid., PG 29:433D.

149. HS 16.39–40. See also *Letter* 227 in which Basil asserts that the ordering in the church is not "merely man's ordaining," but it is done "with the aid of the Holy Spirit."

150. Ibid., 26.61 (Lewis, 119).

151. *The Morals* 80.4 (Clarke, 128); ibid., 60 (Clarke, 117); *De Fide* (Clarke, 96); *De Jud.* (Clarke, 81); *LR* (Clarke, 165); *HS* 16.39–40, 26.61; *Hom.* 3, PG 31:213A.

152. HS 26.61.

153. Ibid.

Although St. Basil often uses as examples Old Testament saints[154] and New Testament martyrs, he does not think that the Spirit is concerned only with these people leaving the rest of believers to themselves. He is convinced that the Holy Spirit fills everybody with his power, and that he distributes his energy according to "the portion of faith" of each person.[155] Basil thinks that every believer receives the Spirit individually as people receive sunshine, and that the grace which is sent forth is "sufficient and full for all mankind, and is enjoyed by all who share it, according to the capacity, not of His [Spirit] power, but of their nature."[156] St. Basil's vision of the Christian life is a community where all people are actively involved in service to God and to fellow believers. Commenting on 1 Cor 12:8–10, he explains that in each of the gifts "the recipient has as much for others' sake as for his own. So that of necessity in the community life the working of the Holy Spirit in one man passes over to all the rest at once."[157] St. Basil is anxious to persuade his readers to support each other and to use gifts for the good of others. Preaching on envy, he explains that some people in the church are more skilled to interpret "the Sacred Scriptures" by "the grace of the Holy Spirit," but everyone in the church benefits from their gift. As St. Basil phrases it, "The benefit is yours and through your brother the gift of doctrine is sent to you, if only you are willing to accept it."[158] He strongly believes that according to the Gospel, it is dangerous for a Christian to live alone because his/her gifts become "useless."[159] Only when people live together, they may "enjoy" their own gifts and even multiply a gift "by imparting it to others and, reap the fruits of other men's gift as if they were *their* own."[160]

Following the Bible, St. Basil repeats that these fruits are "love, joy, peace,"[161] but he pays extra attention to "joy." He believes that God allows all people to experience this "joy" in order to remind them of what they have lost. However, righteous people may have a constant feeling of "divine and heavenly joy" because it is a sign of the presence of the Holy Spirit

---

154. See, for example, *LR* (Clarke, 149).

155. *HS* 9.22. In his *Letter* 105 St. Basil describes the Spirit and his work in the lives of individual believers as follows: "The Holy Ghost, having His subsistence of God, the fount of holiness, power that gives life, grace that makes perfect, through Whom man is adopted, and the mortal made immortal."

156. *HS*, 9.22–23.

157. *LR* (Clarke, 164–65).

158. *Hom. 11* (Wagner, 472).

159. *LR* (Clarke, 165).

160. Ibid. It is singular "his" instead of "their" in the original text.

161. *Ps.* 32, PG 29:324C. Basil refers to Gal 5:22.

in them.¹⁶² This is the reason, St. Basil writes, the Holy Spirit is called the "unction of joy."¹⁶³ As the body (ἡ σάρξ) of the Lord was anointed by the Spirit, so all people who are "sharers of Christ" can partly receive the same anointing.¹⁶⁴ They are given, St. Basil goes on, "a portion" of "fellowship of the Spirit."¹⁶⁵ Through the *koinonia*, they are united to each other and can keep "the concord of one body."¹⁶⁶ At the same time, the Holy Spirit makes believers spiritual through "the fellowship with Himself."¹⁶⁷ As Torrance noted, "In Basil's thought the Holy Spirit is indivisibly linked to and comes from the κοινωνία of the Father and the Son, and is as such the immediate Source of our communion with the Holy Trinity."¹⁶⁸ The activity of the Spirit makes the church perceive union with God not only as a future event, but also as a present experience.

St. Basil explains that through the gift of grace during baptism the Holy Spirit provides a way for a person to receive "the adoption of sons" and to join the community of God's children.¹⁶⁹ In this community where the same Spirit "distributes the gifts according to each recipient's worth"¹⁷⁰ and where he keeps the order,¹⁷¹ believers are supposed to grow and to learn from him that "teaches us who were blinded, and guides us to the choice of what profits us."¹⁷²

According to St. Basil, through the Spirit, believers are nourished in the church, and they are provided with "the food for souls."¹⁷³ This food is "the words of God," which are read in "the Church of God" every time people get together.¹⁷⁴ St. Basil believes that these "words" belong to the

---

162. Ibid.

163. *Ps.* 44, PG 29:405A. St. Basil uses the words "joy" and "gladness" as synonyms. He says that the fruit, which the Spirit grows in believers, is χαρά; and this is the reason the Spirit himself is called the oil of ἀγαλλίασις (extreme joy).

164. Ibid.

165. Ibid.

166. *Letter* 90. In this epistle to the western brothers, St. Basil shows that he includes into "the fellowship of the Spirit" all believers from the East and the West.

167. *HS* 9.23.

168. Torrance, *The Trinitarian Faith*, 315.

169. *HS* 15.36.

170. Ibid., 15.37. See also *Hom.* 3, PG 31:213A

171. Ibid., 16.39.

172. Ibid., 19.50.

173. *Ps.* 59, PG 29:464C. See also the same idea in *Hom.* 2, PG 31:197B.

174. Ibid.

community[175] and they are sent by God as "gifts."[176] In his homily *On Psalm 1* he conveys the idea that the words of the Scripture can be used not only as food but also as medicine.[177] Written by the Holy Spirit, the Scripture contains "common remedies for our souls" in order that all of us as humans can find "healing"—each one for his own moral ills.[178] St. Basil explains that, since the Holy Spirit knows that it is hard to lead "the human race to goodness," he provides this treatment through Psalms. The same way wise doctors use honey to hide the bitter taste of medicine.[179] He calls Psalms "the voice of the Church"[180] because they serve for "the new comers as the first lessons, they make the advanced believers grow, and they make the perfect ones firm."[181] St. Basil repeats this argument in his *Letter 2* when he says that through the study of inspired Scripture a person can find "as from some dispensary, the due medicine for his ailment."[182] All this is done by the Spirit that people can "really teach their souls."[183] For this reason, he is called "the common Corrector of life, the great Teacher, the Spirit of truth."[184]

In St. Basil's thought, salvation is a process of restoration of the image of God. A process when humans gradually receive knowledge of God, which is impossible without the presence of the Spirit.[185] It is a process of progressive illumination inside the community of believers when "souls wherein the Spirit dwells, illuminated by the Spirit, themselves become spiritual, and send forth their grace to others."[186] St. Basil compares this effect with the

175. Literally, St. Basil is saying, "words of God are ours." PG 29:464C.
176. *Ps. 59*, PG 29:464C.
177. *Ps. 1*, PG 29:209A.
178. Ibid.
179. Ibid., PG 29:212B.
180. Ibid., PG 29:213A.
181. Ibid.; translation is mine.
182. *Letter* 2.3.
183. *Ps. 1*, PG 29:212B.
184. Ibid., PG 29:216AB. Under "corrector" Basil meant "one who sets right." See διορθωτής in Lampe, *A Patristic Greek Lexicon*, 373. The idea that "sin is a serious and difficult matter" and that the Scripture is the remedy, which "heals the sick and establishes the sound in more perfect health" also can be found in Basil's homily *Give Heed to Thyself*. See Wagner, 436.
185. HS 18.47; see also ibid,. 15.36; 16.38.
186. Ibid., 9.23. The only problem with this idea in St. Basil is its association with his argument when he proves the divinity of the Holy Spirit. For St. Basil the Holy Spirit is divine because he can grant the divine grace. In the statement quoted above people through becoming spiritual can "send forth grace to others." No doubt, they do not become divine, but still the meaning of this expression is not clear. See this argument in Torrance, *Theology in Reconstruction*, 225.

reflection of sunbeams from a shining surface, which has been cleaned of every impurity. Once a believer is cleansed and indwelled by the Spirit, he becomes a source of spiritual light for others in the community.

There are two important characteristics of the Spirit, which are connected with this "spreading" of spirituality in the community. The Spirit is the one who is holy and who loves people.[187] Consequently, the economy of the Spirit, which is described by St. Basil, presupposes that the basis for this growing illumination or perfection is not only sanctification but also love toward people, love toward our neighbors, or in other words, the relationships of love in the community. This love, St. Basil posits, is the greatest of all things, "which characterizes the Christian."[188] Although the whole Godhead is the source of that love, the role of the Spirit is to communicate with all humans and to dispense the gift of grace to those who have been baptized. According to St. Basil, the Spirit is "to be present in a manner" even with the unworthy who "have once been sealed" in the community through the baptism. The Spirit is "awaiting the salvation which follows on their conversion."[189] Even people who are not converted yet can be considered potential participants of the eschatological community during their earthly life because of the presence of the Spirit. Only after their death in the day of "redemption" or the day of "judgment"

> ... they which have grieved the Holy Spirit by the wickedness of their ways, or have not wrought for Him that gave to them, shall be deprived of what they have received, their grace being transferred to others; or, according to one of the evangelists, they shall even be wholly cut asunder, the cutting asunder meaning complete separation from the Spirit. The cutting asunder, as I have observed, is the separation for aye of the soul from the Spirit.[190]

Using the scriptural idea behind the text of Psalm 6:5, St. Basil confirms that there is not any chance for people to change their destiny "in Hell" "because the succour of the Spirit is no longer present."[191] Conse-

---

187. Ps. 33.5, PG 29:361D.

188. *De Fide* (Clarke, 97). See also *The Morals* (Clarke, 131).

189. HS 16.40. This phrase implies that a person who was baptized is not necessarily converted. The conversion may happen later in his life and the Holy Spirit waits for this event.

190. Ibid.

191. Ibid. St. Basil perceives "the Hell" as an ultimate alternative reality, which opposes the heavenly church. Interestingly enough, in his thought, it is not so much connected with a physical torment as with the spiritual sufferings. First of all, there will be no presence of God and, consequently, no joy in the Spirit and no divine light.

quently, they will be separated from the fellowship with the whole Godhead and with those who live in eschatological communion in the presence of God.[192] In this sense, the ultimate salvation and the ultimate punishment depend on the economy of the Holy Spirit and are strongly connected with life in the community.

CONCLUSION TO CHAPTER 2

In many of his works, St. Basil expresses the conviction that from the beginning of this world the intention of God's work was the creation of an environment in which humans were supposed to live and grow in love. They were created with the ability to have relationship with the Triune God and with each other in order to acquire better knowledge of their Creator that at the end they may attain the mind of Christ. St. Basil believes that their own nature makes them seek the fellowship, which can help them develop in this direction. The community of people could become the best place for the realization of God's plans for all humans who are in need of interpersonal relations. The fact that the first couple broke God's instructions and alienated themselves from him led to the correction of the initial scheme and to the implementation of the actions concerning the salvation of humanity. For this reason, according to the initiative of the Father, the church is born through the Son and formed by the Spirit. In this sense, the historical existence of the church is shaped by the economy of the Trinity. In St. Basil's thinking, it is not the church that saves people through its actions, but it is God the Trinity who creates the church in order to gather all his children, to restore his image in them, and to re-establish the relationships of love. The life of such community is trinitarian in the sense that it stands on three pillars: divine economy of the Father, and the Son, and the Holy Spirit.

In St. Basil's doctrine of the Trinity the primacy of the Father guards his understanding of the church from a one-sided concentration on the Spirit or on the role of Christ. Being inseparably linked with each other, both

---

Secondly, those people who "acted wickedly" await "reproach and shame." As St. Basil put it, "For they will see in themselves their disgrace, and the marks of their sins. And perhaps the shame in which the sinners are destined to live forever is more horrible than the darkness and the eternal fire." See *Ps.* 33.4, PG 29:360–61. The translation is from Bettenson, *The Later Christian Fathers*, 90. St. Basil also believes that "to be alienated and estranged from God is more intolerable even than the punishment that awaits us in hell." He thinks of punishment after death mostly not in terms of a physical but of a psychological pain, and compares it to the "deprivation of light to the eye." See *LR* (Clarke, 155).

192. *De Fide* (Clarke, 95–96).

economies that of the Son and of the Spirit are concerned with the future of humanity. St. Basil insists that Christ assumes human flesh in order to restore the relationship with humanity and to bring peace between heaven and earth. Being both God and human, he provides the way for salvation in a special community, which is his body, where people have the opportunity to attain his likeness. St. Basil emphasizes the idea that this community is constituted by the Spirit. Together with the Father and the Son, the Holy Spirit fulfills the divine plan of salvation through his own operations. He transforms the lives of the people in the church illuminating the believers and leading them up to union with God. The Spirit assembles all who have been saved into a different social reality where he destroys the barriers, which previously separated people on earth. Coming from *koinonia* of the Trinity he creates a new way of fellowship among believers in the church. St. Basil believes that in this community where the Spirit keeps an order the believers are supposed to grow serving each other with the gifts, which they receive from him. Guiding Christians through the process of transformation, the Holy Spirit together with the other Persons of the Trinity waits for their salvation, which will be fully realized only in the age to come. People will be able to live in the presence of the Triune God in their heavenly home that was prepared for them from the moment of their creation.

CHAPTER 3

Trinitarian Communion, φιλανθρωπία, and the Concept of the Church

A RATHER OBVIOUS CONCLUSION from the previous chapter is that the whole economy of salvation is viewed by St. Basil in terms of God gradually leading humanity toward life in community in which at the end we will enjoy fellowship with God in the kingdom of heaven.[1] The trinitarian communion will be revealed to believers through abiding with the Father, and the Son, and the Holy Spirit. The Greek word, which St. Basil uses for this community of people in heaven, is *ekklesia* that usually translated as the church.[2] As we already noticed, St. Basil's understanding of the church is from an eschatological perspective. This leads us to a concept of the church on earth in which the structure should reflect the future relationships of the eschatological community of believers who will abide in God and who will become like God.[3]

We have to pay attention to the fact that in St. Basil's thought there are at least two dimensions of the church: the church here on earth and the church in heaven.[4] This way of thinking makes St. Basil's ecclesiology

---

1. *HS* 9.23, 15.36; *Ps.* 45, PG 29:421CD, 424A.

2. *A Patristic Greek Lexicon*, 429–32.

3. *HS* 9.2. The idea of "becoming like God" in Basil's writings is discussed in Gross, *The Divinization of the Christian*, 190–93.

4. *Ps.* 45, PG 29:421CD, 424A.

extremely complex. The church exists in the world and for the people from the world in order to change this world and bring them to the reality, which is not of this world, where it still can be called the church.[5] Once again, we can see how St. Basil uses an apophatic approach, but this time he applies it to the mystery of the church. He wants his readers and listeners to understand that the earthly church is not the end. The church does not exist only here and now, but in some mystical way continues its existence in the divine realities, which we do not yet know and cannot yet understand.

HEAVENLY DIMENSION OF THE CHURCH

Although the church in St. Basil's thought is divided in two parts—heavenly and earthly—these two parts are not isolated. While there is a distinction between these two dimensions of the church, there is a strong bond between them as well. According to St. Basil, they are not completely separated: the members of the church who have already experienced physical death, some of whom died as martyrs, continue to be in communion with believers on earth. He believes that people from the earthly congregation can call upon the intercession of martyrs to aid them. St. Basil urges believers to glorify them, to call upon them, and converse with them in prayer because these martyrs are still involved in the life of the earthly church.[6] For example, he mentions the miracles that have been effected by the martyr Jullitta.[7] One of the reasons why St. Basil expresses great interest in the relics of martyrs in several of his letters[8] is the belief that they can confer sanctity both on the place they occupy and on those who are gathered there.[9] In his sermon, *On Feast of Forty Martyrs*, St. Basil declares that the prayer of these forty martyrs, in concordance with God, guarantees the presence of God.[10] In St. Basil's understanding, the role of these saints in the life of people on earth is so important that he calls them "the common guards of the human race."[11]

---

5. See this idea in Lossky, *Mystical Theology*, 175.
6. See homilies *InMJ* in PG 31:237–61 and *InSQM* in PG 31:508–25A.
7. *InMJ* 2, PG 31:241AB.
8. The relics of martyrs are mentioned in St. Basil's letters: *Letter 49*, *Letter 155*, *Letter 197*.
9. *InMJ* 2, PG 31:241AB.
10. *InSQM* 7, PG 31:524A. He uses a verse from Matt 18:20 as the basis for this statement.
11. Ibid., 7, PG 31:524C; translation is mine.

For Christians they are "the good partners in problems, the fellow-workers in prayers, [and] the most powerful intercessors."[12]

In the middle of the fourth century, Christians were still persecuted in some places.[13] It was a time when becoming a martyr and passing from the earthly dimension of the church to the heavenly one was not an abstract option. Martyrs were real Christians whom people knew very well.[14] This caused St. Basil to perceive the church as a present historical gathering and as a future one at the same time. He asserts that these saints belonging already to the heavenly dimension of the church still share the burdens of those believers who struggle to finish their journey on earth. Using his words, the "church of martyrs" is a source of "inexhaustible grace" and of "prepared help for Christians."[15]

St. Basil does not explain the structure of the church in heaven in detail, but he gives us some hints, which clarify what people can expect when they get there. One of the descriptions can be found in his homily *On Psalm 114*:

> That is the country of living, in which there is no night, in which there is no sleep, the image of death, in which there is no eating, no drinking, the supports of our weakness; in which there is no disease, no pains, no remedies, no courts of justice, no businesses, no arts, no money, the beginning of evil, the excuse for wars, the root of hatred; but a country of the living, who have not died through sin, but live the true life in Jesus Christ, to whom be glory and power forever.[16]

This is a gathering of the "firstborns" whose names are "written in the heaven."[17] They experience joyful life, and the main source of this joy is the Holy Spirit with which they are constantly filled.[18] St. Basil believes that this heavenly church is similar to an earthly city.[19] The same way, as every city on earth is ruled by a law, this heavenly Jerusalem is ruled by a law. Of course, there is a difference. In heaven, the church is ruled by "the heavenly law," which distinguishes it from any earthly society.[20] This is a community

12. Ibid.
13. *Letter* 155.
14. See *Letter* 197 in which St. Basil affirms the genuineness of the relics of Dionysius.
15. *InSQM* 7, PG 31:521C.
16. *Ps.* 114. See Way, 358–59.
17. *Ps.* 48, PG 29:448C. See also *Ps.* 45.4, PG 29:424A.
18. *Ps.* 45, PG 29:421CD. See also *Ps.* 32.1, PG 29:324B–D.
19. Ibid. See also *InSQM*, PG 31:509B.
20. Ibid.

where "all the manner of life required by the Gospel," which is "a forecast of the life that follows on the resurrection."[21] Therefore, it is possible for believers to fulfill all its rules after they pass to this new life and attain likeness to Christ.[22] According to St. Basil, people on earth are not able to understand or completely imagine the structure of this city because the city of God or the heavenly church is beyond human comprehension.[23]

St. Basil believes that all citizens live in peace and harmony in this heavenly city, which is the final destination for all saints. To all who are "children in Christ" is granted the same place of rest.

> While one has reached his rest another arrives, another hurries on, but one and the same end awaits them all. He has outstripped us on the way, but we shall all travel the same road, and the same hostelry awaits us all.[24]

St. Basil's phrase "settled way of life" from the homily *On Psalm 45* tells us that these citizens will not move from there anywhere else.[25] In addition, his use of the term "heavenly citizenship"[26] implies that this is their homeland to which they belong.[27] It reminds us of the famous Roman citizenship that provided privileges and protection in the ancient world. Christians have hope that someday they will be able to live in this great city called the heavenly church, but until death, they are still on their earthly journey toward their "eternal habitations."[28]

There is an interesting detail in St. Basil's vision of the church in heaven. All faithful people from all ages, all generations, and all nations will live together in this city. This new eschatological community will consist not only of New Testament believers but Old Testament believers as well.[29] As children of God, believers will spend the eternal life in the company of others who lived before them: patriarchs, apostles, martyrs, confessors, and those who were obedient to God from the beginning. All these people are

---

21. *HS* 15.35.
22. PG 31:940C; *LR* (Clarke, 169).
23. *Ps.* 45, PG 29:421CD. See also *LR* (Clarke, 156).
24. *Letter* 5.2.
25. *Ps.* 45, PG 29:421CD.
26. Ibid.
27. See also this idea of heavenly homeland in *InSQM*, PG 31:509B. See also his *Homily* 4 where Basil states, "Your fatherland is the heavenly Jerusalem." See *Hom.* 4, PG 31: 236C.
28. *Letter* 5.2
29. *LR* (Clarke, 149).

called saints and fellow-citizens.³⁰ Christians have to remember that they are not the first representatives of humanity in this heavenly church. St. Basil persuades them to "follow in the steps" of these faithful people who lived in the Old Testament times: king David, Job, the prophet Daniel.³¹ Following the example of these saints, believers can expect for themselves "a life of blessedness" and "joy among the angels in the presence of Christ."³² They will live in the "heavenly Jerusalem, where thousands of angels are found, the assembled first-born, the thrones of apostles, the seats of prophets, the scepters of patriarchs, the crowns of martyrs, and the praises of the just."³³

Although the church in heaven is beyond history, because it continues its existence after the consummation of all things, this is still the same church of God, which he started to create on earth. In St. Basil's thinking, this new life in the eschatological community and fellowship with the Triune God is the greatest reward for all believers from all generations and from all ends of the world. Using a verse from 1 Cor 2:9, St. Basil confirms that this heavenly church is something wonderful that God prepared only for those who love him.³⁴ The idea behind this verse is quite significant for St. Basil's ecclesiology. The church is the place prepared by God where we build the relationships that we will keep even in the eternity after our death. The most important of all is our relationship with God whom we will see face to face in heaven, and who will be visibly present in the church. Next, these are our relationships with our fellow Christians, this future "rejoicing assembly of saints."³⁵

EARTHLY DIMENSION OF THE CHURCH

The eschatological perspective from which St. Basil perceives the destiny of humans and the divine economy shapes his understanding of the church on earth. According to this perspective, the ultimate purpose of the Triune God for humanity is the establishment of a community in which at the end all the

---

30. Ibid. St. Basil does not explain the conditions in which these saints exist right now. He also does not say anything about a pre-existence of the church as some invisible mystical reality, and he does not call the grouping of these Old Testament saints the church. However, St. Basil shares his conviction that this part of humanity, which was faithful to God during their earthly lives, will live in the heavenly church together with all the New Testament martyrs and saints.

31. Ibid.
32. Ibid.
33. *EHB*, PG 31:444C; translation is from Halton, *Baptism*, 87.
34. *Ps.* 45, PG 29: 421CD.
35. *Ps.* 14.4, PG 29:424A.

faithful will be made "partakers of the grace of Christ" and will share "eternal glory."[36] This implies that the hope for such "unseen rewards" should determine their earthly behavior. In one of his homilies, "*On Selfish Wealth and Greed*," St. Basil motivates his listeners to use their wealth here on earth in a proper way and to help those who are in need. He teaches that for their "stewardship of these corruptible things" their reward shall be glory everlasting. In the heavenly church they will become fathers of "a multitude of children," and "mankind from the very beginning will call *them* blessed."[37] In other homilies, he uses negative arguments in order to convey the same idea to his listeners: "The name of dishonest man is not written in the book of living and he does not belong (is not counted among) to the church of firstborns."[38] In this sense, the rewards and lives of believers in the heavenly church depend on their actions and lives in the earthly church. As St. Basil puts it,

> And in the present time that we may live in a way well pleasing to Him by more vigorous avoidance of what is forbidden and the more earnest observance of what is approved, so that, in the future age of immortality, we may be able to escape the wrath that comes upon sons of disobedience and be found worthy of eternal life and the heavenly kingdom promised from the Lord Jesus Christ to all "who keep the covenant and remember his commandments to do them."[39]

St. Basil believes that there is continuity between the earthly reality and the future state of being when believers receive "crowns of righteousness."[40] Although all who live in the heavenly city share the glory, they have different portions because "spiritual glory shall be distributed to each in proportion as he shall have nobly played the man."[41] St. Basil does not have any doubts

---

36. HS 15.36.

37. *Hom.* 6, PG 31: 265D. In the original text it is *thee* instead of *them*.

38. *Ps.* 48. PG 29:448C. Translation is mine.

39. *De Jud.* (Clarke, 89). In a homily on *Ps.* 28, St. Basil also says that "our labor here is our provision for the future life. And that one who here bears glory and honor to the Lord through his good works will treasure up for himself glory and honor according to the just requital of the Judge" (Way, 194). See also *The Morals* 1.5 (Clarke, 101). There can be found the same idea that "after departure from this life there is no opportunity for good deeds," which will be measured by Christ.

40. *Hom.* 6, PG 31:266AB. Similar notion can be found in St. Basil's *Address to Young* where in chapters 8–10 he calls his hearers to earthly life of virtue as preparation for the heavenly life that is to come. See a discussion of this idea in Holder, "Saint Basil the Great on Secular Education and Christian Virtue," 407–10.

41. HS 16.40.

that there are "differences of dignities"—for as "star differeth from star in glory, so also is the resurrection of the dead."[42]

In order to achieve the state of all "fullness of blessing,"[43] people have to begin their process of perfection in the earthly community where they must evolve together with other believers. St. Basil sees this process as a corporate experience because it is intended for all who are longing for citizenship in the heavenly kingdom.[44] "The mystery of salvation," in St. Basil's thought, is perceived as the gradual progress of human education in which they are brought to perfection in their training for godliness[45] where godliness is always connected to love toward others. It starts with elementary, easier lessons, which lead to total self-denial and humbleness.[46] The best example of this love is that which God himself showed to his disciples in order that they could follow and teach others.

> For, behold, the Lord, for the greatness of His love of men was not content with teaching the word only, but that accurately and clearly He might give us a pattern of humility in the perfection of love He girded Himself and washed the feet of the disciples in person.[47]

This kind of attitude toward their "brethren" God expects from all believers in the church. St. Basil uses the examples of "faithful servants," such as Moses or Paul, as sufficient proof that it is possible to reach that "measure of love towards one's neighbor."[48] They manifested this great love through their willingness to sacrifice their lives for the salvation of all their brethren, even though God did not demand it. In this manner, they rejected the individualistic way of thinking and demonstrated the natural human longing for life in community, which God had planted in them.[49]

St. Basil's arguments for the fellowship of love in the church are rather simple. He starts from God's attitude toward humanity and moves to what He had commanded. As we already mentioned in the previous chapter, St. Basil believes that all persons of the trinitarian communion love humanity, and the goal is to bring people to a new stage where they will "abide" in

---

42. Ibid.
43. Ibid., 15.36.
44. See *Hex.*5.6.
45. *HS* 14.33.
46. *LR* (Wagner, 246). See also *HS* 14.33.
47. *LR* (Clarke, 166).
48. Ibid., 158.
49. Ibid., 154. See also *HS* 5.7, "the Father loves the Son."

Christ's love as he abides in his Father's love.[50] The Father wills "that all men be saved and come to the knowledge of truth," and he acts in the history through the Son and the Spirit.[51] The "love to humanity (φιλανθρωπία) of the Saviour" leads him to *kenosis*, the embodiment, and to the sufferings on the behalf of humanity.[52] The love of the Spirit St. Basil demonstrates through his title φιλανθρώπου Πνεύματος—the Spirit who loves humans.[53] Since the ultimate goal of humans is godlikeness, and the love toward people is an essential feature of Godhead, then we come to the conclusion that the immediate goal of all believers is growth in love. This is the reason that one of the main themes to which Basil returns repeatedly is the mutual love among believers.[54]

Throughout his works, St. Basil insists that love is the principle, which holds the church together,[55] and that it is the distinguishing characteristic of the Christian community.[56] He believes that people need to cooperate with each other in order to fulfill God's plan for them and to accomplish what they are supposed to do. In his homily *On Psalm 33* St. Basil explains that since the mind of one person is not able to understand the greatness of God then there is a need for others. They are gathered for the fellowship (*koinonia*) in order to discover together the laws of their Triune Creator. The more they learn how everything works in the universe the more

---

50. Ibid.

51. *SR* (Clarke, 320).

52. *HS* 8.18.

53. *Ps*. 33.5, PG 29:361D. Daley makes an interesting observation in his article concerning the Cappadocian Fathers and their rhetoric of philanthropy, "In the tradition of Hellenistic ethics, the concept was hardly new. Originally identified above all with love of the gods for the human race, the *philanthropia* was also most often seen, in classical literature as a quality to be praised—and thus encouraged— in tyrants and kings." Therefore, he asserts, Basil's plan of action with the aid of two Gregories and other supporters was "to reaffirm the Christian version of the public side of the philosophical and religious life that pagan Hellenism had admittedly failed to realize." See Daley, "Building a New City," 434–38.

54. According to Francis Young, "The spirit of self-sacrificial love for others is at least the mainspring of Basil's teaching." Young, "Cappadocians," 155.

55. *Letter 70*.

56. *De Fide* (Clarke, 97). See also *The Morals* (Clarke, 102, 131). See the same idea in Koschorke, *Spuren der Alten Liebe*, 17. "Liebe und Frieden, so Basilius, sind das himmlische Erbe das der Herr seiner Kirche hinterlassen hat (Joh 13,35; 14,27). Damit stellen sie zugleich die beiden Grundbestimmungen der Kirche dar und sind die Merkmale, an denen der Leib Christi erkannt waren kann" (Love and peace are the heavenly inheritance, which the Lord has left to his Church [John 13:35; 14:27]. Thus, they also represent two basic rules of the church, and they are the features by which the body of Christ can be detected); translation is mine.

they will praise God.⁵⁷ In St. Basil's thought, the knowledge of God, which people have to gain, is closely connected with salvation and their ultimate purpose.⁵⁸ He explains, "What is the goal of our calling—that there is set before us the being made like to God so far as man's nature allows. Now no likeness is possible without knowledge, nor can there be knowledge without lessons."⁵⁹ In this sense, the salvation and the eschatological future of all humans depends on their cooperation with other believers. According to the previous idea from *Psalm 33*, only together are they able to discover "What is God like?" and "What is His plan for them?" This leads us to the concept of the church as a community of believers where people have to keep close relationships with each other in order to learn together as much as possible about God. Consequently, it will help them to understand how they can attain the likeness of God and to create the community, which God the Trinity had intended for them.

According to St. Basil, the foundation for these close relationships among believers should be love toward God and love toward their neighbors because "it is well known to every disciple of Christ that in these two all is contained."⁶⁰ The first of these commandments tells us how we should act in return for all God's gifts. He is so good that he does not ask for any recompense except "being loved in return."⁶¹ The second commandment completes the first and is linked to it,⁶² for the one "who loves his neighbour fulfils love toward God, since God accepts the favor as conferred on Himself."⁶³ All the other commandments join these two and "form an interconnected whole,"⁶⁴ which is based on love.

St. Basil believes that the observance of all commandments is "necessary for attainment of our salvation" because salvation is not only about calling on the name of the Lord.⁶⁵ It is about doing God's will as he wills with a disposition of love towards him.⁶⁶ In other words, it is about our eternal personal relationship with God, which should be based on mutual

---

57. *Ps.* 33.3, PG 29:357AB.

58. See a good analysis on this topic in Aghiorgoussis, "Image as 'Sign' (*semeion*) of God," 19–54.

59. *HS* 1.2, PG 32:69B (Lewis, 18).

60. *Letter* 9.1.

61. *LR* (Clarke, 156).

62. Ibid., 152.

63. Ibid., 158.

64. *LR* (Wagner, 225).

65. *LR* (Clarke, 147).

66. Ibid., 148.

love and our obedience. On the one hand, when "we excel in the love of God" this love "at the same time animates us to the observance of the Lord's commandments." On the other hand, through the fulfillment of the commandments "love itself will be lastingly and indestructibly preserved."[67] Explaining this idea, St. Basil emphasizes that commandments should be considered as the means through which the kingdom of heaven can be attained.[68] However, God did not leave believers alone with this task, but he is "faithful," and he helps them to "keep His commandments by the grace of Christ in the Holy Spirit."[69]

Through the commandments people have the opportunity "to perfect their lives" and "to ascend to God."[70] In this sense, God provides for people the means and conditions in the church, which can help them to attain all the needed knowledge, in order to receive their "crowns of righteousness" and to become a part of the heavenly kingdom.[71]

> So in training us for the life that follows on the resurrection the Lord sets out all the manner of life required by the Gospel, laying down for us the law of gentleness, of endurance of wrong, of freedom from the defilement that comes of the love of pleasure, and from covetousness, to the end that we may of set purpose win beforehand and achieve all that the life to come of its inherent nature possesses.[72]

God also gives them the teachers who can guide them while they are growing in love.

> He has planted for us, so to say, props, in establishing in His Church apostles, prophets, teachers; and raising our thoughts by the example of the blessed in olden times ... He wishes that the clasping of love, like the tendrils of the vine, should attach us to our neighbors and make us rest on them, so that, in our continual aspirations towards heaven, we may imitate these vines, which raise themselves to the tops of the tallest trees.[73]

---

67. *LR* (Wagner, 243).
68. Ibid., 224.
69. *De Fide* (Clarke, 98).
70. *Hom.* 3, PG 31:213A.
71. See also *De Fide* (Clarke 97).
72. *HS* 15.35.
73. *Hex.* 5.6.

What seems very important for St. Basil is the idea that the relationships of love can be practiced by believers despite our human differences.[74] He states that this fellowship (*koinonia*) brings people together in peace[75] even if they oppose each other in the world because of their lifestyle. However, in order to establish and to keep these relationships, St. Basil teaches, they have to forget about their privileges and their riches when they enter the church of God.[76] The church is a community of reconciliation where people can be reconciled not only to God, but to each other as well. This reconciliation takes place among people who in any other circumstances would not be able to communicate at this level. In Basil's words, "through the Church they are habituated to love (*agape*)."[77] This implies that the Triune God structured the church on earth in a way that through love brings people closer to the community in which they will live hereafter, and where the criteria to measure their dignity will be different. It is not their material possessions or their social rank, but their ability to love according to God's commandments that will be considered by God in the community for which they were made originally.

St. Basil teaches that "the love of God is not something that is taught."[78] It is more like a "seed," which humans have from the moment of their creation. He believes that this inherent tendency can be cultivated.[79] Therefore, having within themselves this inclination to love and the ability to keep the commandments, believers are called to develop and nurture this implanted gift. Then the church can become for them "the school of God's commandments" where they are enabled by God's grace "to exercise it with care, to nourish it with knowledge, and to bring it to perfection."[80] Nevertheless, we have to remember that the grace of God and the love of God toward people are the most important conditions for the existence of this "school." It is God the Trinity, who planted the seed of love into humans. He calls people into this special communion, and only because of his love and mercy they can be saved.[81]

---

74. *Ps.* 48, PG 29:433D. In some sense, this idea is reflected in the current popular expression—"reconciled diversity." See Gunton, "The Church on Earth: the Roots of Community," 66.

75. Ibid. Literally, in the text it is "the fellowship of calling," which implies that these people were called to this fellowship by God.

76. Ibid., PG 29:436A.

77. *Ps.* 48, PG 29:433D.

78. *LR* (Wagner, 233).

79. Ibid.

80. *LR* (Clarke, 153). See also the idea of "training ground" in *Hex.* 1.5, 1.6.

81. *Ps.* 32.3, PG 29:329D.

Discussing the idea of God's merciful attitude toward humanity in the homily *On Psalm 32*, St. Basil comes to a concept of the church as a place where sinners can be spiritually healed. He believes that God is a merciful Judge and his intention is to pardon anyone who sincerely repents. The sinner is still able to become a participant in God's generous and gracious gifts, but he or she has to humble themselves, to regret all their dishonest deeds, and to confess openly what they had done in secret. All these actions lead to the most important step: the sinner has to ask "brethren" to work with him/her together in order to receive healing.[82] This way the love of the community works as medicine and helps to restore a lost brother or sister to fellowship in this community and to fellowship with the Triune God. St. Basil even compares Christians with doctors, who "with much compassion by their knowledge of the teaching of the Lord healing the diseases of souls, [have] to win for them health in Christ and perseverance."[83] In this sense, the restoration of God's image in a particular person can be facilitated by other believers and through their friendship. The church then becomes a place where people who recognize their problems can be assisted in their sincere attempts to restore their true identity and dignity. This love, which God the Trinity wants people to have and to practice, transforms them into true humans.[84]

The notion that friendship with God is closely connected with friendship among believers and with the perfection in love can be also found in St. Basil's homily *On Psalm 44*.[85] Once again, St. Basil uses the examples of Moses and of the disciples who were able to reach the highest level of perfection in love here on earth.[86] This kind of love can bind all of them together as friends and sustain their community. At the same time, he asserts that vicious people cannot be friends with saints and with God because a bad disposition of the heart is not compatible with friendship.[87] His conclusion is based on the exegesis of verse John 15:15. St. Basil states that it is possible

---

82. Ibid., PG 29:329D–332AB.

83. *The Morals* (Clarke, 129).

84. In St. Basil's thought, a person without love ceases to be a human because he "becomes more brutish than the brutes." HS 30.78. See this idea in Fedwick, *The Church*, 118. See also the end of the homily *On Psalm 48* where Basil explains that a man who "did not perceive his own dignity but bowed down to the passion of the flesh, 'hath been compared to senseless beasts, and made like to them.'" The translation is from Way, 331.

85. *Ps.* 44.2, PG 29:392A–D. Interestingly enough, the Son of God is called in this passage πατηρ for all creation. See PG 29:392A.

86. Ibid., PG 29:392BC. See also PG 29:392A, the literal translation is "perfect or complete capacity of love."

87. Ibid., PG 29:392CD.

Trinitarian Communion, φιλανθρωπία, and the Concept of the Church

for perfected people to know truly the beloved one [implied the Son of God] and to become his friends.

Already at this point, we can notice that in St. Basil's thought there is a tension in the attitude of the church toward the sinner, which is in fact twofold. The church should give its love and support to the sinners in order to restore them to the community, but the sinner cannot be a part of community because he/she cannot be a friend to God or to saints. Moreover, St. Basil teaches that the sin of one person affects the entire community. He believes that sin does not remain in one soul alone, but "infects also those who have not manifested zeal for good."[88] In this sense, all the believers are interdependent and the whole church suffers when one of them receives the "infection" of sin. St. Basil uses several illustrations from the Old and New Testaments, which support this idea. He starts with the statement that when a person commits a sin it is harmful to the entire community, and that this does not depend on the multitude of sins or their magnitude.[89] Every sin should be judged as disobedience toward God. Using the story of Achan (Jos 7), St. Basil makes a conclusion that his sin

> became the cause of destruction, not only to himself alone, but also to his wife and children . . . And the punishment of sin was already about to seize upon all the people as well, like a flame, (and that too, though they knew not what had happened, nor had they even excused the sinner).[90]

St. Basil comes to the same conclusion when he examines the New Testament text from 1 Cor 5:1–2. The man, who was accused of the sin, "is not only himself handed over to Satan for destruction . . . but involves the whole Church together in those accusations because it had taken no proceedings against the sin."[91] St. Basil wants to warn his readers of the danger linked to sin and the presence of sinners in the community. He reminds them that in the Old Testament the judgment even of sins committed in ignorance was so severe that sacrifice was "necessary for expiation."[92] After this statement, Basil asks the important question: "What should be said about those who knowingly commit sin or who by their silence acquiesce

---

88. *De Jud.* (Clarke, 85).
89. Ibid, 81–82.
90. Ibid, 82.
91. Ibid, 87.
92. *De Jud.* (Wagner, 45).

in the sinful deeds of others?"[93] This way he introduces us to the idea of the necessity of repentance and to the notion of penance for committed sins.[94]

In his *Letter 22*, St. Basil gives a detailed answer to the above question. He explains the important principle, which Christians are supposed to follow in love when they are dealing with a sinner amongst them.[95] First of all, he wants all people in the community to understand that the mistakes and sins of any person should be considered a loss for the whole community. Therefore, "the Christian ought in Christ's love to grieve and be afflicted at his brother's faults."[96] At the same time, Christians cannot be "indifferent or silent before sinners." They have to show such a person that what they did was wrong, but they "ought to do so with all tenderness, in the fear of God."[97] The main idea behind the explanations in the text of this epistle is that the believers have to do all these things "with the object of converting the sinner."[98] After a person is accused of a sin, which he or she has committed for the first time in their life as a believer, they must repent in order to receive a pardon. If they continue to repeat their wrongdoing after the first and second admonition, they must be brought before the authorities. If even after that step the sinner fails to be set right, "he is to be cut off from the rest as one that maketh to offend, and regarded as a heathen and a publican."[99] The only reason for such strict rules or the severe actions is "the security of them that are obedient."[100] Once again, St. Basil reminds Christians of the influence of sin on the community paraphrasing the meaning of Proverb 29:16, "When the impious fall the righteous tremble."[101] The attitude of love toward the sinner should not bring danger to the existence of the whole community. There must be some limits, which do not allow Christians to get

---

93. Ibid.

94. This idea of penitents who should not only repent, but they "need also fruits meet for repentance" can be found in *The Morals* 1.4 (Clarke, 101), where under "fruits" St. Basil means "good deeds," which "please" God. See the next sentence in *The Morals* 1.5 (Clarke, 101).

95. Although this is one of St. Basil's so called "ascetic" epistles, it is possible to use it in connection with life of all Christians who want to follow the way of perfection. The ideas from the ascetic writings can be equally well applied to the church because St. Basil was trying to integrate this practice into the life of the church. See this idea in Meyendorff, *The Byzantine Legacy*, 201. See this thought also in Fedwick, *The Church*, 20–22.

96. *Letter* 23.3.

97. Ibid.

98. Ibid.

99. Ibid.

100. Ibid.

101. Ibid.

into the situation in which love can be abused by the sinner. The structure of the church and its rules should protect its members from the destruction caused by sin.

In his later work, St. Basil describes a penitential system in more detail, which can be found in his 'canonical' letters to Amphilochius.[102] The principles that he applies to life in the church are the same as are mentioned in his earlier *Letter 22*. The goal of penance is the rehabilitation and restoration of the sinner into the church.[103] The stages of recovery were created in order to help him/her not to fall back into their sins. As we already noted, the basis for all actions taken by Christians should be love, which includes both the sinner and the rest of community. All other members are warned by these rules, and they are also guarded from the influence of evil.[104] Through this system and its practice, Christians are reminded that their lives are bound together in the community. The bond is "the law of love,"[105] which includes assistance to a person, who has to "recognize his defects" and who needs someone that "can reprove him" and "set him right with kindness and compassion."[106] This "law of love" calls for cooperation between believers in the fight against sin in the community.

In St. Basil's thought, the church on earth serves as the place where all people learn to live together striving for perfection in love. They are expected to go through the transformation themselves and to help others move in the same direction toward union with the Triune God leaving behind all iniquities, sins, and weaknesses.

CONCLUSION TO CHAPTER 3

Although St. Basil's understanding of the church in two dimensions is rather complex, we can notice a particular logic behind this idea that gives hope to believers on earth. This helps Christians feel supported by the larger *ekklesia*, which includes all the faithful throughout the history of humanity. In this sense, the identity of the members of the church is formed by the understanding that they have different citizenship. They belong not only to

---

102. These are *Letters* 188, 199, 217. See the chronological table of the life and works of St. Basil in Fedwick, *The Church*, 133–55. Accordingly, the *Letter* 22 was written in 368, the *Letter* 188 in 374, and the *Letters* 199 and 217 in 375.

103. *Letter* 217.82.

104. *Letter* 217.84.

105. *LR* (Clarke, 163). Although St. Basil uses this term in a different work, it perfectly conveys his idea of love in these circumstances.

106. Ibid.

a local community, but to the heavenly realm as well. Life in the eschatological community together with the other saints will be their reward from the Triune God when they continue their existence in the divine realities after death.

From what has preceded, we can also conclude that St. Basil describes the church as a community of people who are gathered by God's love (φιλανθρωπία). The trinitarian love toward humanity builds up the community and encourages its members to love each other. God the Trinity structured the life of this community on earth in a way that each person has the opportunity to develop new and better relationships, which lead to reconciliation and peace. According to St. Basil, the church is a place where people may receive healing and recover from their sins. For each woman and man the means are provided to reach the full measure of love and to restore their dignity. In order to fulfill these purposes, Christians have to follow God's commandments or God's "law of love." They must support each other's efforts on the way to their ultimate destiny, their heavenly home, where they will continue to keep these relationships of love with the Triune God and with other members of the church.

CHAPTER 4

Persons of the Trinity and the Metaphors of the Church

ST. BASIL DOES NOT explain the nature and the essence of the church in a systematic way because it was against his method of epistemology and his apophatic approach. In his opinion, the church was created by the Triune God, and it is a mystery like other theological realities. His language of the church is often the language of analogy, which reflects the Eastern mystical way of thinking.[1] In his writings, St. Basil introduces a wide range of metaphors of the church that are closely connected with the Persons of the Trinity. We will try to follow St. Basil's method of interpretation and logic so that we can grasp the broader application of these key metaphors. This analytical approach contributes to the proper understanding of his ideas and can help us to clarify his concept of the church.

---

1. In the writings of the contemporary Orthodox theologians, we still can find similar approaches to the church. As Pomazansky noted in his *Orthodox Dogmatic Theology* the character of the church can be best explained by the biblical metaphors because it is "difficult to embrace in a short verbal formula" and "the life of the Church in its essence is mystical." See Pomazansky, *Orthodox Dogmatic Theology*, 222–24.

GOD AS THE FATHER AND THE CHURCH AS THE MOTHER

St. Basil's idea of the Trinity uses the language of *ousia* and *hypostaseis* to address the question of the distinctness between the three divine Persons. In his opinion, each divine *hypostasis* is "contemplated in the special property."[2] For God the Father this "property" is revealed as his Fatherhood.[3] In his writings, St. Basil expresses the idea that God is the real Father of the whole of humanity, and human parents are only instruments for the procreation of children.[4] Trying to prove Eunomius wrong and suggesting the correct understanding of the Father and the Son in his second book *Against Eunomius*, St. Basil comes to an important conclusion. God can be called our Father in "the original true meaning" of this word because he brought us "through our bodily parents into existence from non-existence" and adopted us through his grace.[5] In St. Basil's thought, this statement is true not only for Christians but for all faithful people, even if they lived before Christ. Using the context of Job 1:18–22 as an example, St. Basil ascribes the words of explanation to Job:

> I was called a father for as long a time as He who made me wished it. He willed, in turn, to take from me the crown of offspring. I do not resist Him. May that which seems good to the Lord prevail. He is the Maker of my children; I am His instrument.[6]

Through such allusions to God's paternity St. Basil shows the attitude of God toward humanity. The key phrase of this passage, "May that which seems good to the Lord prevail," demonstrates his assurance in God's providential activity and care toward his creation. According to St. Basil, God is wise and "He metes out that which is profitable to His servants," and we should "only love the dispensations of His wisdom."[7] In the last paragraph of the homily, St. Basil explains that Job's children who died are not completely dead, but they "live on in the best part of their nature." They have "gone before to await their father." With an obvious joy St. Basil declares, "All of

---

2. *Letter* 214. 4.

3. Ibid.

4. *CE*, 2.2, PG 29:624AB. See this idea in Orphanos, *Salvation and Creation*, 76. See also *Hom.* 21 in Wagner, 502. PG 31:560B.

5. *CE*, 2.23, PG 29:624B. See also *Hom.* 26.2 (DelCogliano, 198). "All are our relatives, all our brothers, all descendants of one father. If you seek your spiritual father, it is he who is in heaven."

6. *Hom.* 21 (Wagner, 502). PG 31:560B.

7. Ibid., 504.

them will stand about Job when the Judge of human life will gather together the universal Church."[8] God is not only creator of this world, but he is the Father whose goal is to keep his children alive and provide for them a place where they will experience "the glory everlasting."[9] This place, St. Basil suggests, is the church universal, which welcomes all children of the Father.

If we look at the images, which describe the involvement of God the Father in the life of the church, we will not be surprised to find that he is perceived by St. Basil as the Father of the church. In poetical language, St. Basil introduces the image of God as a loving parent in his homily *On Psalm 44*.[10] The titles that he ascribes to the church are "the daughter of the King" and "the bride of Christ."[11] These words show the implied logic of the homily: the church is the bride of the Son, and at the same time, she is the daughter of the Father who adopted her through his love.[12] Developing this daughter/bride analogy a little bit further, St. Basil comes to a logical conclusion that the church is the mother (ἡ μήτηρ) of all children of Christ.[13] At this point St. Basil introduces a change to the metaphor because previously the believers were presented as children of God the Father. However, this illustration can help us to understand essential aspects of St. Basil's ecclesiology.

The significance of this motherhood imagery appears to be two-fold. In the first place, the identity of the church is primarily determined by her relations to the Father and to Christ as her bridegroom, rather than by her relation to the believers who constitute the community. In St. Basil's thought, it is not just a human institution, but also a mystical entity that is united with the Father and the Son in a very special way. In the second place, the identity of a believer is connected with the non-biological birth,

8. Ibid., 505.
9. PG 31:564AB. Ibid.
10. *Ps. 44*, PG 29:388A–413D. In English version of the Bible, this is Psalm 45.
11. Ibid, PG 29:412A.
12. Ibid, PG 29:409A.
13. Ibid., PG 29:413C. Traits of, and allusions to, the church as the mother, appear already in the works of other Church Fathers, who lived before St. Basil. It seems that he just followed the method of interpretation, which was common in the church at that time. For example, Eusebius in his *Ecclesiastical History* calls the church "Virgin Mother" of believers when he describes in detail the sufferings of the Christians of Gaul during the persecutions around the year 177. See Eusebius of Caesarea, *Ecclesiastical History*, 429. Also Cyprian in his famous saying use the same imagery: "He can no longer have God for his Father who has not the Church for his mother; . . . he who gathereth elsewhere than in the Church scatters the Church of Christ." See Cyprian, *On the Unity of the Church*, 423. See also Irenaeus, *Against Heresies* 3.24.1 (458), where he says that "where the Spirit of God is there is the Church and . . . those who do not partake of Him" are not nourished "into life from the mother's breasts" implying the church. See similar notion of church's motherhood in *Second Clement*, 107–9, 121.

which happens through the mother-church.[14] From now on, the believers are called "the sons of Christ's bride"[15] and "the sons of the Church."[16] Although St. Basil uses a masculine language in these particular phrases, we can understand from the context of the Psalm that the daughters are included as well. It is especially true for the exegesis of the verse 14, which mentions virgin companions of "the bride."[17]

St. Basil declares that the church is called by God and should forget "*her* people and *her* father's house"[18] and instead she receives "the sons of the Gospel."[19] His interpretation of this phrase is quite important. It shows the role, which the church plays in salvation. There is an interesting nuance in St. Basil's use of the verb λαμβάνω. The church does not produce the children for God, but she *receives* them as a gift from God on account of her obedience.[20] This reminds us of St. Basil's analogy of the earthly parents who are only the instruments because God is the real Father of all people. However, the church is entrusted with a great responsibility—to raise children of God and to guide them until they become mature. For this reason, she feeds them as catechumens with milk, then "weans" them through baptism, and after that provides them "the solid food of dogmata."[21] According to St. Basil, the church as a good mother does her job properly because the deeds of her children are even more incredible than the deeds of Patriarchs.[22] Her

---

14. Following the logic of the Eastern Church Fathers on this "motherhood" imagery Zizioulas introduced a very good term, "ecclesial hypostasis," which characterizes the identity of a believer that he receives through this non-biological birth. On this issue, see Zizioulas, *Being as Communion*, 56–57. See also *Letter* 227, where St. Basil is using similar analogy when he gives the advice: "Do not enter into a dispute with your Mother Church at Nicopolis." He implies the local congregation to which the person belongs.

15. *Ps.* 44, PG 29:413C.

16. Ibid., PG 29:413B.

17. See ibid., PG 29:412D.

18. Ibid., PG 29:408D. St. Basil implies Gentile religions. In the original phrase of the Psalm the pronoun "your" is used instead of "her," and it goes like "forget your people and your father's house."

19. Ibid., PG 29:413B.

20. Ibid. We have to mention that in his homily *Exhortation to Holy Baptism* St. Basil does say that the church goes through the "birth pain" and "gives birth" to Christians through baptism, but it does not contradict the fact that she receives these children from God. See PG 31:425A.

21. *EHB*, PG 31:425A. Probably St. Basil follows here the biblical metaphor of "milk" and "solid food" from 1 Cor 3:3.

22. Ibid., PG 29:413BC.

children that are born "through Christ"[23] become "saints" and "rulers"[24] of the earth.

Following St. Basil's logic, we come to a conclusion that there are some conditions, which the church should fulfill in order to receive the children. She should forget the customs of her old house, which means Gentile culture, humbly accept "the Gospel teaching," and be obedient to God.[25] St. Basil keeps pointing to these particular requirements in this homily because, in his thought, the idea of receiving the Gospel is connected with "abiding in the sound and unperverted doctrine."[26] St. Basil is probably concerned with the preservation of the church's identity and unity in face of the heretical dissensions among believers. Obviously, there is a strong sense of oneness of the church in this imagery. There is only one bride of Christ, which should demonstrate the fidelity to the Gospel and become the mother of believers. Using the vivid language of Psalm 44, St. Basil shows the authority of the church with which she is endowed from God. The story ends with the picture of the mother-church as the queen appointing her children ("sons of the Gospel") as rulers to the different parts of the earth.[27] For these actions, her name will be remembered through all generations, and she will be confessed and praised among the nations.[28] St. Basil clarifies this statement introducing one more metaphor. It is not the church that will be worshiped by all people, but Christ as "her face."[29] Therefore, God will be worshiped and glorified through the church and her actions in history, which become inseparable from the proclamation of the Gospel.

St. Basil mentions again the motherhood of the church in his homily *On the Feast of the Forty Martyrs*. He explains that the city of God (heavenly dimension of the church) where these martyrs will live forever is the heavenly Jerusalem and this city is the mother of Paul and others like him.[30] Thereby, he implies that heavenly church is the mother of all Christians who went through sufferings in this earthly life and kept their faith. In the same paragraph of this homily, he repeats the idea that all these martyrs have "a common Father who is God." This fact makes them members of the same spiritual family—the church. Just as in the case of the children of Job, the

23. Ibid., PG 29:413B.
24. Ibid., PG 29:413C.
25. Ibid., PG 29:409AB.
26. See *Letter* 251.4.
27. *Ps*. 44, PG 29:413C.
28. Ibid., PG 29:413D.
29. Ibid., PG 29:409C.
30. *InSQM* 2, PG 31:509B.

mother-church welcomes her children, whom this world put under trials and murdered for their faithfulness to their Lord and Savior.[31]

One more time St. Basil employs the same metaphor of the mother-church in his homily "*On Detachment from Worldly Goods.*"[32] This homily was preached in reference to a fire, which occurred in the near neighborhood of the church on the previous evening. Upon the careful analysis of this event, St. Basil draws out two conclusions. First, the church as "our common mother" fought together with the Savior against the Devil and won the battle.[33] This means that one of the functions of the church is the protection of her children from "the Foe and his engines of the war."[34] According to St. Basil, for this reason the church was built by Christ as "the fold for His flock." He believes that this kind of event can serve as "the memorials erected by the Savior," which points to "His victory over the fury of the Devil."[35] In St. Basil's thinking, the fact that the church "remained unharmed"[36] shows that she has a special place in the divine plan. Second, the Lord is always present in the church and "He is at His post even now, in our midst."[37] In this sense, the power and the life of the church completely depends on this divine presence and her connection to God. She is honored and recognized as the mother of all believers only when she has an intimate relationship with the Father of her children.

METAPHORS FOR CHRIST AND THE CHURCH

Throughout St. Basil's writings, we can find different metaphors that describe the relationship between Christ and believers in the church: a vine and the branches,[38] the bride and the Bridegroom,[39] the body and its member,[40] brothers [and sisters] in the family of God.[41] Among these metaphors there is one, which occupies a prominent place in St. Basil's thought and was

---

31. Ibid., 4, PG 31:512BC.
32. *Hom.* 21, PG 31: 540CD–564AB.
33. PG 31:556C. See also the translation in Wagner, 499.
34. *Hom.* 21 (Wagner, 499).
35. Ibid.
36. Ibid., 500.
37. Ibid.
38. *Hex.* 5.6; *The Morals* 80.3, 20 (Clarke, 127, 128).
39. *Ps.* 44; *The Morals* 80.18 (Clarke, 128).
40. *Letter* 70.
41. *LR* (Clarke, 167); *The Morals* (Clarke, 128).

mentioned by him many times and on different occasions.[42] This is the well-known biblical metaphor of the church as the body of Christ.[43] Through this metaphor, St. Basil introduces us to fundamental ecclesiological principles. He believes that Christians should see their identity as bound up members of one body, which God unites so that people may live worthy of Christ as their head.[44] This is not so much about the things, which people can accomplish, or about some moral attainment, but is about the relationships, which believers can have with God, with each other, and with the world.

It is very important to mention that when St. Basil uses the metaphor of the body, he does not mean only people from a local congregation or from several communities that are located near each other. He perceives the church as a whole—"we all, the rest, as many as have believed, are the members of Christ."[45] In another place, he asks his readers, "For what could be more delightful than to behold all, who are separated by distances so vast, bound together by the union effected by love into one harmony of members in Christ's body?"[46] Although in his letters St. Basil often uses the plural form οἱ ἐκκλεσίαι instead of the singular ἡ ἐκκλεσία he still thinks of believers in these local congregations as member of only one body of Christ.[47] St. Basil clearly expresses this vision of the church through the recalling of the past: "I thought that I had gone back to the good old times, when God's Churches flourished, rooted in faith, united in love, all the members being in harmony, as though in one body."[48] In St. Basil's thought, this "body" is

---

42. For example, *Letter 70*; *Letter 97*; *Letter 243.1*; *Letter 222*; *Letter 266.1*; *Ps. 44.5*, PG 29:397CD; *De Jud.*, PG 31:660A; *HS* 5.9; *HS* 26.61; *The Morals* 60 (Clarke, 117, 128); *LR* (Clarke, 164). Probably, St. Basil followed the conviction shared by other believers of his time, which originates from Paul's teaching. As Kelly noticed, the conception of the mystical body of Christ "constitutes the core of the patristic notion of the Church and its most fruitful element" in the setting of trinitarian or christological argument. Kelly, *Early Christian Doctrines*, 403.

43. Sometimes St. Basil uses the whole phrase "body of Christ" and even adds explanations, and in some epistles, he just employs the word "body" for a quick reference to the church. See, for example, *Letter 222, Letter 22.3*. Koschorke argues that "body of Christ" is the central image of the church in St. Basil's ecclesiology. See Koschorke, *Spuren der Alten Liebe*, 30.

44. *The Morals* 80.4 (Clarke, 102).

45. *Ps.* 44.5, PG 29:397CD, 400A. The translation is from Smith, *St. Basil the Great*, 112.

46. *Letter 70*.

47. See for example, *Letter 156, Letter 164* and *Letter 243*. St. Basil uses the plural expression mostly in his letters when he talks about the local congregations, and in other works, he uses singular noun referring to the church.

48. *Letter 164*.

gathered throughout the ages,[49] it covers different geographical locations, and it will be kept by God in eternity. In his homily *On Psalm 44*, he explains, "The Church is the body of the Lord and He Himself is the Head of the Church ... Therefore, the saying: 'God hath blessed thee'; that is to say, He has filled thy members and thy body with blessings from Himself for eternity, that is to say, for time without end."[50] Literally, he is saying that the period of time when God will be filling the body with his good things is "endless."[51] Once again, we notice the eschatological perspective in St. Basil's thought. From the quotation above, we can understand that he applies this metaphor to both dimensions of the church: to the eschatological reality and to that which is still in process of realization. Here on the earth it is composed of those who are learning to live in harmony with one another and "in love of Christ, as members of a body."[52] This is the condition on which they will be allowed to join the eternal dimension of the church. Consequently, they may receive eternal life only by being united to their head and to each other. Otherwise, St. Basil believes, their destiny may be completely opposite because "those who are divided and at variance with one another deserve to perish."[53]

Most of the time, when St. Basil uses the phrase "the body of Christ," he demonstrates his care for the unity of the church and for ecclesiastical obedience.[54] He is concerned that the earthly part of the body is struggling and cannot attain its perfection in face of dissensions and divisions. St. Basil declares,

> ... there should be no schisms in the body, but that the members should have the same care for one another, being moved, no doubt, by the one indwelling Spirit. Why has it been thus arranged? I think that such order and discipline may be preserved far more in the Church of God, to which it has been said: "Ye are the body of Christ and severally members thereof," since the one

---

49. We already mentioned in this book that St. Basil sees the Old Testament saints as part of the church. When we discussed the image of the church as the mother, we also noticed that Job's children are included in the church as well.

50. Ps. 44.5 (Way, 284). PG 29:397CD, 400A. See alternative translation in Smith, *St. Basil the Great*, 112.

51. Ibid., PG 29:400A.

52. *The Morals* (Clarke, 117).

53. Ibid.

54. This can be true for all other images, which we mentioned in the beginning, because unity of the church is the theme that had been the main focal point of St. Basil's attention and consideration throughout his life time.

and only true head, that is Christ, clearly holds and unites each to other with a view to the production of harmony.[55]

This organic metaphor of the body points to the important aspect of the corporate life of believers. Christians are called to share in the life of the church as members, while Christ, as their head, acts as the unifying principle. Therefore, the harmony and the unity in the church appear as the mark of Christ's presence among them. St. Basil strongly believes that "where no harmony is preserved, no bound of peace kept, no meekness in the spirit treasured, but divisions and strife and jealousy are found—it would be very presumptuous to call such men members of Christ or say they are ruled by Him."[56] Only cooperation and love among the believers shows that the Lord is present with them.

In his writings, St. Basil draws out his picture of a healthy church. As any living organism, it is supposed to grow and develop. On the one hand, it "having nourishment ministered" from its head "increaseth with the increase of God."[57] On the other hand, "the whole body fitly joined together and compacted by that which every joint supplieth, according to the effectual working in the measure of every part, maketh increase of the body."[58] This means that God and the church work together when each part of the body does work, and it grows and builds itself up in love. Although there is a distinction between clergy and laity, each member contributes to the common activity of the "body," and at the same time, each member receives help from others. St. Basil places clergy "at the top" because they are supposed to exercise their "own watchful forethought for every portion of the body underneath" so that "no part of the body is deprived of due care."[59] He asks those who are entrusted with the authority of the "care of souls" "to keep each other and all together," and to "cherish them as beloved children."[60] St. Basil perceives the structure of the church as hierarchical. However, he insists that all members of Christ's body should be equal in honor, and that nobody should be neglected due to his/her small "gifts."

> That since the gifts of the Spirit are different, and neither is one able to receive all nor all the same gifts, each should abide with sobriety and gratitude in the gift given him, and all should be

55. *De Jud.* (Clarke, 80).
56. Ibid.
57. *HS* 5.9. The modern translation of this phrase is "grows as God causes it to grow." Original quotation is from Col 2:19, which St. Basil is interpreting in this passage.
58. Ibid. The original quotation is from Eph 4:15–16.
59. *Letter* 222.
60. Ibid.

harmonious with one another in the love of Christ, as members of a body. So who is inferior in gifts should not despair of himself in comparison with him that excels, no should the greater despise the less.[61]

In Basil's view, each member of the "body" is precious to the Lord. Following the biblical text from 1 Cor 12:25, he reminds his readers that "whether one member suffereth, all the members suffer with it; or one member is honored, all members rejoice with it."[62] Even when the believer commits sins and does not obey authorities in the church, and must be excluded from the community, he or she still "should be grieved over as a limb cut from the body."[63] St. Basil thinks that it is a painful loss for the body as well as for the person who caused the problems. Both for this person and for the community this loss has eternal consequences. He/she is excluded not only from the local congregation or the earthly church but also from the heavenly kingdom. This person is deprived of their citizenship in this "new Jerusalem" and he/she is lost forever.

The statement above about the grief of the lost "limb" shows that St. Basil, as many of the Church Fathers before him, believes that the true Christian has no life apart from Christ's body, which is the church, because she/he is a member of that body.[64] For this reason, St. Basil explains that life in solitude does not bring any benefits. On the contrary, Christians who live alone and do not "serve the common welfare in a way well-pleasing to God" cannot preserve "their subjection" to Christ.[65] They have "the idle and fruitless life"[66] because they do not exercise their gifts, which in the life of community become "the common property of their fellows."[67] "When brethren live together in community," St. Basil writes, "then there is a stadium for athletic exercise, a method for development, a combined course of training and practice in the Lord's commands."[68] In St. Basil's opinion, those who constitute the church are all interdependent, and they attain their union to God not as isolated individuals, but as the living body. Once incorporated into

---

61. *The Morals* 60 (Clarke, 117).

62. *De Jud.* (Clarke, 80).

63. *Letter* 22.3. About the believers who have sinned, St. Basil says that instead of the members of Christ they become "members of a harlot." See *Ps.* 28 (Way, 197).

64. Ignatius of Antioch, *To Philadelphians* 3.2; Irenaeus, *Against Heresies* 3. 24.1; Cyprian, *On the Unity of the Church* 6. See this idea in O'Grady, *The Church in the Theology of Karl Barth*, 245.

65. *LR* (Clarke, 164).

66. Ibid.

67. Ibid.

68. *LR* 7. The translation is from Bettenson, *The Later Christian Fathers*, 95.

community, the believers became a part of life-giving "body" that maintains the mystical union with Christ as its head. Therefore, to leave this body or break the connection with it means to cut themselves from the source of life. As branches are not able to live without a vine and limbs without a body, so believers cannot live apart from God and from his church. This life as members is a part of the divine plan, which God has for fallen humanity.[69] The Lord himself, Basil posits, "has deigned to style the universal Church of God His body," and he "has moreover granted to all of us to live in intimate association with one another."[70] He provided the opportunity for all people to join this dynamic and living organism "that in the goodly order of *their* Church *they* may keep *their* strength and the foundation of *their* faith in Christ; that God's name may be glorified and the good gift of love increase and abound."[71] Through the church, God unites humanity to himself and to each other forming of them the mystical entity. Their ultimate goal is eternal life together and "the glory of God."[72]

As far as other christological metaphors are concerned, St. Basil uses them to convey similar ideas about the relation between Christ and the church. He repeats his arguments and discusses oneness of the church in connection with Christ as the source of its unity. As the preacher of love par excellence, Basil emphasizes that this union should be "effected by love."[73] Although he does not deal with those metaphors as extensively as he does with the metaphor of the body of Christ, St. Basil adds some important details to the previous picture of the church.

In his homily *On Psalm 44*, St. Basil describes the church as "the one perfect dove of Christ,"[74] which receives the believers in "the right side of Christ's country"[75] because they are known for their good deeds. At the same time, she separates them from the "evil" people.[76] St. Basil goes on to posit that the church, like "a shepherd," is able to make a distinction between "the lambs and the goats."[77] It is obviously an allusion to the Last Judgment from Matt 25:31 when all the nations will be gathered before Christ, and

---

69. Ps. 45, PG 29:421CD, 424A. The ultimate goal of God is to collect all people into a "city," "heavenly Jerusalem."

70. *Letter* 243. See also *HS* 26.61.

71. *Letter* 222.

72. LR 7. See Bettenson, *The Later Christian Fathers*, 95.

73. *Letter* 70.

74. Ps. 44 (Way, 291).

75. Ibid. PG 29:408C.

76. Ibid.

77. Ibid. See Way, 291.

he will separate people from one another. Using this metaphor, St. Basil expresses the conviction that the church has the authority to make this kind of judgment as well. He continues and illustrates this point of view with some more metaphors. In the next sentence, the church is described as "the queen" and as "the soul" who is engaged to her "Bridegroom the Word." He stresses the idea that the church is "not ruled by sin."[78] On the contrary, she is "a partaker" of the kingdom of Christ, and she stays at the right hand of the Savior.[79] In Eastern culture, the place at the right hand is for the most respected and honored persons. This reminds us that according to the biblical testimony, Christ himself sits at the right hand of his Father.[80] Probably, when St. Basil presents the church next to Christ, he follows this biblical metaphor. One more time, he makes clear that the church is defined not by its relation to the existing gathering of believers but from the perspective of the new creation of God. She is called the "perfect dove" and she is presented as "not ruled by sin" because of who she will be in Christ's kingdom. In St. Basil's thought, the identity of the church is completely defined by her eschatological state. Using the same metaphor of "queen" from Psalm 44, St. Basil develops this idea in his *Homily 8* and applies it to the believers. St. Basil asserts that everything that was said about the church can be said about "every soul" because the church as "a whole" consists of individuals.[81] In this sense, the identity of a believer is closely connected with the church, and it can be defined only through his/her participation in the heavenly dimension. St. Basil persuades his listeners to think about the present and the future remembering that they will be rewarded according to their deserts by the righteous Judge.[82]

METAPHORS FOR THE SPIRIT AND THE CHURCH

Although the discussion of the Person of the Holy Spirit occupies a considerable place in St. Basil's teaching, we cannot find many separate metaphors, which describe his work in the church.[83] However, the Spirit is present in

---

78. Ibid. PG 29:408C.
79. Ibid.
80. See, for example, Eph 1:20.
81. *Hom.* 8, PG 31:328B.
82. Ibid., PG 31:328C.
83. In the homily on *Ps.* 44, the Holy Spirit is called "the Scribe" and "the anointing of joy" and in treatise *On the Holy Spirit* in chapter 26, he is compared to a "form" and to a "place" with sanctified people. Unfortunately, all these metaphors do not play such prominent role in St. Basil's thought as the christological images.

christological metaphors where he plays an important role. He indwells[84] the "body" and unites its members with each other.[85] Through participation and the sanctifying work of the Spirit, an assembly of people becomes the church.[86] As the giver and dispenser of life,[87] he supports and shapes the entire life of the "Body."

The Holy Spirit who is the origin of sanctification[88] brings believers to perfection and makes them "spiritual by fellowship with Himself."[89] In St. Basil's view, sanctification is one of the Spirit's main functions because "nothing is sanctified but only by the presence of the Spirit."[90] He illustrates this idea through a metaphor when he compares the Holy Spirit to a "form."[91] St. Basil writes that the Spirit is analogous to a form inasmuch as he "perfects rational beings, completing their excellence" that at the end they become "conformed to the image of the Son of God."[92] Through this work of the Spirit, "the minds of all people who form the Church as the body of Christ will be renewed" and this means "the whole Church will be renewed."[93] St. Basil emphasizes that this means the renewal of the mind "through the Spirit" in everyone who complete the body of the church of Christ.[94] He writes more on this matter in his treatise *On the Holy Spirit* where he maintains that the Spirit "illuminates" the minds of believers. When they "worship in the Spirit," they have their minds "working in the light."[95]

This idea of "renewal" or transformation of the believer's inner being was mentioned once more in St. Basil's homily *On Psalm 32*. Following 1 Cor 12:3, St. Basil affirms that this is the Spirit who enables people to confess that "Jesus is the Lord." No one can worship him if he/she does not have "the right spirit," which "was renewed" inside him or her.[96] St. Basil

---

84. *De Jud.* (Clarke, 80).

85. *HS* 26.61.

86. *HS* 15. See also *Ps.* 32, PG 29:333C. In this homily, Basil asserts, "Everything is sanctified only through the Spirit."

87. *HS* 9.22, 15.35–36.

88. Ibid.

89. Ibid.

90. *Ps.* 32.4, PG 29:333C. See also *HS* 16.38.

91. *HS* 26.61.

92. Ibid.

93. *Ps.* 29, PG 29:308A.

94. Ibid. Interestingly enough that St. Basil uses a little bit different expression this time—it is "the body of the church of Christ."

95. *HS* 26.64 (Lewis, 123).

96. *Ps.* 32, PG 29:325B.

implies that the Holy Spirit "renews" the believers and creates this "right" attitude in them when they receive the ability to confess Christ as their Lord and Savior. Commenting on verse three of the same psalm, St. Basil continues the discussion of this topic. He asserts that when the believers "sing a new song," which is "the teaching of the Lord" in "the renewed spirit," then they "destroy" the old person in themselves and become a new one "day after day."[97] This "new song" is about the incarnation of the Lord, about the mystery of his resurrection, and about "the regeneration and renewal of the whole world," which "became old under sin."[98] In this sentence, we can notice an idea of the transformation, which is available for the whole world through the work of the Spirit in the church. It reminds us that as the Spirit was involved in the creation of the world, so he still plays a leading role in the re-creation of this world in order to bring it to the new state, or to shape it to a new form.

In his homily *On Psalm 44*, St. Basil also uses an interesting metaphor for the Holy Spirit where he is presented as "the Scribe" (Γραμματεύς) because he writes on believer's hearts[99] and because he is wise and teaches everybody.[100] St. Basil also mentions in another homily the role of the Spirit in establishing the truth.[101] As the "Intercessor" or "Helper," and as the Spirit of truth, he calls all people to come together and listen to the preaching (κηρύγμα). Through the prophets and apostles, he assembles everyone who was saved all over the earth until the end of the world (οἰκουμέωη).[102] St. Basil is convinced that "the advice," which is given by the Holy Spirit, leads the believers to "the good end," which is "the blessed end/goal of the human life."[103]

St. Basil develops this idea of the blessed life a little bit further in his homily *On Psalm 61*. Implying the eschatological events, he talks about the Spirit of promise. In St. Basil's opinion, every believer is a servant of a great

---

97. Ibid.

98. Ibid, PG 29:325C. Further insight into St. Basil's understanding of renewal can be found in his *Homily 9*. Interpreting the words from Psalm 50:12—"Create in me a clean heart"—St. Basil explains that it does not mean making "something now but renew what has grown old through evils." Then he adds that the word "make" means not that something was brought out of non-being, but that beings are transformed and that the meaning of improvement has been assigned to the term "creation." See *Homily Explaining That God Is Not the Cause of Evil*, in Harrison, *On the Human Condition*, 69.

99. *Ps.* 44, PG 29:396AB.

100. Ibid., PG 29:396A.

101. *Ps.* 48, PG 29:433A

102. Ibid.

103. *Ps.* 45, PG 29:416A.

king [God], and he/she is called by him to be a member of his household.[104] This means that Christians should be proud of who they are and of the king whom they serve. Those, who received the Spirit of promise, are sealed by him as the accepted children of God.[105]

In the treatise *On the Holy Spirit*, St. Basil introduces one more metaphor for the Holy Spirit where he is called "the place" of those who are sanctified.[106] In St. Basil's opinion, this metaphor means that only in the Spirit as in a special "place" can we have a "vision" of God. Interpreting the story of Moses, he comes to a conclusion that the Spirit is "the special and peculiar place of true worship."[107] The believers are supposed to bring their "sacrifice of praise" and "spiritual" offerings "in spirit and in truth." Then the question arises: "In what place do we offer it?" St. Basil goes on and explains that the Spirit should be perceived as the presence of God in the believer's life.

> It follows that the Spirit is verily the place of the saints and the saint is the proper place for the Spirit, offering himself as he does for the indwelling of God, and called God's Temple.[108]

St. Basil thinks that believers can be called "saints" or "sanctified" because of the presence of the Spirit in them. In this sense, the church is also a place where the Spirit is present inside the Christians and among them. As the body of Christ, and as the place where the Spirit dwells, the church plays a special role in the plan of God for humanity.

TRINITARIAN PERSONS AND OTHER METAPHORS OF THE CHURCH

In St. Basil's writings, there are also metaphors of the church where all three Persons of the Trinity are present at the same time: the city of God, the family of God, and the house of God. The first metaphor was already discussed in detail in the previous chapter. It refers mostly to the heavenly church[109] where believers live together having fellowship with the Triune God and

---

104. *Ps.* 61, PG 477AB.
105. Ibid, PG 477B.
106. *HS* 26.62.
107. Ibid.
108. Ibid., 62–63.
109. See the metaphors of the city in *Ps.* 45, PG 29:421CD. St. Basil believes that this metaphor can be applied to the earthly church as well. See ibid., PG 29:424BD. See also *InSQM*, PG 31:509B.

with each other. Therefore, here we will look at two other metaphors, which St. Basil mentions in his works.

Family of God

An allusion to God's family can be found in many of St. Basil's works. Whenever he calls his listeners and readers "brethren,"[110] it points to their relation as members of one family of God. This metaphor reflects the communal character of the church. It is fellowship of God's children or communion of siblings. Commenting on Psalm 48, St. Basil emphasizes that Christ himself considered humankind as his brethren.

> Though we were not His brethren, but were enemies through wicked works, yet He, being not man alone, but God, after He Himself has given us freedom, calls us brethren. He who redeemed us was, if we consider His nature, neither our brother nor man; but if we regard His gracious condescension to us, He calls us brethren and descends to humanity.[111]

St. Basil asserts that through Christ people "might receive the adoption" into God's family,[112] which means that by faith they might become sons and daughters of God. As we have seen in the earlier discussion, this adoption happens in the mother-church where they are supposed to grow and to learn the teaching of the family that is the Gospel.[113] They are also expected to behave according to the family rules in order to become rulers of different parts of the earth. In this sense, that family has an international character and includes many nations, but at the same time, they constitute one people of God. As Basil writes, "All believers in Christ are one people; all Christ's people, although He is hailed from many regions, are one Church."[114]

St. Basil also reminds his readers that as children of God they should be "formed after the likeness of God, according to the measure granted to men."[115] This means that as Christians, they should keep this family resemblance in order to show to which family they belong and who is their real

---

110. Fedwick is convinced that the term ἀδελφότης is "indiscriminately applied by Basil to both the ascetic community and the local church." See Fedwick, *The Church*, 23. On ascetic community, he refers to *Letters* 223.5 and 257.2 and as applied to the church to *Letters* 133, 135.2, 136.2, and 255.

111. *Ps.* 48.4, PG 29:441B. Translation is from Smith, *St. Basil the Great*, 109–10.

112. *Letter* 261.1–2.

113. See chapter 4 of this book.

114. *Letter* 161.1.

115. *The Morals* (Clarke, 128).

Father. Obviously, this is not about the physical appearance, but about their spiritual condition and behavior. St. Basil picks up this topic in his homily *On Psalm 45* and makes clear, since God is "the Sun of righteousness," the believers will become "children of light" (τέκνα φωτὸς).[116] In his letters, St. Basil refers to non-believers as to "children of disobedience."[117] He believes that their real Father is God,[118] but they do not want to admit this fact in their lives. However, they still have a potential to become children of obedience and to join the family because the goal of God is to embrace all His children, the whole of humanity.

One of the best examples of the connection between this family metaphor and all the trinitarian Persons can be found in St. Basil's homily *On the Feast of the Forty Martyrs*.[119] He starts from the statement that though these martyrs do not have a common homeland, they all belong to the heavenly Jerusalem, which is the city of God.[120] Using the same logic, St. Basil comes to a conclusion that though the human families of these martyrs are different, their spiritual family is the same because God is their common Father.[121] He continues the explanation and asserts that all of them are brothers not as born from the same parents, but as adopted by the Spirit. They are joined together through like-minded love.[122] Then St. Basil mentions another Person of the Trinity, Christ, in the fourth paragraph of this homily when he finishes the story of their unjust trial. According to the existing rules, prisoners had to pronounce their names before public execution. As St. Basil testifies, each of them in his turn said, "I am Christian" (Χριστιανός εἰμι).[123] In order to show their faithfulness to this spiritual family, every one of the martyrs rejected the name given to him at birth and called himself according to the name of their common Savior.[124] St. Basil emphasizes that all of them did not say their family names but named themselves Christians.[125] In this homily, we notice three important features of St. Basil's ecclesiology, which also can be found in other works. First, God is the Father of all humans, and he prepared a special place for those who

---

116. *Ps.* 45.5, PG 29:424D.
117. *Letter* 46, *Letter* 210. St. Basil uses the expression from Eph 2:2.
118. *CE* 2.23, PG 29:624AB.
119. *InSQM* 2–4. PG 31:509BC, 512BC.
120. Ibid., 2. PG 31:509B.
121. Ibid. PG 31:509BC.
122. *InSQM* 2. PG 31:509C.
123. Ibid. PG 31:512B.
124. Ibid. PG 31:512C.
125. Ibid.

believe—the church (here on earth and there in heaven). Second, the Spirit provides a way for them to receive "the adoption of sons."[126] Third, as common Savior of all people, Christ introduces them into a new family with a new name, Christians, which becomes their true identity.

It is very important for Basil to affirm that we are saved not as individuals, but as members of God's family. He believes that Christians have to re-evaluate all their "physical relationships and human friendships" in accordance with the "strictness of the gospel of salvation."[127] Any of these relations, which conflict with the Gospel, should be renounced, and then the believer receives new parents and new brethren instead of the old ones. As St. Basil writes,

> He renounces also all affection of this world which can hinder the aim of godliness. Such a man will consider his true parents those who in Christ Jesus begat him through the Gospel; as his brethren, those who received the same spirit of adoption.[128]

St. Basil believes that when "love of parents or relations" is in "opposition to the commands of the Lord" the words of Luke 14:26 about hatred toward one's parents can be applied.[129] In this sense, the church, as a new Christian family, should become more important for the believer than the real physical family into which he was born. If there is a conflict between these two, the priority goes to the church where the believer will begin to learn a new style of life.

In the family analogy, as in many others, St. Basil stresses the importance of proper relationships in the community: "That it is impossible for them to be counted worthy of the kingdom of heaven who do not imitate in their dealings with one another the equality observed by children among themselves."[130] Although this may refer to Matt 18:3, it still can be applied to the members of one family, the church. Believers are expected to communicate as children of their common Father who equally loves them all. In this sense, the relationships with other children of God reflect the depth and the quality of our knowledge of God. St. Basil also persuades the leaders of the church to become "faithful stewards," and as "fathers and nurses of

---

126. The same idea can be found in *HS* 15.36. See also *Ps.* 61, PG 477B where St. Basil asserts that believers are sealed by the Spirit and accepted as children of God.

127. *LR* (Clarke, 166).

128. Ibid., 167. See also this idea in *CBap* 1, Wagner, 346.

129. *LR* (Clarke, 167). Similar notions can be found in St. Basil's homily *On Psalm 44* where he asserts that "the celestial and blessed love" to God makes the believers forget their relatives and friends. See *Ps.* 41 (Way, 287).

130. *The Morals* 45.1 (Clarke, 112).

their own children, in the great affection of their love in Christ willingly to render to them not only the gospel of God but even their own souls."[131] They should share responsibilities and privileges of the older brethren of the family, which include support and help to "younger" children. This refers to the practical side of their ministry: they should be concerned about the physical and spiritual needs of those who are trusted by God under their care. Following Christ willingly, they are expected to sacrifice their own souls for the sake of their brothers and sisters. Moreover, it is not just a figure of speech but also a reality, which they might face. In his *Letter 240*, Basil reminds the presbyters of Nicopolis about their ancestors, "You are children of confessors; you are children of martyrs; you have resisted sin unto blood. Use, each one of you, the examples of those near and dear to you to make you brave for true religion's sake."[132]

These words determine their identity and their position within society. In this sense, in becoming a member of the church, a believer receives more than he/she, probably, realizes. Christians inherit the family history and the patterns of behavior. There are some expectations that are imposed on them by the family to which they belong. As children of faithful martyrs and confessors who died for their faith, they are expected to follow in the steps of those who are dear to them and to repeat the same acts if they have to. They have the examples, which were set before them: by the oldest brother, Christ; then by the older generation of the family; and then by their parents. Now this is their turn to represent the family and to keep the identity.

House of God

Another remarkable metaphor of the church where St. Basil uses all three trinitarian Persons is the house of God and a courtyard. The main idea behind this analogy connected not so much with the place, but with the presence of God in the church and the understanding of true worship to God. Commenting on the second verse of Psalm 28, St. Basil explains what he means by this metaphor: "the house of the Lord" is the church of the living God.[133] He affirms that there is only one holy courtyard (or house) of God where believers can worship him.[134] Previously, it was the Jewish synagogue, but after they had sinned against Christ, their house became empty.[135] This

---

131. Ibid., 80.18 (Clarke, 129).
132. *Letter 240*.
133. *Ps.* 240, PG 29:288C.
134. Ibid, PG 29:288A.
135. Ibid, PG 29:288B. In the same paragraph of this homily, St. Basil implies that

is a very important remark, which tells us about Basil's understanding of the church. Jewish people still have their synagogues as the place of their worship, but according to St. Basil, God is no longer present there. Therefore, St. Basil concludes, the church, as the holy house of the Lord, is the place where the true worship happens.[136] In this sense, a gathering of people in a place can be called the church only if the presence of God is there.

In the same homily, St. Basil makes another interesting statement about the believers who are present at the church. Many, he says, may have an outward appearance of being praying people, but they are not really present at the courtyard because their minds are occupied with worthless things and their thoughts are moving around.[137] Consequently, they are "neither worshiping the Lord, nor present at the holy house."[138] Thereby, St. Basil comes to a conclusion that to be in the church means to have a special condition of the mind when fellowship with the Triune God becomes the present experience. In St. Basil's thought, the whole Trinity is involved in ecclesial activity. He develops this idea in his homily *On Psalm 29* where he asserts that the metaphor of the house implies the church, which is built by Christ.[139] Recalling 1 Tim 3:15, St. Basil repeats that "God's house" is "the Church of the living God." Furthermore, he explains that "through the Holy Spirit" the process of renovation takes place,[140] which actually means "the renewal of the mind" in everyone who constitutes "the body of Christ."[141] Although St. Basil talks about a house or courtyard, he does not perceive

---

Jews lost the right to be in God's court because now they are outside of it. Similar idea can be found in St. Basil's homily *On Psalm 48* when he says, "Israel which followed the flesh was called a fool" and "the houses" of such fools are "their sepulchers forever." Then he adds, "He who is dead through sins does not dwell in a house." See *Ps.* 48 (Way, 322–23). It is worth mentioning that the same images, the church as the house of the Lord and believer's lives as houses built on the rock, were used by Origen in his commentaries to affirm that the OT prophecies about the chosen people of God "prefigure Christ and anticipate their fulfillment in his church." This was done in order to prevent the Jews to use the messianic texts in their own interest. See Timiadis, "The Trinitarian Structure of the Church and Its Authority," 121–58.

136. Ibid. PG 29:288A.
137. Ibid. PG 29:288B.
138. Ibid. PG 29:288C; translation is mine.
139. *Ps.* 29, PG 29:308A. See also *HS* 7.16: through Christ and by Christ the grace of God is effected for us that we have access to his "household." Similar notion can be found in his *Hom.* 4 where St. Basil explains that "through the blood of the Only-begotten" people were called back to become again the members of God's household. *Hom.* 4, PG 31: 224A.
140. *Ps.* 29, PG 29:308A.
141. Ibid.

the church so much as a place, but as a gathering of people.[142] At that time, two very important conditions are met: First, God is present among these people; second, the minds of believers, which means their attitude and intentions, are transformed and renovated because of the activity of the Holy Spirit in the body of Christ.

St. Basil returns to the topic of the renewal of human nature by God in his homily *On Psalm 61*. In this case, human beings are considered as the buildings, which are under God's reconstruction.[143] St. Basil reminds his listeners that, on the one hand, the nature of human beings is under sin and therefore "it should be destroyed."[144] On the other hand, St. Basil continues, after the renewal made by the one who has built it in the beginning, it may become secure, indestructible, and steadfast.[145] Quoting the verse from 1 Cor 3:9, he repeats that humans are "God's field and God's building."[146] Although this building has been damaged by "the enemy," our Creator repairs all the destruction. Therefore, St. Basil concludes, the destruction was necessary because of sin, but "great is the resurrection through immortality."[147] The church at the end will consist of this kind of "renewed buildings," which were fixed by God as the true owner of his field. Using the verses from Eph 2:20–22, St. Basil confirms this idea in *The Morals* when he says that we are "builders of God's temple, sharing the soul of each one so that he fits harmoniously on to the foundation of the apostles and prophets."[148] God builds his church through repairing every little part of his temple, every human soul that constitutes this house of God.

St. Basil develops this metaphor of the church as a house in his *Homily 3* where he explains how this "great house" functions. He speaks of "a great variety of pursuits" in this house, which is "the church of the living God."[149] Although St. Basil calls people hunters, travelers, architects, build-

---

142. The word "church" in the meaning of a group of people was also used by St. Basil in his homily *On Forty Martyrs*. Even these forty believers he calls "the church of martyrs" and explains furthermore that God is present among them referring to Matt 18:20. See *InSQM* 7, PG 31:521C. The same idea can be found in his seventh homily on *Hexaemeron* 7.6 where St. Basil explains that his goal is "to make all *he* says turn to the edification of the Church." Obviously, he means people and not the building or place by the word "church."

143. *Ps.* 61, PG 29: 473C.

144. Ibid. PG 29:472C.

145. Ibid.

146. Ibid.

147. Ibid.

148. *The Morals* 80 (Clarke, 129).

149. *Hom.* 3, PG 31: 205BD–208AB.

ers, farmers, shepherds, athletes, and soldiers, he implies different spiritual tasks for those "who are united in labor for Christ's Gospel."[150] Accordingly, the "architect should lay the firm foundation of faith, which is Jesus Christ and let the builder look to his materials."[151] The same way, "a hunter" has to take good care that his "prey does not elude" him, so that having captured them with the word of truth the hunter "may bring back to the Savior those who have been wild and savage by iniquity."[152] "A shepherd" is in charge of "pastoral duties" and he is supposed "to bring back that which is lost, to bind up that which was broken, to heal that which is diseased."[153] Also "a farmer" has his own responsibilities in this common "house" of the Lord. He "digs around unfruitful fig trees and administers remedies that will provide fecundity."[154] A soldier should "labor with the gospel, war a good warfare against spirit of wickedness."[155] All of them are doing the work, which has to be done in that "house" in order that the church can exist and function properly. St. Basil believes that every Christian can fulfill at least one of these ministries: "Every one of us, indeed, who is instructed in the Holy Scripture, is the administrator of some one of those gifts which, according to the Gospel, have been apportioned to us."[156] As in everyday life, people have to work and maintain their own households so they are expected to carry out their duties in God's house, the church. Their talents and skills could be different, but for everybody God prepared a gift with which the believer can serve to the Lord and to others.

CONCLUSION TO CHAPTER 4

The vivid metaphors and images, which St. Basil uses throughout his works, enable us to see his concept of the church in a new light and at the same time to keep the trinitarian perspective. The picture, which emerges from the analysis of these metaphors, clarifies the dominant themes in St. Basil's ecclesiology.

Several metaphors, such as motherhood of the church, or belonging to the body of Christ, or incorporation into the family of God, clearly reveal to us St. Basil's idea that the Christians cannot be imagined as separated from

---

150. Ibid. (Wagner, 437–38).
151. Ibid.
152. Ibid., 437.
153. Ibid.
154. Ibid.
155. Ibid., 437–38.
156. Ibid., 436–37.

the church because there is no salvation outside this special community. At the same time, the Fatherhood of God gives hope to all people that they are equally included in his plan of salvation.

Almost all of these metaphors—the household and its keepers, the brotherhood and the family, the body and its members, the building under reconstruction—emphasize a sense of the corporate nature of the Christian life. These words describe not something static, but dynamic and alive. In these metaphors, both God and the community are at work. The church, as the active part of these metaphors, is supposed to grow, to develop, and to become complete. It always goes through the process of transformation and change in order to become the perfect body, the loving family, and to bring the good fruits of faithful service. In St. Basil's thought, all these metaphors include at least one Person of the Trinity that reminds believers that they are never left alone. As the loving Father and the eldest brother, God leads his people toward eschatological reunion. Being present in the church in the Person of the Holy Spirit, he creates a new social reality where believers have to learn the new way of life.

CHAPTER 5

Inward Life of the Church
Education and Transformation through Praises and Prayers to God the Trinity

AFTER DEALING WITH THE general concept of the church in the previous chapters, the exploration of St. Basil's ideas of sacraments and worship will lead us into his understanding of the inward life of the church. In his works, he pays considerable attention to liturgy in the Christian community, especially in regard to corporate learning and transformation. We will look from St. Basil's point of view at different acts and rituals that all Christians are supposed to go through individually and together with other believers.

LITURGY AND TRINITARIAN TEACHING

A universal tradition of Eastern Churches attributes to St. Basil the so-called *Liturgy of St. Basil*, which is still employed in Churches of Byzantine rites throughout the year.[1] Although many scholars suggest that as time went on this liturgy underwent some changes, most of them agree that the core of it actually goes back to St. Basil.[2] In addition to this famous work, there are

---

1. An influence of this Liturgy is illustrated by its adoption by the patriarchal see of Constantinople and by its spread over the whole East, as well as to Sicily and Italy. Later in the ninth century, it was translated into Slavonic by St. Cyril and St. Methodius. See Quasten, *Patrology*, 226–27.

2. For discussions of the authenticity of "The Liturgy of St. Basil the Great," see a

different original texts, which bear witness to St. Basil's liturgical practice and theology: his *Letters, Homilies, Monastic Rules* and especially his treatise *On the Holy Spirit*, which has its origin in liturgical changes.³ All his ideas about the liturgy, especially several of his beautiful and profound prayers, can become for us one more source for a study of St. Basil's approach to the life of the church because in his writings doctrine, ethics, and worship are inextricably woven.

In order to understand better St. Basil's liturgical ideas, we have to go back to the christological and pneumatological disputes and their influence on the liturgy. The fourth century is marked by divisions within the Eastern part of the church.⁴ The rise of Arianism touched the most important question of the church's life—the person of Jesus Christ, Son of God, the Lord and Savior. Thereby, these disputes led to other questions, such as professions of faith and liturgical prayers. Later on, when the Person and the divinity of the Holy Spirit were brought to discussion in the church, it became a matter of vital importance for believers to understand how to pray or what kind of words to use. Should the Son be honored equally with the Father? What should be the position of the Spirit in the prayer? How do liturgy and prayers have to be organized? One of the problems was that Arians appealed to the traditional doxology, customary in that time in the church: Glory to the Father through the Son in the Holy Spirit. The words "through the Son" in Arian theology pointed to his lower stage than that of the Father. This interpretation of the doxology brought the "orthodox" theology of the church to the adaptation of a new doxology, which could not be misunderstood or wrongly interpreted.⁵ St. Basil started using a new liturgical formula beside the old one: Glory to the Father *with* (μετὰ) the Son *together with* (σὺν) the Holy Spirit. He was convinced that the old doxology was not erroneous, but in the new one St. Basil wanted to emphasize the equality of the Persons inside the Trinity and to support the "orthodox" views in the trinitarian controversies in the church.⁶ In this sense, this dox-

---

very good article of Bebis, "Introduction to Liturgical Theology of St. Basil the Great," 273–85. See also Hutcheon, "Sacrifice of Praise," 3–23. As Orlov said in his book, the problem with the text of liturgy was that it was "always alive and grew throughout the centuries." See Orlov, *Liturgiya Svyatogo Vasiliya Velikogo*, 1; translation is mine.

3. St. Basil introduced the new doxology in order to support his views against those who refused to rank the Holy Spirit with the Father and the Son. In this treatise, he provides the arguments for this change.

4. St. Basil describes this situation in his work *HS* 30.78.

5. See more on the history of liturgy and its development in Jungmann, *The Early Liturgy*, 188–98.

6. This conclusion can be made from the content of his book *On the Holy Spirit*. See, for example, his statement about both doxologies in *On the Holy Spirit* 27.68: "[N]ot

ology was the logical consequence of his trinitarian theology. Defending his trinitarian views, St. Basil employed both Scripture and "unwritten mysteries of the church," which were "delivered" "in a mystery by the tradition of the apostles."[7] Thereby, St. Basil used previous liturgical practices of the church in order to support his theological views and at the same time to justify the use of the new doxology, which, from his perspective, reflected the proper trinitarian ideas.

This whole story of the development of a new doxology brings us to a conclusion that in St. Basil's thought the liturgy was not merely a time of prayer and worship. It was also the time of religious education when the congregation was able to learn proper theological statements and beliefs. A notable feature of St. Basil's *Liturgy* is clearly trinitarian expressions. It consists of the great hymns of praise where the words of glory and honor to the Persons of Trinity are repeatedly recited.[8] In addition, we can notice that the whole service is organized as a corporate action where all who are present have to participate.

One of the best examples of St. Basil's liturgical prayers, which show his theological vision of the Trinity, is his Eucharistic prayer before the consecration of the gifts.[9] Different poetic devices and techniques were used there in order to convey to people in the church the mystery of trinitarian relationships. Beginning with the address to the Father and through the personal praises to each trinitarian hypostasis, St. Basil's *Liturgy* leads his hearers to the important theological point that God is

---

that they are opposed in mutual antagonism, but that each contributes its own meaning to true religion."

7. HS 27.66. As Florovsky explains, the phrase "unwritten mysteries" means not something "in secret," but the form of rites and liturgical usage. Most of the times the term "mysteries" refers to the rites of baptism and Eucharist. See Florovsky, *Bible, Church, Tradition: An Eastern Orthodox View,* 86. More information on the idea of "written'" and "unwritten" tradition, see De Mendieta, *The "Unwritten" and "Secret" Apostolic Traditions in the Theological Thought of St. Basil of Caesarea,* 1965. For another opinion about the tradition in St. Basil, see the article by Hanson, "Basil's Doctrine of Tradition in Relation to the Holy Spirit," 241–55.

8. See Neale and Littledale, *The Liturgies of SS Mark, James, Clement, Chrysostom, and Basil, and the Church of Malabar.* See also *The Orthodox Liturgy: Being the Divine Liturgy of S. John Chrysostom and S. Basil the Great.* See similar idea in Behr, *The Nicene Faith,* 317.

9. St. Basil's exposition of the trinitarian theology in this liturgy is compatible with the theological vision that we can find in his other writings, which modern critical scholars consider as authentic. For example, in his famous work *On the Holy Spirit.* See the textual correspondences of St. Basil's anaphora with *On the Holy Spirit* in the article by Hutcheon, "Sacrifice of Praise," 17–18.

> the Master of all things, the Lord of heaven and earth, and of every creature visible and invisible . . . the Father of our Lord Jesus Christ the great God and Savior . . . by Whom the Holy Ghost was disclosed: the Spirit of truth, the grace of adoption . . . the fount of sanctification, by whom every reasonable and spiritual creature empowered serveth Thee and sends up to Thee the everlasting doxology.[10]

By providing to the attendees in the church this kind of liturgical text, St. Basil hopes that through the celebration and worship they will become edified and will be able to withstand heretical attacks. That understanding of the liturgy finds expression in his fourth homily *On Hexaemeron* when St. Basil describing the divine act of creation compares the beauty of the ocean with the worship and praises, which a community offers to God. According to St. Basil, the proper liturgy should not be shadowed by heresy or troubled with any kind of ill-intentioned claims. Only the worship of believers who are guided by Christ and remain faithful to Him will be approved by the Lord.

> If the Ocean is good and worthy of praise before God, how much more beautiful is the assembly of a Church like this, where the voices of men, of children, and of women, arise in our prayers to God mingling and resounding like the waves which beat upon the shore. This Church also enjoys a profound calm, and malicious spirits cannot trouble it with the breath of heresy. Deserve, then, the approbation of the Lord by remaining faithful to such good guidance, in our Lord Jesus Christ, to whom be glory and power for ever and ever.[11]

Similar understanding of interconnectedness between the knowledge of God the Trinity and worship is demonstrated by St. Basil when he discusses the divinity of the Holy Spirit. He is convinced that God bestows this knowledge of himself only on true worshippers. St. Basil implies that they believe in God the Son and the Spirit. Thereby, the words "to worship in spirit and in truth" are interpreted by St. Basil almost literally where truth means the orthodox teaching about God.

> For it is not said through the Spirit, but by the Spirit, and "God is a spirit, and they that worship Him must worship Him in spirit

---

10. The Greek text is the canonical one from Vaporis, ed., *The Divine Liturgy of Our Fathers among the Saints Basil the Great*, 23–25. The English translation is from Neale and Littledale, *The Liturgies of SS Mark, James, Clement, Chrysostom, and Basil, and the Church of Malabar*, 129–30.

11. *The Hex.* 4. 7, PG 29:93C.

and in truth," as it is written "in thy light shall we see light," namely by the illumination of the Spirit, "the true light which lighteth every man that cometh into the world." It results that in Himself He shows the glory of the Only begotten, and on true worshippers He in Himself bestows the knowledge of God.[12]

In his *Letter 235*, St. Basil explains the idea of the knowledge of God, "Knowledge is manifold—it involves perception of our Creator, recognition of His wonderful works, observance of His commandments and intimate communion with Him."[13] In St. Basil's thought, this "intimate communion" implies the act of worship and later in this epistle he affirms, "The statement that God shall be known from the mercy seat means that He will be known to His worshippers. And the Lord knows them that are His, means that on account of their good works He receives them into intimate communion with Him."[14] Therefore, St. Basil's position is that the proper understanding of God is a fundamental point for a believer's communication with God and vice versa—proper worship leads to the right knowledge of God.[15] St. Basil is anxious to persuade his readers that those who reject the knowledge of the Spirit's divinity cannot offer true worship to God. He writes, "Such an one has no part in the true worship. For it is not possible to worship the Son but by the Holy Spirit, nor is it possible to call upon the Father but by the Spirit of adoption."[16] St. Basil elaborates this discussion in his treatise *On the Holy Spirit*. He emphasizes one more time, "Even in our worship the Holy Spirit is inseparable from the Father and the Son. If you remain outside the Spirit you will not be able even to worship at all."[17] This idea is so important to St. Basil that in one of his letters he uses the term "true worshippers" for those believers who worship the Holy Spirit as God.[18] Therefore, in St. Basil's opinion, the believer is defined as a Christian by his worship to God—the Father, Son and Holy Spirit. For this reason, St. Basil wants people in the

---

12. *HS* 18.47. St. Basil returns to this discussion in *HS* 26.64.

13. *Letter* 235.3.

14. Ibid.

15. We may clarify a little bit more what does it mean for St. Basil "the knowledge of God." As St. Basil emphasizes in his *Letter* 234.1, "The word to know has many meanings. We say that we know the greatness of God, His power, His wisdom, His goodness, His providence over us, and the justness of His judgment; but not His very essence." He goes on further and explains the connection between the knowledge and worship. *Letter* 234.3. See more on this topic in Bonis, "Problem concerning faith and knowledge," 27–44.

16. *HS* 11.27 (Lewis, 59).

17. *HS* 26.64.

18. *Letter* 50.

church to pay close attention to prayers, which they repeat during worship, and to other texts, such as the creed or doxologies. He insists that their minds should be completely devoted to God when they are present in the church.

> The time which you lend to God is not lost: he will return it to you with large interest . . . Deliver your heart, then, from the cares of this life and give close heed to my words. Of what avail will it be to you if you are here in the body, and your heart is anxious about your earthly treasure?[19]

Similar ideas about acquiring the proper understanding of God through worship can be found in other works of St. Basil. Commenting on the words, "In the temple of God all shall speak his glory," he reminds his readers, "Wretched men, who leave their homes and run to the temple, as to enrich themselves somewhat, do not lend their ears to the word of God . . . and even become a hindrance to the others."[20] Therefore, they are in danger and can be condemned together with "those blaspheming the name of God." For this purpose, St. Basil appeals to Christians to use their reason and their ability to think in order to glorify God and win the glory to themselves.

> Let the tongue sing, let the mind interpret the meaning of what has been said, that you may sing with your spirit, that you may sing likewise with your mind. Not at all is God in need of glory, but He wishes you to be worthy of winning glory.[21]

St. Basil pays extra attention to the educational function of psalms, which people sing together during worship in his homily *On Psalm 1*.[22] Admitting in the beginning that it is difficult for the human race to learn about virtue or the "upright life," St. Basil explains the role of the Holy Spirit in this process of education in the church. When the beautiful melody is used, the teaching and the word of God can be received by believers much easier and without resistance.

> The delight of melody He [the Spirit] mingled with the doctrines[23] so that by the pleasantness and softness of the sound

---

19. *Hex.* 3.1. St. Basil insists that the teaching in the church is the words of the Lord himself with which he addresses people when the message is proclaimed "through mouths of His servants." *Homily 8.8*, Schroeder, *On Social Justice*, 86.

20. *Ps.* 28, PG 29: 301C (Way, 209–10).

21. Ibid., PG 29:304A (Way, 210). St. Basil believes that not to have the knowledge of God is equal to "the death of soul." See *Hom.* 13, PG 31:423C.

22. This also reflects the liturgical practice of Scripture readings from the Psalms.

23. We have to mention that in the Basilian sense, the term *"dogmata"* was not yet

heard we might receive without perceiving it the benefit of the words... Therefore, He devised for us these harmonious melodies of the psalms, that they who are children in age or, even those who are youthful in disposition might to all appearances chant but, in reality, become trained in soul...

... the wise intention of the teacher who contrived that while we were singing we should at the same time learn something useful; by this means, too, the teaching are in a certain way impressed more deeply on our mind. Even a forceful lesson does not always endure, but what enters the mind with joy and pleasure somehow becomes more firmly impressed upon it.[24]

In this sense, worship could become one more tool, which God uses in order to train his children for the life according to the Gospel and to guide them into the right direction. This also includes the knowledge of God, which he wants to reveal to his people and to the world. St. Basil is convinced that through the psalms even an ignorant person can spread the Gospel all over the place where he lives.

For, never has any one of the many indifferent persons gone away easily holding in mind either an apostolic or prophetic message, but they do chant the words of the psalms, even in the home, and they spread them around in the market place.[25]

Therefore, we can come to the idea that the liturgy is developed in a way that participants are able to receive the important information. Through repetitive pattern, they have the opportunity to memorize some ideas and doctrines. Afterwards, they can share this information with other people. St. Basil gives a whole list of "good things," which people can learn from Psalms:

---

a term with "a strict and exact connotation." See Florovsky, *Bible, Church, Tradition: An Eastern Orthodox View,* 86. It "mainly comprises the liturgical and sacramental prayers and customs, and the implied theological doctrines." See De Mendieta, *The "Unwritten" and "Secret" Apostolic Traditions,* 40. See also De Mendieta, "The Pair ΚΗΡΥΓΜΑ and ΔΟΓΜΑ in the Theological Thought of St. Basil of Caesarea," 129–42.

24. *Ps. I*, PG 29:212B (Way, 152). PG 29:213A (Way, 153). In addition to this quotation about the usage of "harmonious melodies of the psalms," we have to mention that St. Basil was also interested in ecclesiastical music. Similarly, as he was attacked for using the new doxology, so he was accused of liturgical innovations for using a form of music that previously was unheard of in the church. See *Letter* 207.2–3. On this issue, see also Karavites, "Saint Basil and Hymnology," 203–14. See also Waddell, "Identifying Authorities and Pastoral Practice in the Early Church," 48–59.

25. *Ps.* 1 (Way, 152).

> Therein is perfect theology, a prediction of the coming of Christ in the flesh, a threat of judgment, a hope of resurrection, a fear of punishment, promises of glory, an unveiling of mysteries; all things, as if in some great public treasure, are stored up in the Book of Psalms.[26]

One more function of psalms, which St. Basil mentioned in this homily, is their ability to "form the friendship, unite those separated, conciliate those at enmity."[27] St. Basil is strongly convinced that people in the church cannot still consider each other as an enemy when they "utter the same prayer to God." Therefore, the participation in liturgical singing, "psalmody," brings about "choral singing, a bond, as it were, toward unity, and joining the people into a harmonious union of one choir."[28] Through offering up the praises together, the believers are brought to a condition when the psalm becomes "the voice of the Church."[29] Excellent descriptions of such unity in worship can be found in St. Basil's *Letters* 207.3 where he shares his experience of the vigil service:

> Among us the people go at night to the house of prayer, and, in distress, affliction, and continual tears, making confession to God, at last rise from their prayers and begin to sing psalms. And now, divided into two parts, they sing antiphonally with one another, thus at once confirming their study of the Gospels, and at the same time producing for themselves a heedful temper and a heart free from distraction. Afterwards they again commit the prelude of the strain to one, and the rest take it up; and so after passing the night in various psalmody, praying at intervals as the day begins to dawn, all together, as with one voice and one heart, raise the psalm of confession to the Lord, each forming for himself his own expressions of penitence.[30]

Although St. Basil discusses a lot the educational function of psalms and prayers, it appears that he is concerned not only about this purpose of the liturgy. As we mentioned earlier,[31] St. Basil places the emphasis on the believer's relationships with the living God. He believes that God himself is

---

26. Ibid., 153. PG 29:213B.
27. Ibid., 152. PG 29:212CD.
28. Ibid.
29. Ibid., 153. PG 29:213A.
30. *Letter* 207.3.
31. See the previous discussion of relation between the knowledge and "intimate communion with God" in this chapter. See also the discussion of the image "house of God" in chapter 4 of this book.

always present in the church among his people.³² This means that during the worship the believers communicate in their prayers with God, who is not distant, but the one who is actively involved in this liturgy. God does not stay away from his people, but he pays close attention to every need of the believers present in the community. St. Basil is convinced that the time of liturgy gives the believer the opportunity to show his/her faithfulness and thankfulness to God and to become a blessing or a hindrance to others in the church when they receive the teaching.

The earthly liturgy can also serve as an image of the worship in heaven where people and angels will join together in the common praise of their Creator and Redeemer.³³ The liturgy in the church is a foretaste of the kingdom that awaits the Christians.³⁴ In this sense, the future of the person present at the liturgy depends on his attitude toward God: whether he glorifies God and builds the relationships with him through the prayer and worship or ignores him.³⁵ The same way it depends on his attitude toward his fellow worshipers: whether he joins them in unison or serves as a stumbling block for their sincere prayers.

Prayer is an important part of the liturgy and the Christian life in general. As St. Basil admits in one of his letters, "I know that communion in prayer brings great gain."³⁶ According to St. Basil, these liturgical prayers are organized in a way that they are supposed to remind the community as a whole about their common "old country" where they came from, about their common Savior, and their common future destiny after the resurrection.

> Thus we all look to the East at our prayers, but few of us know that we are seeking our own old country, Paradise, which God planted in Eden in the East. We pray standing, on the first day of the week, but we do not all know the reason. On the day of the resurrection (or "standing again," Greek. *anastasis*) we remind

---

32. See St. Basil's words about God's presence in the church in *Hom.* 21: "He is at His post even now, in our midst" (Way, 500). See the same idea that God "sees the affections of those entering" and "the prayer of each is manifested" to him in *Ps.* 28, PG 29:301C (Way, 209).

33. See *LR* (Clarke, 149); and *Ps.* 45.4, PG 29:424A. In his *Letter* 2.2, St. Basil wrote about the experience of devoted worship, "What state can be more blessed than to imitate on earth the choruses of angels?"

34. As St. Basil noted, "On the day of the resurrection we remind ourselves of the grace given to us by standing at prayer . . . because the day seems to us to be in some sense an image of the age which we expect." *HS* 27.66.

35. See this idea in *Letter* 221 where following the Bible, St. Basil asserts that "Christ's worshippers" will be honored and "be made famous and glorious by Him before all" because this is the destiny of those who honor God.

36. *Letter* 150.2. See more about the prayer in *The Morals* 56 (Clarke, 115–16).

ourselves of the grace given to us by standing at prayer, not only because we rose with Christ, and are bound to "seek those things which are above," but because the day seems to us to be in some sense an image of the age which we expect.[37]

As part of liturgy, these prayers and practices related to them unite the church in its action as a single whole and lead the people to the understanding of who they are and where they are going. St. Basil noted that this "upright attitude of prayer" makes their minds "to dwell no longer in the present but in the future." "Moreover," St. Basil goes on, "every time we fall upon our knees and rise from off them we show by the very deed that by our sin we fell down to earth, and by the loving kindness of our Creator were called back to heaven."[38] In some sense, these corporate actions and prayers during the liturgical service help the believers to develop a certain understanding of the church as the one and indivisible entity, which experiences the presence of God and fulfills his plan. At the same time, the believers are able to learn the foundational principles of the church's faith, which, according to St. Basil, is the heritage from the apostles. Repeated throughout the service, the affirmative movements and words draw people's attention to the important theological statements and ideas in order to encourage them to remain faithful to their common goal in times of doubt and heretical attacks.

BAPTISM—ENTERING THE CHURCH

In many of his works, when St. Basil discusses the rite of baptism, he provides his readers with the arguments that the foundation of Christian baptism is trinitarian.[39] Since he writes during the continuing christological and pneumatological struggles, it is understandable that he feels the need to defend the trinitarian doctrine of the church. In addition to that, in the passages concerning baptism, St. Basil mentions other important ideas, which reflect his understanding of the church and her role in the life of believers.

Baptism is the rite whereby a believer becomes the member of the church. For St. Basil it is not a mere official procedure or a physical washing, but "the mystery"[40] through which the person is initiated into the com-

37. HS 27.66. "The day of resurrection" means Sunday in this context.

38. HS 27.66.

39. See his treatise *On the Holy Spirit,* chapters 10, 12, 15, 16, 26, 28. See also *Exhortation to Holy Baptism,* PG 31:423–44; *De Fide* (Clarke, 96); *Letter* 159.2; see about baptism of heretics and schismatics in *Letter* 188 and *Letter* 199.20.

40. HS 27.66. From the context we can understand that St. Basil uses this word

munity of those who received the new life. In St. Basil's words, baptism is "the beginning of life," and "the day of regeneration the first of days," the day in which "the utterance uttered in the grace of adoption was the most honorable of all."[41] This is the day when the believer enters not only the community of people whom he or she probably knew before the rite. This person is introduced into relationship with God the Trinity who makes this rite legitimate. As St. Basil explains, "The God who gave, the Son who received, and the Spirit who is the unction."[42] St. Basil emphasizes this idea in his homily *Exhortation to Holy Baptism* where he uses the analogy of human friendship. In order to have good relationships with people, we have to do what is pleasing to them. In order to enter fellowship with God, we have to accept baptism.[43] In this way, the rite of baptism can be considered as twofold. It is performed in the church by people and by God and, therefore, includes both human and divine activity at the same time. St. Basil believes that people are regenerated through God's grace given in baptism, and their salvation is "established through the Father and the Son and the Holy Ghost."[44] Therewith, the church administers the rite and the church is responsible for the fulfillment of all the requirements in order to help people become Christians.[45]

> Whence is it that we are Christians? Through our faith, would be the universal answer. And in what way are we saved? Plainly because we were regenerated through the grace given in our baptism. How else could we be? And after recognizing that this salvation is established through the Father and the Son and the Holy Ghost, shall we fling away "that form of doctrine" which we received? Would it not rather be ground for great groaning if

---

"mystery" with the meaning "the sacrament," but not something unknown. There is a mystical notion in it, which includes God's action and God's grace, but the main meaning of the word "mystery" is the rite through which the believer has to go in order to join the church. Interestingly enough, the Orthodox Church still uses this word for the sacraments. This is the official language and the official term of the contemporary Orthodox scholars. See Michael Pomazansky, *Orthodox Dogmatic Theology,* 255–307.

41. *HS* 10.26.
42. *HS* 12.28.
43. *EHB,* PG 31:433C.
44. *HS* 10.26. St. Basil also believes that after baptism the human "soul" becomes "suitable henceforward as a dwelling place of God in the Spirit." What is more, "God is sitting in the soul which shines from its washing, as if He making it a throne for Himself." See *Ps.* 28.8 (Way, 210–11).
45. Interesting that in the early church the rite of baptism was "essentially corporate, presided over by bishop, assisted by his clergy, and with the faithful involved." See Fisher, "Baptism: 1. Patristic," 56.

we are found now further off from our salvation "than when we first believed," and deny now what we then received? Whether a man has departed this life without baptism, or has received a baptism lacking in some of the requirements of the tradition, his loss is equal.[46]

According to St. Basil, if the rite of baptism performed in the church lacks "in some of the requirements of the tradition" then it is considered equal to not having baptism at all. St. Basil thinks that salvation of the person depends on the tradition, which was kept in the community of faith. It is important whether it was delivered without mistake or some customs were rejected. In the second case, he asserts that the rejection leads to the injury of "the Gospel in its very vitals" when it becomes "a mere phrase and nothing more."[47] Therefore, the role of the church is to keep the traditions and the proper teaching in order to help people obtain their salvation and eternal life.

As the preacher who consistently reminds his listeners about the importance of education and the knowledge of God, St. Basil emphasizes that this is the church who calls people together through her "high preaching." She teaches the catechumens with "milk," which is "the words of instructions,"[48] in order to prepare them for baptism. In the church, they become the disciples of the Lord before they are "accounted worthy of holy Baptism."[49] Later on, after the rite is performed, it is the church again who feeds them with "the solid food of dogmata."[50] In this case, baptism serves as the crucial moment when people become "enlightened," and they obtain

---

46. *HS* 10.26.

47. *HS* 27.66. Most of these important customs, which people might reject, St. Basil mentioned in this passage from *On the Holy Spirit* when he discusses the "unwritten traditions" of the church except the trinitarian formula, which is mentioned many times in other passages of this treatise. Concerning the rite and prayers of the administration of baptism, he describes more than seven actions: a) the sign of the cross on catechumens; b) the renouncement of Satan and his angels; c) the blessing of baptismal water; d) the blessing of the oil of chrism; e) the blessing of the catechumen who are to be baptized and the anointing with oil; f) the baptismal formula in the name of the Father, and of the Son, and of the Holy Spirit; g) the triple complete immersion in the baptismal water. More on this subject in De Mendieta, *The "Unwritten" and "Secret" Apostolic Traditions*, 60–61.

48. *EHB*, PG 31:425A.

49. *CBap* 1 (Wagner, 339). Teaching the disciples of the Lord is one of the important ideas in St. Basil. For him "a disciple . . . is one who comes to the Lord for the purpose of following Him, that is, to hear His words, to believe in Him and obey Him as Master, King, Physician, and Teacher of truth, in the hope of gaining eternal life." *CBap* 1 (Wagner, 340–41).

50. *EHB*, PG 31:425A.

the ability "to contemplate God,"[51] and to receive the knowledge of God in the church. Once again, we see the cooperation of God-church activity in baptism. The church invites people through the preaching and provides the instructions. Through the Holy Spirit, God changes, regenerates, and enlightens those who are baptized in order to prepare them for the new portion of teaching, which they receive in the church. As St. Basil explains,

> ... in baptism two ends were proposed; on the one hand, the destroying of the body of sin, that it may never bear fruit unto death; on the other hand, our living unto the Spirit, and having our fruit in holiness; the water receiving the body as in a tomb figures death, while the Spirit pours in the quickening power, renewing our souls from the deadness of sin unto their original life. This then is what it is to be born again of water and of the Spirit, the being made dead being effected in the water, while our life is wrought in us through the Spirit. In three immersions, then, and with three invocations, the great mystery of baptism is performed, to the end that the type of death may be fully figured, and that by the tradition of the divine knowledge the baptized may have their souls enlightened.[52]

Also through the "mystery" of baptism, people are allowed to receive this special teaching of "unwritten tradition," which they lacked before. Now the community of believers accepts the baptized person as one of them and shares the knowledge, which was kept in secret.[53] St. Basil clarifies that the church guarded this information from the beginning in silence because "what is bruited abroad randomly among the common folk is no mystery at all."[54] He continues the explanation, "This is the reason for our tradition of unwritten precepts and practices, that the knowledge of our dogmas may not become neglected and contemned by the multitude through familiarity."[55] In other words, St. Basil thinks that there is a necessity of preserving the

---

51. *EHB*, PG 31:423C. Actually, in this homily, St. Basil says that one who is not baptized is not enlightened and is not able to perceive or see God.

52. *HS* 15.35.

53. Historians and scholars usually call this "secret" information the *disciplina arcani*. These were certain practices and formulas used during the rite of baptism and Eucharist. There were some things or words that had to be kept secret from all non-baptized—the heathen and the catechumens. During the service, they had to leave the church after the lesson, before the celebration of Eucharist or the actual baptismal rite took place. See Jungmann, *The Early Liturgy: to the Time of Gregory the Great*, 159.

54. *HS* 27.66.

55. Ibid.

sanctity of the Christian mysteries, and the church is the authority, which can protect it and keep it for only those who belong to her.

In his homily *Exhortation to Holy Baptism*, St. Basil uses several illustrations with the language of "belonging" to some group of people in order to show the importance of church membership and the connection between the rites of this earthly community and eternal life in the heavenly kingdom. This means that through the baptism, a person joins not only the earthly group of people who administers the rite, but the heavenly dimension of the church where all the saved will live afterwards. First of all, St. Basil asks rhetorical questions in order to remind his unbaptized hearers that they do not belong to the Christian community yet: "When will you become Christian? When will we get to know you as ours?"[56] Then St. Basil continues and asserts that the baptism allows people to receive a gift, which is the way to the heavenly kingdom, and which is open for those who are not afraid to obey and go through the rite.[57] In the next sentences, St. Basil illustrates his point of view with the example of Jewish people who used circumcision as the sign of belonging to the people of God. Recalling the words from Genesis 17:14,[58] he persuades his hearers to accept baptism because as the Jews were not counted among their people if they did not go through circumcision so his listeners do not belong to the "sharers of the resurrection" if they do not go through the rite of baptism.[59] Defending the necessity of baptism further on in this homily, St. Basil uses the following metaphors: a distribution of gold, a freeing of slaves, and a cancelling of debts.[60] All these actions from the social life of the world look like incredible blessings, and St. Basil makes use of them in order to explain the advantages enjoyed by those who receive baptism and join the church. St. Basil also uses the analogy of citizenship to emphasize the importance of belonging to the church. He is trying to persuade the hearers to "transfer *themselves* totally to the Lord" and to "give *their* names to be enrolled in the Church" as those, who live in the city, register themselves into the number of citizens. St. Basil urges them to inscribe themselves "in this book in order to be transcribed in the one above"[61] implying that their membership in the earthly church equals citizenship in the heavenly city.

56. *EHB*, PG 31:425B.
57. Ibid. PG 31:425C.
58. Ibid. PG 31:428A.
59. Ibid. Similar idea of "the circumcision without hands" or "the circumcision of Christ" can be found in *HS* 15.35.
60. Ibid. PG 31:429A–D.
61. Ibid. PG 31:440A.

One of the most interesting illustrations, which St. Basil provides in this homily, is drawn from military life—an army's use of password during warlike activities. This password or "an agreed sign" (τὸ σύνθημα) helps "the friends" not to mix with the enemy and separate easily from them.[62] Therefore, St. Basil implies that through baptism the believer receives the sign of God[63] that from now on she or he belongs to him together with the other people in the church who become their friends. On the contrary, all the others are considered on the side of the enemy. St. Basil insists that "nobody will recognize you, whether you are ours or the enemy" if with these "mystical symbols" you do not prove "the friendship" with us.[64] He continues explaining that this sign is more like a seal or "a mark" (σφραγίς) of God's ownership upon the believer.[65] In addition, St. Basil compares this sign with the blood on the top and sides of the doorframe from the story of Exodus 12:23–29 when the firstborns from the sealed Jewish families survived the plague.[66] The main meaning of this seal or mark has an eschatological orientation. St. Basil asks the direct question, "How will you be able to return to Paradise, if you do not bear the seal of baptism?"[67] He is convinced that people will be recognized by God as his and allowed to participate in the heavenly life of the church only if they received this mark in the earthly church during their earthly life. He is trying to convey the idea that the postponement of baptism is dangerous, especially in a case of unexpected death when people die unbaptized and, therefore, unsealed.[68] This seal serves as the testimony of their faith and obedience. St. Basil stresses the idea that the trinitarian faith of a person is a fundamental point for receiving baptism and the seal of salvation or God's ownership.

> Faith and baptism are two kindred and inseparable ways of salvation: faith is perfected through baptism, baptism is established through faith, and both are completed by the same names. For as we believe in the Father and the Son and the Holy Ghost, so are we also baptized in the name of the Father and of the Son

---

62. Ibid. PG 31:432B.

63. Ibid. Actually, St. Basil describes this sign with the words from Ps 4:7 as "the light of the Lord's face."

64. Ibid. PG 31:432BC.

65. Ibid. PG 31:432C.

66. Ibid. St. Basil repeats the same idea and the story from Exodus in *HS* 14.31.

67. Ibid. PG 31:428C.

68. Ibid. PG 31:436C. Actually, the aim of the whole homily is to convince the hearers not to postpone their baptism, because without baptism they were not bound by the rules of the church and its penitential regulations. See Mayer, "Ecclesial Communion: The Letters of St. Basil the Great revisited," 229.

and of the Holy Ghost; first comes the confession, introducing us to salvation, and baptism follows, setting the seal upon our assent.[69]

Therefore, through baptism people receive the right to join the community of the faithful here on earth and in the future in the heavenly realm after their death. In some sense, through these arguments St. Basil defends the idea that there is no salvation outside the church.[70] This reasoning leads St. Basil to the necessity of answering the question: who then belongs to the church? On the one hand, the answer is obvious—those who accepted the baptism in the church. On the other hand, everything becomes more complicated in face of divisions and schisms brought in by the groups of heretics and schismatics. In his writings, St. Basil is trying to work out the solution to this problem and to decide whose baptism could be accepted as legitimate and whose baptism should be rejected as not genuine. For St. Basil this is the question of vital importance because, as we can see from the previous discussion, he believes that the eternal destiny of people depends on the properly administered baptism.

Discussing this topic in his *Letter 188*, St. Basil mentions three groups of people who separate themselves from the church: heretics, schismatics, and unlawful congregations. First, he provides the explanation of the differences between these groups, and then on this basis, he gives the opinion of "old authorities"[71] concerning the legitimacy of their rites of baptism. After that he shares his own thoughts about which of them can be considered as part of the church. Following the "old authorities" of the church, St. Basil applies the name "heretics" to people who are "altogether broken off and alienated in matters relating to the actual faith."[72] Schismatics could be named as those "who had separated for some ecclesiastical reasons and questions capable of mutual solution."[73] The last term on the list is "unlawful

69. *HS* 12.28.

70. The previous discussion on this issue is in chapter 4 of this book.

71. Under "old authorities," St. Basil implies the previous generations of faithful Christians who already made the collective decisions about this kind of groups. Many of these decisions were written down in the church canons, which were accepted by the Councils of the church. St. Basil also suggests that in dealing with some groups the further decisions have to be made the same way. See his *Letter* 199.47. He writes, "Wherefore, if this be determined on, more bishops ought to meet together in one place and publish the canon in these terms, that action may be taken without peril, and authority given to answers to questions of this kind."

72. *Letter* 188.1. For better understanding of the historical background, see the footnotes to this letter in Bettenson, *The Later Christian Fathers*, 84–85. See also Guitton, *Great Heresies and Church Councils*, 11–95.

73. Ibid.

congregations," which means that they were held, according to St. Basil, by "disorderly presbyters or bishops or by uninstructed laymen."[74] As an example, St. Basil provides the consequence of events that could bring these people to separation: commitment of crime, the discharging of ministerial functions, the refusal to submit to the canons, and, as a result, the organization of unlawful assembly. In the next sentence of the same letter, St. Basil gives another definition of schism—"the disagreement with members of the Church about repentance."[75] Therefore, the separation of schismatics and unlawful gatherings has to do more with discipline than with the doctrines and faith. Most of the times these people or their leaders do not want to submit to canonical authority and, in this sense, this is more the question of penitence. From the context of the letter, we can suggest that the right confession of faith was preserved in these groups. Nevertheless, St. Basil still thinks that baptism of some schismatics should not be accepted by the church as valid and effective.[76]

In the beginning of the letter, he introduces his reader to the suggestion made by the older generation of Christians that the rest of believers have to admit the baptism of schismatics, on the ground that "they still belonged to the Church." "As to those who assembled in unlawful congregations," Basil continues, "their decision [old authorities] was to join them again to the Church, after they had been brought to a better state by proper repentance and rebuke, and so, in many cases, when men in orders had rebelled with the disorderly, to receive them on their repentance, into the same rank."[77] However, St. Basil is convinced that "those who had apostatized from the Church had no longer on them the grace of the Holy Spirit, for it ceased to be imparted when the continuity was broken."[78] Although St. Basil is aware that baptism of some schismatics is accepted in the other geographical locations, he still does not allow them to join the church under his authority.[79] As he explains,

74. Ibid.

75. Ibid.

76. We have to mention that on this issue St. Basil has a different opinion than some other contemporary bishops in the church. This conclusion can be made from the further reading of this letter and his *Letter* 199. See a short summary of Basil's views on the baptism of schismatics and heretics in Ericson, "Reception of Non-Orthodox into the Orthodox Church," 72–75.

77. *Letter* 188.1.

78. Ibid. In some sense, St. Basil even acts contrary to canon 8 of the Council of Nicaea but he seems to be very strict on this point. See also his *Letter* 199. See notes on the canon 8 of Nicaea in Bright, *The Canons of the First Four General Councils of Nicaea, Constantinople, Ephesus, and Chalcedon*, 29–38.

79. Ibid. For example, in this letter concerning the Cathari, St. Basil says,

... they who were broken off had become laymen, and, because they are no longer able to confer on others that grace of the Holy Spirit from which they themselves are fallen away, they had no authority either to baptize or to ordain. And therefore those who were from time to time baptized by them, were ordered, as though baptized by laymen, to come to the church to be purified by the Church's true baptism.[80]

Therefore, we can conclude that in St. Basil's understanding, there is only one church, which alone possesses the right to confer the grace of the Holy Spirit. This grace cannot be transferred to any other gatherings of people through the divisions made by human efforts. All these schisms and divisions do not do any good to those who left the church because they lost the grace. This means that they lost the ability to baptize and to ordain people for ministry. In this sense, they cannot function even as a part of the church. Although they can still preach about faith, they are not able to provide salvation, in St. Basil's opinion, because their baptism is not valid. Once again, we can notice how St. Basil defends the unity and authority of the church through promoting the idea that there is no salvation outside the church.

As was mentioned earlier, in the case of schismatics, there were disagreements with other Christians on the issue of discipline and submission to canonical authorities, but this does not imply any false teaching or doctrinal controversies at least in the beginning of schism. On the contrary, St. Basil posits that the disagreement of heretics had to do with "the actual faith in God." This means that the improper understanding of creedal statements and the wrong profession of faith makes the church reject the baptism of heretics altogether.[81] In St. Basil's thought, this "actual faith" is always connected with the trinitarian confession.

"Nevertheless, since it has seemed to some of those of Asia that, for the sake of management of the majority, their baptism should be accepted, let it be accepted." However, in his *Letter* 199.47, he adds that he re-baptizes Novatians (Cathari are followers of Novatian) on the same ground as Encratitae, Saccophori, and Apotactitae. "All these I re-baptize on the same principle. If among you their re-baptism is forbidden, for the sake of some arrangement, nevertheless let my principle prevail."

80. Ibid. This passage also shows St. Basil's belief that baptism could be administered in the church only by an ordained priest. St. Basil grounds his arguments on the unity of the church and from this he deduces the unity of baptism. It seems that he follows Cyprian's opinion on this matter. See *Letter 69, Cyprian to Magnus*. Hamman, *Baptism*, 56.

81. Ibid.

> As we were baptized, so we profess our belief. As we profess our belief, so also we offer praise. As then baptism has been given us by the Saviour, in the name of the Father and of the Son and of the Holy Ghost, so, in accordance with our baptism, we make the confession of the creed, and our doxology in accordance with our creed.[82]

St. Basil is convinced that only through administration of baptism in the name of the Trinity the faith of the person leads to salvation. For St. Basil, the rejection of invocation of one of three Persons of the Holy Trinity during the baptism is compatible with the rejection of the Christian faith. His argument is that, according to the Gospel, our Lord himself taught his disciples to baptize in the name of the Father, and of the Son, and of the Holy Spirit.[83] St. Basil also believes that in some cases heresy could lead to eternal damnation as it happened to the Pepuzenes[84] because "blasphemy against the Holy Ghost admits of no forgiveness."[85] Therefore, St. Basil concludes, "For those who have not been baptized into the names delivered to us have not been baptized at all."[86]

The example of practical application of this belief can be found in St. Basil's *Letters* 199.20 where he discusses the particular case of a woman that rejected the heretical teaching and returned to the church. St. Basil stresses the idea that people while in heresy should be considered as those "who have not yet put on Christ's yoke" and "do not recognize the laws of the Lord." Therefore, St. Basil insists that they have to be received in the church

---

82. *Letter* 159.

83. *De Fide* (Clarke, 96). In the first book *Concerning Baptism*, St. Basil states, "Thus, baptized in the Name of the Holy Spirit, we were born anew. Having been born, we were also baptized in the Name of the Son, and we put on Christ. Then, having put on the new man according to God, we were baptized in the Name of the Father and called sons of God." *CBap1* (Wagner, 386–87).

84. *Letter* 188.1. According to St. Basil, they are "plainly heretical, for, by unlawfully and shamefully applying to Montanus and Priscilla the title of the Paraclete." In so doing, they "outraged the Holy Ghost by comparing Him to men," and they have "to be condemned for ascribing divinity to men." Pepuzenes belonged to a sect (later half of second century) who "were apocalyptic enthusiasts claiming special inspiration of the Spirit." See Bettenson, *The Later Christian Fathers*, 84n6.

85. Ibid. Similar idea of blasphemy against the Holy Spirit can be also found in St. Basil's *Letter* 159.2: "All who call the Holy Ghost a creature we pity, on the ground that, by this utterance, they are falling into the unpardonable sin of blasphemy against Him."

86. Ibid. We have to mention that St. Basil is aware that this statement is in some sense in disagreement with the New Testament evidence when apostles baptized in the name of the Lord or in Christ only. He provides some explanations on this issue in *HS* 12.28, but he still comes to a conclusion that the trinitarian formula is the criterion of the authenticity of baptism.

as catechumens. In addition, they have remission of all their sins "from their faith in Christ" including all their previous misunderstandings. St. Basil goes on and explains, "As a general rule, all sins formerly committed in the catechumenical state are not taken into account. The Church does not receive these persons without baptism."[87] From this statement, we can conclude that St. Basil considers heretics as those who do not know God and his law and, in this sense, equal to pagans.

It is obvious that all these divisions and schisms undermine unity of the church.[88] Also of the great importance for St. Basil is the inability of these groups to safeguard the true baptism and its effectiveness and, therefore, the salvation of people who join their gatherings. The consequences of these heretical divisions are very dangerous and lead to the destruction of the eternal destiny of many people. In St. Basil's opinion, trinitarian faith and baptism is a fundamental point of Christian communion with God. As he explains, "So we believe, and so we baptize into a Trinity of one Substance . . . If we keep this faith [in Trinity], we show love towards Him and are counted worthy to abide in Him."[89] On this ground, heretics are not able to have true relationships with God because of their faith discrepancy, which contradicts the "actual faith" in the Holy Trinity. In addition, according to St. Basil, they are deprived of the grace of the Holy Spirit, which can be granted only to those who received the true baptism of the church.

In St. Basil's thought, the idea of grace conferred in baptism is connected to the idea of human free will.[90] In his treatise *On the Holy Spirit*, St. Basil implies that in baptism, a baptized person is not saved completely, but God through the church provides the opportunity for this person to work out his salvation with the help of God's grace.[91] Only on "the day of redemption" in heaven will the grace of the Spirit be "bestowed in more abundant and perfect measure"[92] on the righteous. The meaning of this concept of grace in St. Basil's writings refers to the economy of salvation, performed

---

87. *Letter* 199.20.

88. See St. Basil's opinion of heretical divisions in his *Hom.* 23.4. PG 31:596B–D. See also his *Letter* 263 to the Western part of the church on this issue.

89. *De Fide* (Clarke, 96).

90. As will be shown in this chapter, St. Basil believes that humans have the ability to accept or to reject the grace of the Holy Spirit.

91. *HS* 16.40. This idea of grace was kept and developed by the Orthodox Church. See Lossky, *Mystical Theology*, 196–216. See also Pomazansky, *Orthodox Dogmatic Theology*, 257–61. As Pomazansky nicely phrased it in his book, "Those who enter the Church have entered into the Kingdom of grace." St. Basil also provides a list of benefits accomplished by the death of Christ and conferred in baptism in his homily *EHB* 5, PG 31:433A.

92. Ibid.

both by the Son of God and by the Holy Spirit with the understanding that God the Father is involved in everything. St. Basil connects the rite of baptism to what is done by Christ and what Christians are supposed to do as the result. Following the biblical teaching, St. Basil asserts,

> All we who were baptized into Christ Jesus were baptized into His death. We were buried therefore with Him through baptism into death; knowing this, that our old man was crucified with Him, that the body of sin might be done away, that we should no longer be in bondage to sin.
>
> [To be born again means] to put on the new man, which is being renewed unto knowledge after the image of Him that created him; as it is written: As many of you as were baptized into Christ did put on Christ.[93]

He is convinced that the ultimate goal of every Christian is to become Christlike.[94] In order to accomplish this task, a person through baptism has to be born of the Spirit. In some sense, a believer should become spiritual because "he should be, according to the measure given him, that very thing of which he was born [Spirit]."[95] St. Basil means that through baptism the believer receives "the measure of grace," which makes him able to acquire the qualities of a real Christian.

> What is the mark of a Christian? To be cleansed from all pollution of flesh and spirit, in the blood of Christ, to perfect holiness in the fear of God and love of Christ, and not to have spot or winkle or any such thing, but to be holy and without blemish.[96]

At the same time, St. Basil believes that people have the ability to reject this grace of the Spirit even after the baptismal rite "by the wickedness of their ways."[97] In this sense, he perceives this grace as the presence of the Spirit in the life of those who accepted baptism.

In Basil's opinion, grace does not guarantee salvation and those who were "sealed by the Spirit for the day of redemption" have to "preserve pure and undiminished the first fruits which they received of the Spirit."[98] Furthermore, being assisted by grace, they have to learn the Christian way of

---

93. *The Morals* (Clarke, 130). St. Basil follows here Rom 6:3, 4, 6 and Gal 3:27.

94. *HS* 1.2, 9.23. See also *LR* 8 (Clarke, 169).

95. *The Morals* 20.2; 80.22 (Clarke, 107, 130). St. Basil uses the verse from John 3:6 to support his opinion.

96. *The Morals* (Clarke, 130).

97. *HS* 16.40.

98. Ibid.

life, which means spiritual growth in love toward God and their neighbors.⁹⁹ As St. Basil insists, ". . . be enrolled in the Church . . . Take instructions, learn the constitution of the Gospels—vigilance of the eyes, control of the tongue, mastery of the body, humility of mind, purity of thought, and an end to anger."¹⁰⁰ Therefore, the church is the place where this growth begins with baptism and where it continues afterwards. Regenerated through grace given at baptism, every human receives the opportunity to become completely transformed in the image of God. St. Basil reminds his readers that "those who have grieved the Holy Spirit by their evil ways, or have not increased the talents they were given, will be deprived of what they have received, and their share of grace will be given to others; . . . they will be separated from the Spirit forever."¹⁰¹ However, this separation takes place only after the physical death of the person. Until then the life of the baptized is penetrated by the Holy Spirit, and she or he has a chance to return to God.

> At present, before the day of judgment comes, even though the Spirit cannot dwell within those who are unworthy, he nevertheless is present in a way with those who have been baptized, hoping that their conversion will result in salvation. On the day of judgment, however, He will be completely cut off from the soul that defiled His grace.¹⁰²

St. Basil believes that even if a true conversion did not take place before the rite, the grace given at baptism will be present with the person throughout his life while he stays in the church.¹⁰³ Later on, this idea of grace, which is received at baptism and which assists humans in acquiring their salvation, became one of the arguments in support of infant baptism. It is possible to make a conclusion from the passage cited above that if the Holy Spirit awaits the conversion of an adult who has been baptized, then he might await the conversion of an infant as well. It should be noted, that St. Basil never formulated this conclusion in his writings, and his position on infant baptism is not very clear.

---

99. *The Morals* (Clarke, 131). Several times in this passage, St. Basil gives the answer to the question "What is mark of a Christian?" At the end, he comes to a conclusion, "To love one another, even as Christ also loved us . . . to see the Lord always before him."

100. *EHB*, PG 31:440A. Translation is from Halton, *Exhortation to Holy Baptism*, 84. See the same idea of the church as "the school of God's commandments" in *LR* 2 (Clarke, 153). See similar idea of learning and transformation in *CBap 1* (Wagner, 358–59).

101. *HS* 16.40 (Anderson, 66).

102. Ibid., 67.

103. As we have seen earlier, St. Basil thinks that, even if a Christian leaves the church, he loses this grace because there is no salvation outside the church.

St. Basil does not mention directly the baptism of infants in any of his works, but there are some phrases, which could be interpreted in a way that infants and little children are allowed to receive baptism.[104] For instance, there are passages where he persuades his hearers not to postpone their baptism and to receive it as early as possible, and where he argues that Jews do not put off circumcision, and they perform it on the eighth day.[105] The implied logic is that believers in Christ should not put off "the circumcision made without hands."[106] In another passage, St. Basil proposes to his hearers that the young are to guard their youth with "the bridle of baptism."[107] Here is St. Basil's argument: "Who has guaranteed you the full term of old age? Who can guarantee the future so confidently? Do you not see infants snatched away, and those in prime of life carried off?"[108] From St. Basil's writings, we also can get a picture that infants and children were present during the service. In his *Homily 8*, he says that newborn infants are being brought into the congregation and "they should be present there indeed" but with their parents.[109] Also children who have left their books at school join their voices with the congregation. They do the responses together with adults as a kind of pleasure and fun, "making our grief into a holiday."[110] However, it is not obvious from the context whether these children and infants were previously baptized or not. On the evidence given in the homily, it is impossible to decide how long they stayed with the congregation, and when they were supposed to leave the church worship.[111]

Although, as we can see, St. Basil insists on baptism of young people, it still does not mean that he suggests this should happen as soon as a baby

---

104. The book by Wall, *The History of Infant Baptism*, is quite helpful. The author collected the short abstracts from the original writings of Church Fathers about infant baptism including the writings of St. Basil, and he provides *pro* and *contra* arguments based on these works. For background information, see also Jeremias, *Infant Baptism in the First Four Centuries*.

105. *EHB*, PG 31:428A. *HS* 15.35.

106. *HS* 15.35.

107. *EHB*, PG 31:432C.

108. *EHB*, PG 31:436C (Halton, 83).

109. *Hom. 8*, PG 31:309CD, 312A. In this homily, St. Basil mentions that the infants were brought to the church and left there alone without their parents. The reason is unclear, but he rebukes the parents for doing such things.

110. Ibid., PG 31:309C.

111. If there were any hints in St. Basil's homily that they stayed for Eucharist, we could conclude that they were baptized. Many scholars who support the idea of infant baptism do not discuss the infant Eucharist, but these two rites in the Eastern Church go together and cannot be separated. See Jewett, *Infant Baptism & the Covenant of Grace*, 41–42.

is born. He himself was baptized as an adult. Although he grew up in a Christian family, the practice of infant baptism was not common at this time.[112] If we look more closely at the text, we can notice that St. Basil's hearers "have been catechized in the word from their childhood."[113] This means that they started to attend the church when they were children, but they are not yet baptized. The other observation might be that if these people have reasons to postpone their own baptism, probably, they would not baptize their children either. One more argument could be taken from St. Basil's description of the baptismal ceremony. The list of actions from the rite implies that those who receive baptism should be of responsible age. They were supposed to say some words, lift their hands to heaven, stand on their feet, bend their knees, speak the confession aloud, give adherence to God, and renounce the enemy.[114] Therefore, it is possible for children to accomplish this ceremony, but not for infants.

On the basis of discussed arguments, we can come to several conclusions concerning infants and children in the church: First, St. Basil considers children and infants worthy to be present during the liturgy; second, they were part of the communal life and they received "the word" or instructions from an early age; third, St. Basil does insist on early baptism and on this ground children could be allowed to receive baptism at the age when they are able to follow the ceremony; fourth, since baptism on death-bed was an accepted practice,[115] the same could be provided for a very sick infant.

Although St. Basil in his writings talks of baptism upon personal profession of faith, we also have to take into consideration that there is evidence of the baptism of infants from the second century on.[116] We do not have evidence that St. Basil practiced infant baptism, but this possibility cannot be excluded because of his serious attitude toward the rite and his belief that salvation of everybody should be secured through true baptism. In St. Basil's understanding, baptism is an important step in the life of a believer and the life of the church. This is the moment of the establishment of a

---

112. This observation can be also supported by the historical fact that only later when Augustine of Hippo provided the theology for infant baptism, it became common practice. See Wright, *What Has Infant Baptism done to Baptism?*, 12. See also Fedwick, "A Chronology of the Life and Works of Basil of Caesarea," 6.

113. *EHB*, PG 31:425B.

114. Ibid., PG 31:436C. In the following centuries when baptism of infants became common practice, the words were said for them or instead of them.

115. Ibid.

116. Both Tertullian in his *De Baptismo* 18.4 (200–206 AD) and Cyprian in his *Letter to Fidus* (AD 251–53) discussed baptism of infants. See the abstracts from both writings in W. Wall, *The History of Infant Baptism*, 41–50; 61–73. See also the translation of Tertullian's treatise in Hamman, *Baptism*, 30–49.

new relationship with God and admission to the community of his people since in baptism the adoption takes place.[117] All humans are supposed to accept baptism in order that they may receive their salvation and enter the life eternal in the heavenly church. Both a new spiritual birth of a Christian and his/her spiritual growth happens in the church and through the church's actions including the baptismal rite and the teaching.

EUCHARIST—MAINTAINING THE LIFE OF THE CHURCH

In St. Basil's time the Eucharist was part of the liturgy, which revealed who really belonged to the community of faithful and who stayed outside.[118] This is another "mystery" of the church, which is available only for people that went through regeneration, enlightenment, and adoption in baptism. They are accepted by the community on the ground of their public profession of faith in the Holy Trinity and the fulfillment of all the requirements prescribed by the "unwritten tradition"[119] of the church concerning baptism. The Eucharist is the next step, which happens immediately after baptism and is closely connected to it.[120] This is fellowship of Christians who once were sealed by the grace of God and who continue their journey together in the right direction. St. Basil points out, "What is the mark of a Christian? To be cleansed from all pollution . . . to be holy and without blemish, and so to eat the body of Christ and drink his blood."[121]

---

117. HS 10.26, 15.35. EHB, PG 31: 425A, 433A. Several times St. Basil talks of grace of adoption received in baptism—υἱοθεσίς χάριγμα.

118. Non-baptized participants of the service and catechumens were not allowed to take part in the Eucharist and they had to leave the congregation before that rite usually took place. See Jungmann, *The Early Liturgy*, 159.

119. In his treatise *On the Holy Spirit*, St. Basil explains that what was practiced before by other faithful believers came down to the next generation not as "written teaching" but as "mystical tradition." For example, in the preface and conclusion of the Eucharist they added some words not written in the gospel. These words, he implies, were delivered secretly only through the practice of the first Christians to St. Basil's contemporaries as the "unwritten tradition." See HS 27.66. St. Basil testifies that this tradition was delivered to him personally "by one [Dianius, bishop of the Cappadocian Caesarea] who spent a long life in the service of God, and by him *he* was both baptized, and admitted to the ministry of the church." Therefore, he uses the same form, rule, and terms as the presbyters before him. See HS 29.72.

120. After the baptism and the triple immersion in water, the bishop laid his hands on the baptized and signed them with the chrism on the forehead. Then they were allowed to receive the communion for the first time. See the whole procedure in Fisher, "Baptism," 56.

121. *The Morals* 80.22 (Clarke, 130).

This participation in the "mysteries" from the beginning identifies the believers: who they are, what they are supposed to do, to whom they belong, and where they are going. In his writings, St. Basil clearly describes the main characteristics of those who are counted worthy to "eat the bread and drink the cup of the Lord": First, they are marked as the Christians; second, they are supposed to become "holy and without blemish"—to become Christlike; third, they belong to this community of people with whom they partake communion, and where "they love one another;" fourth, they hope "to see the Lord" with whom they are in communion as well.[122] According to the sequences of the rites in the church, the believers receive their identity at baptism and they reaffirm it through the following Eucharist. The difference between these two "mysteries" is that baptism, as initiation into the Church, happens only once,[123] and the Eucharist should be practiced repeatedly.

When one of the ladies[124] asks St. Basil of the frequency with which the Eucharist could be partaken, he answers that "it is good and beneficial to communicate every day, and to partake of the holy body and blood of Christ."[125] As the basis for this statement, he uses the words of the Lord himself from the Gospel: "He that eats my flesh and drinks my blood has eternal life."[126] In the following sentence, St. Basil asserts that nobody will doubt that "to share frequently in life, is the same thing as to have manifold life."[127] Then he shares that his own custom is to communicate four times a week, "on the Lord's day, on Wednesday, on Friday, and on the Sabbath, and on the other days if there is a commemoration of any Saint."[128] The whole

---

122. See all these points in his *The Morals* 80.22 when St. Basil answers the questions "What is the mark of a Christian?" and "What is the mark of those who eat the bread and drink the cup of the Lord?" (Clarke, 130–31).

123. As we have seen earlier, in St. Basil's opinion, true baptism happens only once and after that even if the believers commit sin the grace of God still stays with them and waits for their repentance. St. Basil believes that there should be taken some penitential procedures but not re-baptism. See his canonical letters concerning sins committed by Christians. For example, *Letter* 217, and *Letter* 188. As St. Basil himself put it, "We do not, as is the fashion of the Jews, wash ourselves at each defilement, but own the baptism of salvation to be one." *HS* 15.35.

124. The letter is addressed to the Patrician Caesaria, but unfortunately, there was not preserved any historical information who this lady was.

125. *Letter* 93. This is the most interesting fragment of Eucharistic material, which is found in St. Basil writings. Although there were some debates about the authenticity of the letter, the contemporary scholars agreed that there appear no worthy reasons for doubting St. Basil's authorship. Fedwick listed this letter as authentic in *Basil of Caesarea: Christian, Humanist, Ascetic*, xxi.

126. John 6:54. See *Letter* 93.

127. Ibid.

128. Ibid. Saturday was the day of foretasting of resurrection, Wednesdays and

passage implies that Christians should participate in the Eucharist as often as possible. Although St. Basil does not give the exact reason why communion should be received frequently, we can understand that he considers it as a source of eternal life or, in St. Basil's words, "manifold life." Therefore, we can see the logic in St. Basil's thinking that baptism is the new birth of a Christian[129] and the Eucharist may be perceived as some spiritual nourishment, which should be partaken often in order to support believer's life.[130]

After such an encouragement to take communion daily, the question could arise whether this mean that people have to go to the church every day in order to receive the Eucharist. In the same *Letter 93*, St. Basil explains that "in times of persecution to be compelled to take communion in his own hand without the presence of a priest or minister is not a serious offence."[131] He does not say here that it is possible or acceptable to perform "the mystery" of Eucharist without priest.[132] What he really means is that after the bread and wine were consecrated during the liturgy in the church, they could be taken home and then partaken in portions when it is convenient for the believer. St. Basil is convinced that after the mysteries are completed, the participants can use the elements of the Eucharist when they feel a need.

> ... when the priest gives the portion, the recipient takes it with complete power over it, and so lifts it to his lips with his own hand. It has the same validity whether one portion or several portions are received from the priest at the same time.[133]

The ground for legitimacy of these actions is the customary practice, which was held by the Christians at Alexandria and in Egypt. St. Basil points especially to a long tradition in the deserts where "all the solitaries" kept the communion at their homes.[134] Therefore, in his understanding, the Eucharist is both public and private. The first and the most important part of the

---

Fridays were days of fasting. In this context, the term "saint" means martyr. See Bebis, "Introduction to the Liturgical Theology of St. Basil the Great," 281–82.

129. St. Basil uses this analogy for baptism in *HS* 10.26.

130. The title of chapter 3 in St. Basil's book *On Baptism* mentions this idea of nourishment: "That he who has been regenerated through Baptism should thenceforth be nourished by participation in the Holy Mysteries." See *CBap* 1 (Wagner, 386).

131. *Letter 93*. The context of the letter actually implies that the daily communion can be taken without presence of the priest not only in a case of persecutions.

132. On the contrary, he even believes that it is not allowed to celebrate the mystery and "the holy things" in a common house except in an emergency. *SR* 310 (Clarke, 350).

133. *Letter 93*. See a footnote 2332 to this epistle, "The custom of the reservation of the Sacrament is, as is well known, of great antiquity . . . Abuses of the practice soon led to prohibition."

134. Ibid.

mystery when the wine and bread are prayed over and consecrated should be done only by a priest and during the public service when the whole congregation is present.[135] This corporate act of giving thanks (εὐχαριστία) and praise to the Lord is the time when the believers communicate with God as the church. The second part of the mystery when this bread and wine are distributed among the believers is more private. According to St. Basil, the recipients take it "with complete power over it," and they are allowed to keep it and use it again afterwards, because "the recipient, participating in it each time as entire, is bound to believe that he properly takes and receives it from the giver."[136] The idea is implied that these elements now can help to maintain the believer's life, and the person may use them for this purpose privately. This shows one more time St. Basil's opinion about the importance of receiving this bread and wine often. It seems that for him these consecrated elements of the Eucharist themselves possess something that provides strength for the believers and leads to the eternal life. There is a notion in St. Basil's writings that during the rite and especially the Eucharistic prayer the transformation of bread and wine happens.[137] He does not say directly that they become the real body and blood of Christ, but he uses these words "body and blood" in his writings.[138] St. Basil is also convinced that the words, which the priest says, have "great importance to the validity of the ministry."[139] It is only after the priest "has completed the sacrifice and given it" to the participants, they may use it as a special bread and wine.[140]

---

135. This is the core element of the *Liturgy of St. Basil*, which was kept and celebrated throughout the centuries.

136. *Letter* 93.

137. According to text of the *Liturgy* that bears the name of St. Basil, during the Invocation of the Spirit on the Holy Gifts a priest is supposed to say the following words: "[T]hy Holy Spirit may come upon us and upon these gifts set forth, to bless, hallow, and declare this bread indeed the precious body of our Lord and God and Savior Jesus Christ, and what is in this cup the precious blood of thy Christ." Unfortunately, we cannot be sure that these were the exact words St. Basil used during the mystery. If he used them, then this is proof that he believed in the complete transformation of the Holy Gifts. The text is from *The Orthodox Liturgy Being the Divine Liturgy of S. John Chrysostom and S. Basil the Great*, 73.

138. We can suggest with a high probability that St. Basil followed the common belief of the church that the bread and wine really turned into the Lord's body and blood, which communicate immortal life. In the previous centuries, this was used as an argument against the Docetists' denial of the reality of Christ's body. See historical background in Kelly, *Early Christian Doctrines*, 197–98.

139. HS 27.66.

140. PG 32:485AB. Jackson uses in his translation of the *Letter* 93 a word "offering" instead of "sacrifice," which is slightly different. The use of the term "sacrifice" (θυςία) is very interesting, but a comparatively shortage of texts about the Eucharist in St. Basil's

His words indicate that a change or conversion takes place, and the bread and wine are affected by the administrated rite in a way that now they can support the lives of the believers.[141]

Though it seems that participation in the Eucharist is helpful and will do only good to the believer, there is a condition to it. Following the biblical teaching, St. Basil asserts, "He who approaches the communion without consideration of the manner in which participation in the body and blood of Christ is granted is in no way benefited; but he that partakes unworthily is condemned."[142] In St. Basil's opinion, the community of faithful has the right to decide who is worthy to take part in the Eucharist and to apply the penitential rules to unworthy ones.[143] In the situation when sin is committed openly, St. Basil believes that the church has the opportunity to protect the members from condemnation and to discipline them at the same time. This exclusion from the "mystery" is considered as a punishment, because the believer is cut off from the source of life. However, this action leads to the correction of the person and in the end to the restoration of fellowship with people and with God the Trinity,[144] which is the ultimate goal of every Christian.

The whole structure of the Eucharistic service is created in a way that reflects the importance of the special relationship between the participants.[145] Many things they have to do together in unison—to "sing hymns unto the Lord,"[146] to say words in response, to confirm with "Amen," to reaffirm their faith through reading of the creed, and to offer praises to God. These liturgical acts manifest their unity in love. In order to enter into fellowship with the Holy Trinity the believers participating in the liturgy should exist in love with those who are present in the church. Hence, during the Eucharistic

writings makes it almost impossible to understand which meaning of this term he is using. See different suggestions and options of this meaning in Hallburton, "The Patristic Theology of the Eucharist," 248–49.

141. Later on, the Eastern Orthodox Church developed and completely accepted the idea that during the Eucharist the bread and wine are changed into the real body and blood of Christ by the coming down of the Holy Spirit. See Pomazansky, *Orthodox Dogmatic Theology*, 279. See also Ware, *The Orthodox Church*, 290–91.

142. *The Morals* 21.2 (Clarke, 108). See the same idea in *CBap 1* (Wagner, 389).

143. See, for example, his *Letter* 188, *Letter* 199, and *Letter* 217.

144. As we mentioned earlier in this chapter, the whole liturgy has a completely trinitarian orientation. See Hutcheon, "A Sacrifice of Praise," 3–23.

145. Although we cannot be sure about the particular words of *the Liturgy*, most scholars agree that the main elements and the core of *the Liturgy* were kept from St. Basil's time. Therefore, an analysis of these elements concerning the communal aspect can be helpful.

146. See *The Morals* 21.4 (Clarke, 108).

service in response to the exhortation "let us love one another," there follows the, so called, "Kiss of Peace."[147] This holy kiss is an expression of agape love among believers as followers of Christ who brought them this peace. Another great part of the Eucharistic service, which demonstrates the bond of Christians, is the commemoration of all the members of the church.[148] These prayers for the departed and the living remind the believers that someday they will meet each other at God's table in the heavenly kingdom.

We can notice that though the Eucharist happens here and now among the believers, it looks back to the past and forward to the future at the same time. On the one hand, St. Basil believes that the faithful believers do this in order to keep "in perpetual memory him who died for them and rose again."[149] During the service, they recite the mighty acts of God and the whole salvation history.[150] On the other hand, the meaning and the effects of the Eucharist are more effective than just that of a memorial ceremony.[151] St. Basil is convinced that "participation in the body and blood of Christ is necessary for eternal life."[152] This "mystery" reminds the believers where they came from, and what Christ has done for them, and why they should be thankful. At the same time, it points to their future and directs them to the one whose "body and blood" they partake. In one of the rules of his *Moralia*,[153] St. Basil alleges the consequences of communion with the words from John 6:53–54 about the resurrection. The Eucharist helps the Christians to move from the state of corruption to the resurrection through partaking the flesh and blood of their resurrected Lord. From now on, they are called "to perfect holiness in the fear of God and love of Christ."[154] For this reason, God through the church provides help to his children that "they who live may no longer live to themselves but unto Him."[155] Therefore, St. Basil believes that the "mysteries" are given by God to assist the growth of believers into Christ. Only in the church may they have this communion of love. On this basis, those who separate themselves from the church cannot take part in the true Eucharist. As we have seen earlier, in St. Basil's theology,

---

147. *The Orthodox Liturgy*, 63. See more about this part of the eucharistic liturgy in Cope, "Kiss of Peace," 250–51.

148. *The Orthodox Liturgy*, 77, 81.

149. *The Morals* 80.22 (Clarke, 130). See also ibid., 21.3 (Clarke, 107).

150. For example, the prayers from the *Liturgy* that bears the name of St. Basil in *The Orthodox Liturgy*, 62, 68.

151. St. Basil uses the word ἀνάμνησις. PG 31:740B.

152. *The Morals* 21.1 (Clarke, 107).

153. Ibid., 21.2 (Clarke, 108).

154. Ibid., 80.22 (Clarke, 130).

155. Ibid., 21.3 (Clarke, 108).

there is only one true church, and all heretics do not belong to another part within the church, but they completely "cut themselves off from the whole Church,"[156] from her love, from the true teaching, and from her "mysteries." Unity of the church is one of the principal themes of the Eucharistic service. The Christians offer up a special prayer for this unity in faith and life. Nevertheless, there is an understanding in St. Basil that this unity comes only through their love of God and their love of other Christians, which is closely connected to the right profession of their faith in the Trinity and their participation in the true "mysteries" of the church.

PENANCE—RESTORING TO THE CHURCH

The penitential system in the church plays an important role in the liturgical life of Christians, because it is created in order to prevent some believers from taking part in liturgy and to let them know that they are in danger of losing their salvation and life eternal. The authority of the ecclesiastical canons is grounded in their communal acceptance and, in St. Basil's thinking, these rules have "the force of law" in the church. He believes that they "have been handed down to us by holy men."[157] This means that the previous generation of faithful believers in the church together worked out the system that prescribes what shall be done with those who are guilty of different sins.

Among the writings of St. Basil, there are several letters, which contain ecclesiastical regulations concerning penitential discipline and which provide the information for better understanding of the liturgical life of the church in the fourth century.[158] They explain in detail who, for whatever reason, and for how long should be restraint of participation in liturgy and the Eucharist.[159] St. Basil describes four degrees of the separation of the penitent from the assembly of faithful during the liturgical service: weeping, hearing, kneeling, and standing.[160] First of all, until the sinners do not

---

156. *Letter* 204.7.

157. *Letter* 160.2.

158. These are three so-called Canonical *Letters* 188, 199, 217. In some other letters St. Basil also discusses the rules or customs of the church: *Letters* 160 (about unlawful marriage), 53 (about receiving money from candidates for ordination), 54 (about the ordination of unworthy men), and 287 and 288 (about excommunication).

159. From these canonical letters we can conclude that the existing system of penitential discipline was wholly public and there is no sign of a sacrament of private penance at that time.

160. For example, see *Letter* 217.75. St. Basil does not create his own penitential system, but he follows the existing tradition in Asia Minor. The same states of separation had been mentioned in Gregory Thaumaturgos work *Epistula canonica*. See Quasten,

give up their wrongdoing, they are not allowed even to enter the place where the Christians have their worship services. After believers admit the sin in their lives and cease sinning, they are able to start the process of restoration to communal life. The first step is a state of *weeping* when the person has to stay outside the church building near the doors begging the other Christians to pray for him. Next is the state of *hearing*, and the penitents have the permission to listen to Scriptures and to instructions together with the catechumens and have to leave immediately afterwards. At this stage of penitential punishment, they are not allowed to pray with the community as a part of them. The third degree is *kneeling*, which gives the people an opportunity to pray on their knees during the liturgy. Lastly, the state of *standing* comes when they are allowed to stay with others during the whole service, but they still do not participate in communion. Only after all these stages of repentance are completed, can believers be admitted to the Eucharist. In St. Basil's *Letter 217*, we can find an example of the duration of the different periods while these states of separation are applied.

> The intentional homicide, who has afterwards repented, will be excommunicated from the sacrament for twenty years. The twenty years will be appointed for him as follows: for four he ought to *weep*, standing outside the door of the house of prayer, beseeching the faithful as they enter in to offer prayer in his behalf, and confessing his own sin. After four years he will be admitted among the *hearers*, and during five years will go out with them. During seven years he will go out with the *kneelers*, praying. During four years he will only *stand* with the faithful, and will not take part in the oblation. On the completion of this period he will be admitted to participation of the sacrament.[161]

According to canons, the severity of discipline in some sense is equal to the heaviness of sins committed by the believer, and the length of these periods varies for different sins. They may last for several years and sometimes until the end of life.[162] What was important for St. Basil is not the length of time but the "the fruits of repentance" or "the manner of penance."[163] He is convinced that "it is necessary that those who repent should weep bitterly

---

Patrology, 234.

161. *Letter* 217.56. However, nothing more is said about how the penitents were supervised or how the process was carried on in practice, and how these people were kept out from the liturgy.

162. For example, *Letter* 217.73.

163. *Letter* 217.84. See also *SR* 13 (Clarke, 235).

and show from the heart the rest of the things proper to repentance."[164] In St. Basil's opinion, through the discipline penitents are winning their salvation. Therefore, "the mere giving up of sins is not sufficient for them," but "they need also fruits meet for repentance."[165] The examples of such fruits are given in St. Basil's homily *On Psalm 32* when the repentant is expected to destroy the consequences of committed sin by works of righteousness opposed to it:

> Have you reviled? Bless. Have you defrauded? Make restitution. Have you been intoxicated? Fast. Have you made false pretensions? Be humble. Have you been envious? Console. Have you murdered? Bear witness, or afflict your body with equivalent of martyrdom through confession.[166]

The repentance should be genuine and sincere. In this case, St. Basil asserts, "Worthy repentance always brings with it a firm hope of forgiveness."[167] It should not be only regret, or awareness of one's sinfulness, or acknowledgment of wrong actions. Rather it is a strong desire and a firm intention for correction, which are followed by the fulfillment of all practical steps, prescribed by the church.

Interestingly enough, the basis of forgiveness is not the work done by the repentant, but "God's mercies and the greatness of God's compassion."[168] St. Basil states very clearly that the remission of sins "set forth in the blood of Christ" and the number and greatness of sins should not be a reason for despair. He is convinced that "it is impossible to measure the mercy or number the compassions of God," and "if the manner of our repentance is worthy," then even the multitude of sins might be forgiven.[169] However, in order to join the Christian community again as equals, penitents are supposed to follow the rules and meet all the requirements.

The baptism of believers is the point after which the church authorities have to deal with post-baptismal wrongdoings. Only to Christians may they

---

164. *The Morals* 1.3 (Clarke, 101).

165. Ibid., 1.4 (Clarke, 101).

166. *Ps.* 32.2 (Way, 229–30).

167. *SR* 58 (Clarke, 251). As an example of a real penitence, St. Basil uses the people of Nineveh and others in his *Homily* 8, PG 31:316.

168. *SR* 13 (Clarke, 235).

169. Ibid. In order to support his idea St. Basil refers to Isa 1:18 and to the parable of prodigal son. See also St. Basil's attitude toward the former sinners in his *Letter* 112, "Yet another plea that I ought to urge is this, that we do not chastise transgressors for what is past and gone, (for what means can be devised for undoing the past?) but either that they may be reformed for the future, or may be an example of good behavior to others."

prescribe the canonical discipline in order to keep them saved. Obviously, all the sins committed prior to baptism were remitted during the sacrament or, as Basil calls it, the mystery. Afterwards, in a case of sinful actions, the Christian who committed a sin has to go through ecclesial punishment, which looks severe and shameful. There are also social consequences closely related to it when almost all communications with the offender are suspended.[170] This is one of the reasons, why some people decided to postpone their baptism. It seems that they were not sure about their faith and their ability to avoid sinful behavior. Therefore, they were afraid that at some point in their Christian life they would have to go through the penitential procedure. St. Basil rebukes them for such attitude, because he believes that his hearers do not want to give up their sins and the earthly pleasure related to them. He ascribes the list of sins and the following words to the representative of those who delay receiving baptism:

> Leave me alone. I will use my body to enjoy what is shameful, I will wallow in the mud of pleasure, I will bloody my hands, I will plunder what belongs to others, I will walk in wickedness, I will curse and swear. And I will receive baptism when I finally cease from sin.[171]

In St. Basil's opinion, these people will go through the punishment anyway, but it will be "the torment for eternity."[172] Their sinful life will lead to the commitment "to fire because of the pleasures of the flesh."[173] On the other hand, baptism will keep them saved for enjoyment of heavenly blessings. Consequently, we can come to a conclusion that in St. Basil's thinking, the temporary ecclesial punishment will help the Christians avoid eternal punishment, which is much more severe than any earthly one that the church can use. St. Basil shares with the hearers his concerns that they could be lost forever if they continue to choose sinful pleasures instead of the life proper to Christians who are loved and corrected by the community. As Basil admits, "I am driven to tears when I see that you prefer deeds of wickedness to the great glory of God and that you exclude yourself from the blessed promises in clinging to sin and seductive lust and thus lose sight of the blessings of that heavenly Jerusalem."[174]

---

170. *Letter* 288.
171. *EHB,* PG 31:433B (Halton, 82).
172. Ibid., PG 31:444B.
173. Ibid.
174. Ibid. (Halton, 87).

There is an obvious contrast between the destiny of those, who belong to the community, and those, who are in a state in which they "choose rather to serve the pleasures of the flesh than to serve the Lord and refuse to accept the Gospel life."[175] St. Basil elaborates this idea in his canonical letters in order to convince the readers to follow the ecclesial rules. He is convinced that for the faithful ones there is a bright future when they see the glory of God and when all the promises of the Lord will be fulfilled. At the same time, the opposite group will experience the wrath of God and everlasting damnation.

St. Basil believes that each person who committed sin can be "made good through penitence," and these rules are helpful for the believer because at the end he will "receive the loving-kindness of God."[176] At the same time, these penitential actions serve as an example for other believers in the church.[177] As St. Basil says in one of his letters when he discusses a case of bribery among the church ministers, "I hope then that what I am writing about it may be taken by the guilty as medicine, by the innocent as a warning, by the indifferent, in which class I trust none of you may be found, as a testimony."[178] There is a notion in St. Basil's writings that the penitential system fulfils several functions: a) a discipline for wrong doers and the renewal of their spiritual condition, b) a warning to other Christians and their edification,[179] c) a restoration of sinners to "the communion of the body of Christ."[180] It is not a punishment in a strict sense but pedagogical and healing acts of the church, which are applied when needed to those who have sinned.

In St. Basil's understanding, the main goal of the penitence is to help the believers not to lose their salvation. He perceives all sins from an eschatological perspective because they have eternal consequences: "the end of sin is death" and "the end of the commandment of God is eternal life."[181]

---

175. *Letter* 217.84.

176. *Letter* 217.74.

177. *Letter* 287.

178. *Letter* 53. This word "medicine" can lead to the idea of sin as a spiritual disease, which is noted in the Orthodox thinking. Hence, the penance is seen as a means of spiritual healing. See, for example, Pomazansky, *Orthodox Dogmatic Theology*, 292.

179. See, for example, *The Morals* 11.2–3 (Clarke, 104). St. Basil asserts, "When some have incurred the judgment of God's anger, the rest ought to fear and correct themselves."

180. *Letter* 217.82.

181. *The Morals* 10.1 (Clarke, 104). Although St. Basil discusses in canons only the punishment for greater sins, he strongly believes that all sins without repentance lead unto death. In this sense, it is "impossible to observe this distinction" between sins. Even a smaller sin is disobedience to God, and if a person does not repent, then he

Inward Life of the Church

The role of the church is to guard the believers from harm caused by sin and to provide them with rules, which may correct the behavior of sinners and protect the faithful from the influence of committed sin. In St. Basil's thought, we see the idea of the solidarity of all members: if one member commits a sin, this has its impact on the entire community.[182] As illustrations, he uses the examples of Achan (Joshua 7:1–27) and of Zimri (Numbers 25:6–15) from the Old Testament when the sufferings of the whole nation were caused by a sin of just one person.[183] In these stories, the judge or the priest had to take an action in order to stop God's wrath or the plague and to save the community from the destructive consequences of sin. St. Basil believes that in his time the church and her ministers may act as God's representatives because they are given from God "the power of loosing and binding."[184] Using this allusion to Matt 16:19, Basil justifies the ecclesiastical practice of imposing and remitting penalties for sin. He asserts that when the penitent "exercises penitence with greater zeal," the bishop has the authority to "lessen the period of punishment."[185] On the contrary, in a case of disobedience to the existing ecclesiastical rules, the believer could be "excluded from participation in any of the ordinary relations of life."[186] Through penitence, the church gives to the sinner the second chance for repentance. It is the opportunity to regain the salvation, which could not be repeated.[187]

> When public punishment fails to bring a man to his senses, or exclusion from the prayers of the Church to drive him to repentance, it only remains to treat him in accordance with our Lord's directions—as it is written, "If thy brother shall trespass against thee . . . tell him his fault between thee and him; . . . if he will not hear thee, take with thee another;" "and if he shall" then "neglect to hear, tell it unto the Church; but if he neglect to hear even the

---

"shall not see life." See *SR* 293 (Clarke, 342). Therefore, no sin can be considered harmless, and all sins are subject to repentance (though not always the public penance is involved). As St. Basil noted, even "sinning in ignorance is not without danger." See *The Morals* 9.5 (Clarke 104).

182. This was discussed in chapter 3 of this book in a part concerning "the earthly church."

183. *Hom.* 8, PG 31:316A.

184. *Letter* 217.74. This is also an allusion to Matt 23:4.

185. Ibid.

186. *Letter* 288.

187. St. Basil believes, "He who has been corrected for his former sins, and counted worthy of forgiveness, if he sins again prepares for himself a judgment of wrath worse than the former judgment . . ." See *The Morals* 11.2–3 (Clarke, 104).

Church, let him be unto thee henceforth as an heathen man, and as a publican." Now all this we have done in the case of this fellow ... Henceforth let him be excommunicated.[188]

This is the worst scenario that could happen to a person, because in this situation, according to St. Basil, he "becomes altogether food for the devil."[189] In this sense, when community excludes somebody from their fellowship this person is excluded at once from the heavenly kingdom and transferred to the realm of the devil. On this ground, any penitence could be thought of as means of salvation, which the church is using for her children. Although this looks like a very bleak prospect for the sinners, there is always the possibility to receive forgiveness and to become re-established to the community of faithful. The process of restoration and the punishment itself seems a severe task, which is hard to accomplish. On the other hand, these detailed canons show an incredible grace of God and optimism.[190] According to these rules, any sin can be forgiven, and a person is able to receive a remission of sin even in a case of murder, adultery or idolatry committed after baptism.[191] St. Basil believes that even such sin as the denial of Christ can be forgiven, but those who "sinned against the mystery of salvation, ought to weep all *their* life long, and *are* bound to remain in penitence, being deemed worthy of the sacrament in the hour of death, through faith in the mercy of God."[192]

St. Basil believes that Christians should not be indifferent or neutral to the destiny of people who are in danger to see "the awful judgment" in "the terrible day of the retribution of the Lord."[193] Faithful believers are supposed

---

188. *Letter* 288.

189. Ibid.

190. St. Basil does not mention any ecclesiastical censure for lesser sins, which the Christian may commit daily, and which are hard to avoid. Public penance that he discusses was used by the community for grave sins.

191. We have to mention that in the last decades of the second century such sins as adultery, homicide and idolatry (or apostasy) were treated in practice as irremissible. See Kelly, *Early Christian Doctrines*, 217. In the light of these facts, St. Basil's rules do not look so severe, but on contrary, they show the mercy to the sinner.

192. *Letter* 217.73. We can notice that St. Basil's attitude toward the apostates who denied Christ is different than toward those who do not want to recognize the Trinity. According to the canons, which St. Basil discuss in his letters, in case of apostasy there is still possibility of forgiveness provided through the penitential procedure, although it is a lifelong punishment. However, these groups of people who do not believe in the Trinity, because they have denied the divinity of the Son or of the Holy Spirit, are not considered Christians at all, and penitential rules cannot be applied to them. Therefore, the only way for them to receive salvation is to be re-baptized after a proper confession.

193. *Letter* 217.84.

to support their brothers and sisters in their battle against sinful inclinations. St. Basil's appeal to the church is clear, "Let us above all pray that we may do them good, and rescue them from the snare of the evil one."[194] In this sense, the penitents have to be accompanied by the activity of the church community, which should try to preserve them from death eternal. Therefore, in St. Basil's thought, sin and the following penitence is not the private affair of the person who is guilty, but it has an ecclesial aspect. On the one hand, the community can experience the wrath of God if it tolerates sin among its members because this sin affects everyone. On the other hand, the role of the Christian community is to protect its members from eternal punishment and not to let them perish in their sins. Hence, the remedy is not a complete separation and exclusion of the sinner from fellowship of the faithful believers, but the proper saving actions of the church with regard to the sinners, which lead to a progress in the spiritual condition of the sinners and to the remission of the sins. Consequently, the assigned penitence is the one of these saving acts of the church that are followed by ecclesial prayers. This involvement of the community and other Christians is an essential part of the penitential process, which brings the believer to restoration into full membership and which actually means regaining fellowship with God the Trinity and life eternal.

CONCLUSION TO CHAPTER 5

The discussion of the liturgy and the Christian mysteries reveals to us the inner life of the Christian community. In St. Basil's thought, it is closely connected with the trinitarian teaching. In his opinion, the liturgy as a corporate act of worship fulfills a very special function. The reciting of psalms and common prayers, consisting of proper theological statements, leads to the right knowledge of God as the Father, Son and Holy Spirit. Consequently, this brings the believers to communion with God whom they may know and worship together as "true worshipers."

St. Basil strongly believes that God is present in his church during the service, and he is involved in the liturgy when the Christians offer to him their praises and participate in liturgical singing. According to St. Basil, this participation creates a bond of unity between all believers who join their voices with others in the church. In a sense, it reflects the common praise, which will be offered to their Creator in heaven. Therefore, awaiting this eschatological experience, Christians receive the opportunity to improve their

---

194. Ibid.

relationships with the Triune God and with their fellow worshipers here on earth when they are gathered together during the liturgy.

St. Basil is convinced that in order to join the future assemble of saints, the believers have also to participate in the mysteries that are part of the liturgical practice. Through baptism in the name of the Father, Son and Holy Spirit, Christians after regeneration and illumination receive the opportunity to participate on a regular basis in the second mystery, the Eucharist, and this opens for them a secret "unwritten" tradition. Both these mysteries affirm the right of the believers to join the church not only here on earth but in the heavenly kingdom as well.

In order to preserve believers for life eternal and to protect them against sinful inclinations, St. Basil insists on using penitence. In his opinion, it is better for Christian to abstain from the liturgy for a while during this earthly life than not to join the heavenly assembly of saints in the future. Therefore, this kind of discipline supported by ecclesial prayers may serve as an act of restoration of the believer to fellowship with the community and with the Triune God as well.

CHAPTER 6

Unity of the Church and Trinitarian Confession

FROM THE PREVIOUS CHAPTERS, we notice that two main streams of thought form the foundation for St. Basil's actions and his understanding of the church: the eschatological perspective and his dogmatic teaching, which is thoroughly trinitarian. In St. Basil's thought, the church is created by the Triune God in order to bring his children to a life in harmony where all the faithful enjoy heavenly peace and eternal fellowship with each other and their Creator. Accordingly, the eschatological union should be the main goal of every believer in the world. This way of thinking shaped St. Basil's position as a Christian leader and made him a strong advocate of the unity of the church. In his attempts to promote this unity, St. Basil has often been perceived as a person of action whose thoughts were directed toward maintaining communication among divided Christians and communities. All his efforts at negotiations with different people and leaders in the church may be seen in the context of convictions, which motivated his actions.[1] In the

---

1. The intention here is not to attempt to discuss all the events during St. Basil's episcopate, but to highlight some key themes and relationships, which may reveal to us the complex context of St. Basil's thoughts about the church. For historical background to this correspondence, see chapters 7 and 8 in Rousseau, *Basil of Caesarea*. See also chapter one in Lietzmann, *The Era of the Church Fathers*. For an overview of different theological views of that time, see in Jevtich, "Between the 'Niceaena' and the 'Easterners,'" 235–52. For theological background, see also chapters 8 and 9 in Ayres, *Nicaea and Its Legacy*. A very good overview of the existing cultural and political relationships is given in the article of Van Dam, "Emperor, Bishop and Friends in Late Antique

course of this battle for unity, the trinitarian confession becomes for St. Basil the criterion for deciding who belongs to fellowship of the church.

BASIL'S ATTITUDE TOWARD A CURRENT SITUATION— THE CHURCH AND CHURCHES

Throughout his works and especially in the epistles, St. Basil equally uses both terms "the church" and "the churches" in regard to the Christian communities in the world.[2] Although it brings some ambiguity to our reasoning, we can understand from the context that for St. Basil there is only one true church of God, which is the Mother of all believers, the bride of Christ and his body. It makes itself known in the world through the presence of local "members" of this body, which are also called "churches."[3] This bodily metaphor includes both the congregations and the individual believers who are separated by distances, but united by God for the fulfillment of his purpose.

> Our Lord Jesus Christ, Who has deigned to style the universal Church of God His body, and has made us individually members one of another, has moreover granted to all of us to live in intimate association with one another, as befits the agreement of the members. Wherefore, although we dwell far away from one another, yet, as regards our close conjunction, we are very near.[4]

In this sense, the universal church of God is spread over different places geographically, but it still exists as one entity in the Spirit who enables the communication. It may include a variety of individuals from many locations, but as "believers in Christ," they are "one people," and as "Christ's people," they are "one Church."[5] St. Basil describes this union between Christians as the gift of the Spirit in his epistle to Peter, bishop of Alexandria,

> The sight of the eyes brings about bodily friendship, and long companionship strengthens it, but genuine regard is the gift of the Spirit, Who unites what is separated by long distances, and

---

Cappadocia," 53–76.

2. See, for example, Letter 113, Letter 243, Letter 154, Letter 154, Letter 30, Letter 264.

3. The discussion of metaphors "the mother" and "the body" see in the chapter 4 of this book.

4. *Letter* 243.1.

5. *Letter* 141.1.

makes friends known to one another, not by bodily qualities, but by the characteristics of the soul.[6]

St. Basil's ideal vision is the church, which is united by the Triune God in love. He persistently recalls throughout his writings the good "old times" when "God's churches flourished, rooted in faith, united in love, all the members being in harmony, as though in one body."[7] St. Basil believes that fellowship in the Spirit and love among its members should help these local parts to keep in touch with one another. In his thinking, the life of each part and all of them together should point toward an eschatological community where the perfect unity will be attained.[8] "For is there anything more pleasing than the idea of peace?" St. Basil asks in his letter, "Is anything more suitable to the sacred office, or more acceptable to the Lord, than to take measures for effecting it?"[9] Using the same metaphor, which identifies the church with the perfect body of the Lord, St. Basil asserts, "The greatest of goods consists in the knitting together of the members of Christ's body."[10] Unfortunately, St. Basil's writings reveal to us the sorrowful reality in which he lives: the church on earth requires healing and restoration.

> We live in days when the overthrow of the Churches seems imminent; of this I have long been cognisant. There is no edification of the Church; no correction of error; no sympathy for the weak; no single defence of sound brethren; no remedy is found either to heal the disease which has already seized us, or as a preventive against that which we expect. Altogether the state of the Church (if I may use a plain figure though it may seem too humble an one) is like an old coat, which is always being torn and can never be restored to its original strength.[11]

The dysfunction of its members caused by the schisms and separations is a sign of a sickness, which leads to destruction. Comparing the state of the Christian communities with his own sick body, St. Basil admits in the

---

6. *Letter* 133.
7. *Letter* 164.
8. *Ps.* 45.4, PG 29:424A.
9. *Letter* 156.
10. Ibid. See also his *Letter* 114 where St. Basil asserts, "The one great end of all who are really and truly serving the Lord ought to be to bring back to union the Churches now 'at sundry times and in divers manners' divided from one another."
11. *Letter* 113. See similar description of the situation in his *Letter* 90.2 to the bishops of the West. We have to mention that St. Basil describes the troubles, which were found mainly in the Eastern part of the church. See a short overview of the events in Radde-Gallwitz, *Basil of Caesarea*, 135–37.

letter to Eusebius of Samosata, "The churches are in somewhat the same condition as my body, no good hope shining on them, and their state always changing for the worse."[12] In many other epistles, St. Basil often uses the images of a ship or a boat, of continual storms, and of potential shipwreck when he appeals for help in the face of heresy and schism.[13] For example, in his letter to the bishops of Italy and Gaul St. Basil beseeches them to "reach out a helping hand to the Churches that are being buffeted by the storm," because "if they be abandoned, they suffer complete shipwreck of the faith."[14] The most impressive metaphor of a naval battle, which describes the present condition of the church, is given in St. Basil's treatise *On the Holy Spirit*. It is fought by people who "cherish a deadly hate against one another," because of old quarrels and lack of love:

> Look, I beg you, at the picture thus raised before your eyes. See the rival fleets rushing in dread array to the attack. With a burst of uncontrollable fury they engage and fight it out. Fancy, if you like, the ships driven to and fro by a raging tempest, while thick darkness falls from the clouds and blackens all the scenes so that watchwords are indistinguishable in the confusion, and all distinction between friend and foe is lost. To fill up the details of the imaginary picture, suppose the sea swollen with billows and whirled up from the deep, while a vehement torrent of rain pours down from the clouds and the terrible waves rise high. From every quarter of heaven the winds beat upon one point, where both the fleets are dashed one against the other.[15]

St. Basil continues and gives more details about the state of the battle: the disorder and confusion is tremendous; friends no longer recognize friends; some combatants become traitors and others desert in the midst of the fight. Most of them are confused because of howling winds and different kind of noises from crashing vessels, from boiling surf, and from the yells of the combatants, who do not allow them to hear a word from admiral or pilot. The tragedy is that many of the participants do not pay attention to the fact that while they fight for power in the church, "their ship is actually settling down into the deep."[16]

In this passage, St. Basil mentions one of the main reasons for divisions and problems in the church, "Jealousy of authority and the lust of individual

---

12. *Letter* 30.
13. See, for example, *Letter* 81, *Letter* 82, *Letter* 90, *Letter* 91, *Letter* 161, *Letter* 210.
14. *Letter* 243.
15. *HS* 30.76.
16. Ibid.

mastery splits the sailors into parties which deal mutual death to one another . . . the men are all smitten with the incurable plague of mad love of glory."[17] Later on in the same chapter, he explains that this kind of people "reject the government of the Holy Spirit and divide the chief dignities of the Churches."[18] Developing this idea in one of his letters, St. Basil comes to a conclusion that divisions and fights among Christian communities lead to separation of these churches from God himself. St. Basil cannot accept the situation and asks other faithful believers, "Pray to the Lord yourself, and join all Christ's noble athletes with you in prayer for the Churches, to the end that . . . *God may be reconciled* to his own Churches and restore them to their ancient peace."[19] This reconciliation would only happen among the believers if they communicate with each other as the servants of one God and the Ruler of the church.

A similar way of thinking may be found in St. Basil's work *On the Judgment of God* where the division in the church is considered as a sign that God does not rule the churches. Comparing the history of Israel from the book of Judges to the present day divisions, St. Basil brings his readers to the idea that all these things happen in the church "because of neglect of the one great and only King and God of all."[20] He also believes that such discord and quarreling among the members of the church is the result of people turning away from God. This happens when leaders of the church abandon the teachings of the Lord and claiming to themselves authority in dealing with certain questions, making their own private rules, "and wishing to rule over against the Lord rather than be ruled by Him."[21] Further on, St. Basil uses an example of a swarm of bees that "according to the law of their nature," follow "their king in good order."[22] This illustrates his point that disagreements and divisions show a lack of obedience to a common head. He forms the conclusion,

> For if those who obey one command and have one king are characterised by good order and agreement, then all discord and divisions is a sign that there is no one to rule. In the same fashion such disagreement as regards both the commandments of the Lord and one another, if found in our midst, lays us open

17. Ibid.
18. *HS* 30.77.
19. *Letter* 164; emphasis added.
20. *De Jud.* (Clarke, 78).
21. Ibid.
22. Ibid.

to accusation that we have either deserted our true King . . . or else have denied Him."[23]

St. Basil thinks that all the examples of harmony among the animals are put forth by God as instructions and warnings. In the "dreadful day of judgment they will be brought forward by him unto the shame and condemnation of those who have not profited by the instruction."[24] This statement is followed by a long excursus into the definition of sin as disobedience. Previously, however, St. Basil makes it very clear that the mutual dissensions in the church is disobedience to God. He is convinced that the discord is dangerous and fatal for the church. Therefore, there is "the necessity of harmony on the part of the whole Church of God together, according to the will of Christ in the Holy Spirit."[25] His vision of the church is obviously trinitarian in this sentence, which underlines his doctrinal position one more time.

The unity of the church for St. Basil, first of all, means "the communion of faith,"[26] which is connected with "abiding in the sound and unperverted doctrine."[27] In St. Basil's opinion, the trinitarian confession is fundamental to the identity of Christians, and he makes it a criterion for the authenticity of faith.[28] He emphasizes that heretics do not belong to the church due to "their disagreement concerning the actual faith in God"[29] implying that they do not accept all the Persons of the Trinity on equal basis. On the contrary, St. Basil thinks that some of schismatics may still be considered as part of the church, because the reason for their separation is not the rejection of proper doctrines, but the sinful behavior of the local leaders.[30] Hence, irreconcilable disunity among the believers is caused mostly by dogmatic disagreements.[31] He strongly believes that people who "alter the doctrine of the Lord, not being rightly instructed in the word" do not belong to the community, but they "mix themselves with the sound body of the Church" in order "to spread their pernicious errors secretly among

---

23. *De Jud.* (Clarke, 78–79).
24. *De Jud.* (Wagner, 40).
25. *De Jud.* (Clarke, 81).
26. *Letter* 133.
27. See *Letter* 251.4.
28. See, for example, *Letter* 125, which Eustathius of Sebaste was to sign. See also *De Fide* (Clarke, 90, 95–96) where St. Basil calls trinitarian teaching "the saving confession."
29. *Letter* 188.
30. Ibid.
31. See also *Letter* 191 where St. Basil affirms that "since agreement in the faith is established among us, there is nothing further to prevent our being one body and one spirit."

purer souls."[32] They are not the members of the body, but they only pretend to be such. In reality these people, actually, destroy the unity of the church because they were "corrupted by the teaching of the evil one."[33] Often the separations happened when these kinds of teachers got power in the communities. According to St. Basil, the consequences of the doctrinal divisions are damaging:

> The doctrines of the Fathers are despised; apostolic traditions are set at nought; the devices of innovators are in vogue in the Churches; now men are rather contrivers of cunning systems than theologians; the wisdom of this world wins the highest prizes and has rejected the glory of the cross. Shepherds are banished, and in their places are introduced grievous wolves hurrying the flock of Christ. Houses of prayer have none to assemble in them; desert places are full of lamenting crowds.[34]

St. Basil is concerned even more with the future of the church. If the older believers lament experiencing this discord, they at least know the past, which was filled with love and agreement. The younger generation is the one for whom we should feel sorrow because "they do not know of what they have been deprived."[35] St. Basil admits that in the beginning he "reckoned silence more profitable than speech" in this situation, but then he "was drawn in the other direction by love, which 'seeketh not her own,' and desires to overcome every difficulty put in her way by time and circumstance."[36] Therefore, peace among Christians and reconciliation of all separated groups of believers becomes one of the main goals in his life.[37] Using an example of "the children in Babylon" from the book of Daniel, St.

---

32. *Hex.* 5.5. See similar thinking in *De Fide* (Clarke, 97–98) where St. Basil says that such "false prophets" want to "steal away the simple-minded."

33. Ibid. See similar idea in St. Basil's homily on *Ps.* 48 (Way, 323). The one who "has given his attention to deprived doctrines" and "has perverted the meaning in the Scripture" does not live in the church, but he "hews out in the rock a sepulchre for himself."

34. *Letter* 90.2.

35. Ibid.

36. *HS* 30.78. Similar notion can be found in his *Letter* 244.8 where St. Basil shares that he was restored after "a very violent fever," and he became aware that the only reason for recovery was the wish of the Lord to let him see "the Churches at rest after the storm which they had previously suffered." This meant for him that God expects him to take part in the reconciliation process.

37. See *Letter* 128.1. As St. Basil writes in this epistle, "I have been unable to give any adequate and practical proof of my earnest desire to pacify the Churches of the Lord. But in my heart I affirm that I have so great a longing that I would gladly give up even my life, if thereby the flame of hatred, kindled by the evil one, could be put out." See also his *Letter* 114.

Basil explains that he feels obligated "to support the cause of true religion."[38] For this reason, he believes he needs help from other believers that they may be together with one another and proclaim the truth with all the boldness.

Evidently, there should be criteria of orthodoxy, which can help draw a line between the groups with the right doctrine and heretics. In several of his epistles, St. Basil mentions the *Nicene Creed* as such criterion.[39] He believes that this creed, which affirms the Trinity, can serve as a tool, which not only helps to check the orthodoxy of a particular community or a leader, but it also, in case of heterodoxy, gives them a chance to change their beliefs and to join the church.

> Both men whose minds have been preoccupied by a heterodox creed and now wish to change over to the congregation of the orthodox, and also those who are now for the first time desirous of being instructed in the doctrine of truth, must be taught the creed drawn up by the blessed fathers in the Council which met at Nicaea. The same training would also be exceedingly useful in the case of all who are under suspicion of being in a state of hostility to sound doctrine, and who by ingenious and plausible excuses keep the depravity of their sentiments out of view. For these too this creed is all that is needed. They will either get cured of their concealed unsoundness, or, by continuing to keep it concealed, will themselves bear the load of the sentence due to their dishonesty.[40]

In this epistle, St. Basil adds some explanations to the statements of the *Creed*, which serve the following functions: "some for the correction of what had been corrupted, some as a precaution against errors expected to arise."[41] The goal of St. Basil is not to accuse those believers who do not confess the proper doctrine and cut them off from the church, but to allow them to admit their mistakes and bring them back into the communion of the faithful. "Our duty," St. Basil says, "rather to have regard to them in accordance with the old law of love, and to write to them with one consent, giving them all exhortation with pity, and to propose to them the faith of the fathers, and invite them to union."[42] From all these actions made on the behalf of the church two results are expected. If the heretics change their opinion, then reconciliation may happen, and if they reject fellowship and

---

38. *HS* 30.79.
39. *Letter* 113, *Letter* 114, *Letter* 125, *Letter* 140, *Letter* 159, *Letter* 251, *Letter* 204.6.
40. *Letter* 125.1.
41. Ibid., 3.
42. *Letter* 128.3.

the proper faith, then they will be recognized as "the real authors of the war."[43] From his side, St. Basil is open to having close communion with as many people as possible because he believes that "nothing is so characteristically Christian as being a peacemaker."[44] The only requirement, which he thinks is necessary for maintaining the fellowship in the church, is the acceptance and confirmation of the *Nicene Creed*.

> Let us then seek no more than this, but propose to all the brethren, who are willing to join us, the Nicene Creed. If they assent to that, let us further require that the Holy Ghost ought not to be called a creature, nor any of those who say so be received into communion. I do not think that we ought to insist upon anything beyond this.[45]

St. Basil is convinced that by deeper communication and mutual experience the believers will be able to learn other things as well because the Lord "will grant it."[46] This means that all these things, which God requires them to know, the Christians can acquire if they live in peace and listen to each other. The best example of such relationships in the church for St. Basil is from the ancient times

> . . . when the sufferers from unsound disputation were few, and all lived in peace, "workmen" obeying the commandments and not "needing to be ashamed," serving the Lord with simple and clear confession, and keeping plain and inviolate their faith in Father, Son and Holy Ghost.[47]

According to St. Basil's thinking, this peace, obedience, and a "plain" trinitarian confession create a foundation for unity. Therefore, he thinks that the restoration of these factors will bring the healing of the church. His vision for the future is to govern the churches through mutual accommodation by "the ancient kind of love, receiving as our own members brothers coming from the other side, sending as to our kin, and in turn receiving as from our own kin."[48] St. Basil believes that this used to be "the boast of the Church" in the past. He also convinced that this fellowship could be reestablished once again through the meetings and dialogues with "the men of

---

43. Ibid.
44. *Letter* 114.
45. *Letter* 113. Basil adds similar explanations about the Holy Spirit in his *Letter* 125.
46. Ibid.
47. *Letter* 172.
48. *Letter* 191.

like mind" from different communities who are willing to restore the church and renew its condition.[49]

AUTHORITY IN THE CHURCH—GOD AND HUMANS

One of St. Basil's principles for unity in the church is based on his perception of the existing essential relationships of the Triune God. He calls the Christians to look at the divine Persons who are perfectly united in will and knowledge and try to keep the same kind of fellowship among believers for the wellbeing of the church. St. Basil uses the immanent life of the Triune God, the inner order in which God lives and which was revealed to humanity as the best example that believers should follow.

> Again, when the only begotten Son of God, our Lord and God Jesus Christ, through Whom all things were made, Himself cries: "I am come down from heaven, not to do mine own will, but the will of the Father that sent me," and "I do nothing of myself," and "I have receive a commandment, what I should say and what I should speak"—and when again the Holy Spirit distributes great and marvellous gifts and works all things in all men, and speaks nothing of Himself, but whatever things He hears from the Lord that He speaks,—how it is much more necessary that that the whole Church of God should strive earnestly to keep the unity of the spirit in the bond of peace.[50]

Therefore, St. Basil is convinced that the trinitarian concordance of the divine will serves as a model for all Christian communities. At the same time, in his writings he perceives the church as one body that consists of many members around the world and in which unity is grounded in the economy of the Trinity.[51] This means that, on the one hand, St. Basil is totally aware that God himself creates the church and sustains its unity. He has no doubt that the restoration of "vigorous life" and peace in the church

---

49. Ibid.

50. *De Jud.* (Clarke, 81). See also St. Basil's explanation of cooperation of divine Persons in *HS* 16.38; see *HS* 18.46–47 for the concept of *koinonia* inside the Trinity. See *De Fide* (Clarke, 96).

The idea that St. Basil applied inter-trinitarian relations to the relationship of Christians to each other is discussed by Rusch in his article "Basil the Great views of the unity of the Church." Analyzing St. Basil's vocabulary, which he uses for inter-trinitarian communion and for fellowship of believers, he argues, "Basil is responsible for a decisive step of grounding Christian unity in the unity of the Triune God." See Rusch, "Basil the Great views of the unity of the Church," 287.

51. This question was detailed in chapter 2.

is a "heavenly and saving gift of Christ."[52] On the other hand, he believes that the human labor is necessary to reconcile all Christians with each other and "to renew laws of ancient love."[53] Consequently, he puts a lot of effort into conversations with the leaders of the church through the exchange of letters and visits. His main goal is to make Christians keep the sound faith, to think together with each other or to change their opinion and attitude in order to constitute one body. As St. Basil acknowledges, "For peace's sake there is no trouble that I will not undertake, no act, no word of humility that I will shrink from; I will reckon no length of journey, I will undergo any inconvenience, if only I may be rewarded by being able to make peace."[54]

From St. Basil's epistles, we notice that he does not believe in the authority of one superior bishop in the church, but rather he facilitates unity communicating with many bishops and leaders.[55] Although St. Basil treats some of them with more respect and honor due to their influence on other Christians and their role in the church,[56] he still emphasizes throughout his works that the true bishop and the real head of the church is Christ himself.[57] It should be observed, however, that St. Basil believes in the hierarchy in the church and he highly estimates the role of local clergy and the bishops.[58] In his vision, they are expected to function "like the head at the top" and like "the eyes," which exercise their own "watchful forethought" for

---

52. *Letter 70*. See also *Letter 264*, where Basil asserts that God himself will bestow peace on the church.

53. Ibid.

54. *Letter 97*.

55. Several scholars agree on this issue. See, for example, Fouyas, *St. Basil and the Roman See*, 5. See also Krivoshein, *Ekklesiologia sv. Vasiliya Velikogo*. See similar opinion of Lukas Vischer in chapter 3, "Die Kirche," of his book: Vischer, *Basilius der Große*, 52–72. In St. Basil's view, all bishops are successors of the Apostles. See, for example, *Letter 197.1* where he explains to Ambrose, bishop of Milan, that it is the Lord himself transferred him "from the judges of the earth to the throne of the Apostles."

56. Of course, St. Basil regards some bishops as the first in honor, such as the bishop of Alexandria Athanasius (see *Letter 66* and *Letter 80*). For example, St. Basil believes that Athanasius is able to be "a Samuel to the Churches" and to restore strength to the church of Antioch by concord "being able to control some" and "to reduce others to silence." See *Letter 66*. Also in another epistle, he calls him "blessed Father Athanasius" and admits that he considers himself "bound to follow the high authority of such a man." See *Letter 204.6–7*. St. Basil's relationships with the influential bishop of Rome Damasus are rather complicated (St. Basil wrote to him one epistle [*Letter 70*], but even this one is written without address). On this issue, see a very helpful article by Taylor, "St. Basil the Great and Pope St. Damasus," 186–203. See also the historical and theological review of all relationships at that time in Behr, *The Nicene Faith*, 104–17.

57. See *Letter 50*; *HS* 5.9; *The Morals* 80.4; *Ps.* 44.5; PG 29:397CD.

58. *Letter 222*, *Letter 227*.

local people in order that "the hands" and "the feet" may do their work.[59] This implies that the ministers[60] should fulfill their responsibilities and do not "exalt themselves" over their people but "rather use *their* rank as an opportunity for practicing humility toward them."[61] This is possible on the ground that the aim of the leader is "to bring all to a perfect man, to the measure of the stature of the fullness of Christ."[62] Consequently, the mature Christians will respect their clergy and through this kind of relationship the proper ecclesial order and authority will be kept.

According to St. Basil's thinking, the authority of the bishop, or a Christian leader, comes from God, and it is not simply a human decision, but "the ordinance of God."[63] He is convinced that the appointments in the church and all the things concerning the leadership happen with the help of the Holy Spirit. St. Basil expresses this belief in his epistle to the clergy of Colonia:

> Do not look at this as merely of man's ordaining, nor as having been originated by the calculations of men who regard earthly things. Believe that those to whom the anxious care of the Churches belongs have acted, as they have, with the aid of the Holy Spirit; impress this inception of the proceedings on your hearts and do your best to perfect it.[64]

It seems that people in the church choose who will be a new minister, but "the inception" of their decision is in the Spirit. In this sense, St. Basil's concept of ecclesial administration is closely related to the idea of distribution of spiritual gifts among the members of Christ's body. He strongly believes that the ordering of the church is effected through the Holy Spirit because he gives in the church "first Apostles, secondarily prophets, thirdly teachers. . . ." and "this order is ordained in accordance with the division of the gifts that are of the Spirit."[65] It is evident from other epistles that St.

---

59. Letter 222. See also *The Morals* 80.15 (Clarke, 128).

60. Fedwick noticed in his book that the most common word in St. Basil's terminology for the leader of the church is προεστώς. He also argues that this term is flexible and maybe used in a different context. The best translation of προεστώς is "leader who cares" or "leader in the care of others." See Fedwick, *The Church*, 46–47.

61. *The Morals* 70.24 (Clarke, 123). In *The Morals*, St. Basil usually reinforce his point with the gospel quotes. In this case, he uses Matt 24:45–50 to support the idea of a minister as a faithful servant to his people.

62. *The Morals* 70.31 (Clarke, 123).

63. Letter 227. See also *Letter* 197, where Basil asserts that it is God, who "in every generation selects those who are well-pleasing to Him" and makes them his leaders.

64. Ibid.

65. HS 16.39. See also *The Morals* 60.1 (Clarke, 117).

Basil has no doubt that this is God, who gives the ministers to believers in their communities. For example, he is anxious to persuade his friend, the bishop of Iconium, that God himself "from age to age chooses them that please Him, distinguishes vessels of election, and uses them for the ministry of the Saints."[66] Also in his consolatory letter to the church of Neocaesarea, he reminds his readers that the Lord had always been faithful and from the time of Gregory, "the great champion" of their church, he set over them one "wakeful" bishop after another.[67] They have no need "to despair" of the next one, because, St. Basil affirms, "the Lord knows who are His" and "He may bring into our midst those for whom peradventure we are not looking."[68] However, St. Basil does not want Christians to be careless and unthoughtful. In a similar situation, due to death of the bishop, he calls the Church of Parnassus to raise themselves to "the necessary management of the Church" that "the holy God may give heed to His own little flock," and may grant them "a shepherd in accordance with His own will."[69] We are led, therefore, to the conviction that the ultimate authority in the church always belongs to God as also revealed in the titles of Christ and the work of the Spirit.[70] At the same time, the ministers in the church are endowed with power in order to fulfill "the special and chief work."[71] God gives them the authority to teach those entrusted to them "all that is ordered by the Lord in the Gospel and through His apostles, and whatsoever is consistent with this."[72]

Once again, we notice how Basil shows the cooperation of divine and human activity in the church. Previously, we have seen that in the mystery of baptism and now we can observe a similar pattern of thinking in the process of ordination for ministry. St. Basil does not call it mystery, but he conveys the idea that God has chosen the leaders whom the church, as a community of the faithful, ordains for the special task using prescribed regulations. First, he leads his readers to a conviction that God provides people with talents and ability to rule and guide the congregation.[73] Then St. Basil asserts that Christians should check the qualities and distinctive characteristics of those

66. *Letter* 161.1. This epistle was written on the consecration of a new bishop who previously was not confident in his ability to minister.

67. *Letter* 128.2.

68. Ibid.

69. *Letter* 62.

70. As we mentioned earlier, Christ is called "the true bishop" and "the head of the church." The Spirit brings order in the church and distributes the gifts.

71. *The Morals* 70.11 (Clarke, 121).

72. Ibid., 70.6 (Clarke, 121).

73. This is exactly the order in which the Rules in his *The Morals* are written: first the Rule 60.1 about the gifts and then the Rule 70.2 about the ordination.

who will be entrusted with the authority in the church before the rights and obligations are imposed on them. Thereby, God's intentions should be confirmed by the human actions. St. Basil reminds his Chorepiscopi,[74]

> According to the ancient custom observed in the Churches of God, ministers in the Church were received after careful examination; the whole of their life was investigated; an enquiry was made as to their being neither railers nor drunkards, not quick to quarrel, keeping their youth in subjection, so as to be able to maintain "the holiness without which no man shall see the Lord." This examination was made by presbyters and deacons living with them. Then they brought them to the Chorepiscopi; and the Chorepiscopi, after receiving the suffrages of the witnesses as to the truth and giving information to the Bishop, so admitted the minister to the sacerdotal order.[75]

The last words should not go unnoticed. The term "sacerdotal order"[76] tells us that this person from now on is required to play a special role in God's plans for the community. Among many responsibilities of the leaders, the most important one is "to bring others to the peace that is in Christ."[77] This peace should be a result of proper use of spiritual gifts, which should lead to harmonious life "with one another in the love of Christ."[78]

Responsibilities of God's fellow servants and peace in a local community

The characteristics and responsibilities of the church leaders and the bishop in particular can be found in many of St. Basil's works. They are described very precisely in *The Morals* where St. Basil explains how Christians are

---

74. "Chorepiscopi" means bishops of smaller cities, which were located near the capital of provinces (for example, Caesarea).

75. *Letter* 54. St. Basil believes that the Christians should not be "easy-going as regards ordinations," and they should not "approach them without circumspection." See *The Morals* 70.2 (Clarke, 120). St. Basil is also convinced that the ordination can be done only in the church and by the church. On the contrary, the gatherings held by disorderly presbyters or bishops, or by uninstructed laymen should be called "unlawful congregations." *Letter* 188.1.

76. The Greek: τῷ τάγματι ἱερατικῶν. It can be also translated as "the priestly order." As Deferrari noticed that in the Latin Church the priesthood (including bishops), diaconate, and subdiaconate are called "sacred" orders because "they have immediate reference to what is consecrated." See *Letter* 54 (Deferrari, 1:342–43).

77. *The Morals* 50.1 (Clarke, 114).

78. Ibid., 60.1 (Clarke, 117).

supposed to function as a community.[79] Showing the roles of the ministers, he often supports his statements with the passages from the Scripture.[80] In this way, St. Basil provides a biblical framework for the key aspects of his understanding of the relationships between the clergy and the laity. Many of these verses, which he chooses, remind the ministers of servant leadership, which should be reflected in their lives.[81] As "shepherds," they are expected to lay down their lives for their people if it helps to "impart to them the gospel of God."[82] Clarifying the meaning of the statement, St. Basil adds that as "fathers and nurses," ministers in the community should be willing to render to people not only the gospel, but "even their own souls."[83] As "doctors," they are called to heal the diseases of their souls and to win for them health in Christ.[84] They are supposed to be "planters of God's branches" and "builders of God's temple," but all these actions must be done in "the great affection of their love in Christ."[85] In St. Basil's view, if the bishop wants his Church to bloom like "a vine with good works," he should be like "a wise husbandman and good servant giving meat in due season to his fellow-servants."[86] The ministers of God should do their work as "wise and trusty stewards."[87]

Although St. Basil insists that the leaders should act more like servants in order to provide care and support for their people, he believes in the necessity of hierarchy in the church. Throughout his writings, he uses many different metaphors to demonstrate the importance of the bishops for the local communities. In the homily *On Psalm 28*, St. Basil compares them with a ram, "an animal capable of leading, one which guides the sheep to nourishing pastures and refreshing waters."[88] He asserts that such are those

> . . . who are set over the flock of Christ, since they lead them forth to the flowery and fragrant nourishment of spiritual doctrine, water them with living water, the gift of the Spirit, raise

---

79. See, for example, *Letter* 81; *Ps.* 28.2; *Letter* 246; *The Morals* 60–80.

80. *The Morals* are structured this way when St. Basil reflects on various passages of the Scriptures and derives from them principles he applies to the duties of clergy and laity.

81. See, for example, scriptural support for the rule 70.24 in *The Morals*.

82. *The Morals* 80.16 (Clarke, 129).

83. Ibid., 18 (Clarke, 129).

84. Ibid., 17 (Clarke, 129).

85. Ibid., 20, 21 (Clarke, 129).

86. *Letter* 161.2.

87. Ibid.

88. *Ps.* 28.1 (Way, 195).

them up and nourish them to produce fruit, but guide them to rest and to safety from those who lay snares for them.[89]

St. Basil is convinced that the leaders are "entrusted with the preaching of the Gospel," and, in this sense, they are the guarantors of the teaching of the right doctrine.[90] As "an eye in a body," they are able "to discern between good and evil" and guide the members of Christ.[91] In his epistle to Amphilochius, the bishop of Iconium, he expresses the idea that a good bishop as "a skilful pilot" who may "rise in mind above every wave lifted by heretical blasts" and "keep the boat from being whelmed by the salt and bitter billows of false doctrine."[92] In St. Basil's opinion, the ability to teach and "rightly handle the word of truth" is so significant that believers must receive these kinds of leaders as "if they were the Lord."[93] Reinforcing the central concern of the statement, he explains in the next rule that "those who do not obey the envoys of the Lord dishonor not only them but also Him Who sent them."[94] Interestingly enough, at the same time, he urges the hearers to test what their teachers say.[95] St. Basil thinks that the believers who were already instructed in the Scriptures should "receive what agrees with the Scriptures and reject what disagrees" and decline dealings with those who persist in the wrong teaching.[96] Therefore, a bishop in the community has the authority to represent Christ as long as he faithfully bears witness to him and to his Gospel.

In order to discern whether their bishop is trustworthy or not, St. Basil recommends to those Christians who have "little knowledge of Scripture" to pay attention to "the stamp of sanctity in the fruits of the Spirit" of the leader.[97] They are supposed to receive only those ministers who show these "fruits" but reject those who do not. This means that the bishop has to show by deeds whatever he teaches by words. St. Basil insists in his rules that the minister "should make himself an example to others of every good thing,

---

89. Ibid.
90. *The Morals* 70.1, 70.5 (Clarke, 120–21).
91. *The Morals* 80.15.
92. *Letter* 161.2.
93. *The Morals* 72.3 (Clarke, 125).
94. Ibid., 72.4 (Clarke, 125).
95. Ibid., 72.1 (Clarke, 124).
96. Ibid. See also the similar idea in *The Morals* 70.37, where Basil asserts that "he who is set over the word" must be judged by "the very people who are entrusted to him" (Clarke, 124).
97. *The Morals* 72.2 (Clarke, 125).

practicing first what he is teaching"[98] because it is "unlawful to put constraint upon others to do what man has not done himself."[99] One of the best examples of the fruits of the Spirit, which should be present in the life of the bishop, we can find in St. Basil's description of Dianius. St. Basil admits that he counted him "among the most illustrious in virtue."[100] From his childhood, he used to look up to "the man as majestic in appearance, magnificent, and possessing great sanctity of aspect."[101] After reaching the age of reason, St. Basil testifies, he rejoiced in his company

> ... coming to learn the simplicity, nobility, and generosity of his character, and all the other qualities peculiar to the man—his gentleness of soul, his lofty spirit combined with mildness, his decorum, his control of temper, and his cheerfulness and affability mingled with dignity.[102]

Drawing the portraits of exemplary bishops, St. Basil often lists the characteristics, which may qualify them as the best ministers and so can be practiced by others. About Musonius he writes that this bishop was "a pillar and support of the truth; a stay of the faith of Christ; a protector of his friends; a stout foe of his opponents; a guardian of the principles of his fathers; an enemy of innovation; exhibiting in himself the ancient fashion of the Church."[103]

In St. Basil's understanding, the leader entrusted with the authority from God should make his life "a shining model for the observance of every commandment of the Lord," so that people under his guidance could not find any excuses to think that the Lord's commands are impossible to fulfill.[104] In this sense, a spiritual growth of lay people and their obedience to a minister flows from his ability to live out what he teaches. So, St. Basil asserts, "the example of his actions may afford more effective instruction than any words."[105] What is really required from a bishop is to embody the

---

98. Ibid., 70.10 (Clarke, 121). See also *Letter* 246.

99. Ibid., 9 (Clarke, 121).

100. *Letter* 51 (Deferrari, 1:325). Another description of an exemplary minister can be found in the *Letter* 81 where Basil introduces a presbyter of the church saying that he is a leader "of steadfast character, skilled in canons, accurate in the faith, who has lived up to this time in continence and ascetic discipline," "a man of poverty," who "by the labor of his hands gets a living with the brethren who dwell with him."

101. *Letter* 51 (Deferrari, 1:325).

102. Ibid.

103. *Letter* 28.1.

104. LR 43 (Wagner, 319).

105. Ibid.

Gospel in his life that others can learn and imitate. As Basil so eloquently argues,

> If, indeed, the goal of Christianity is the imitation of Christ according to the measure of His Incarnation, insofar as is conformable with the vocation of each individual, they who are entrusted with the guidance of many others are obliged to animate those still weaker than themselves, by their assistance, to the imitation of Christ, as the blessed Paul says: "Be ye followers of me, as I also am of Christ."[106]

This embodiment of Christ's teaching in the life of the minister brings him to a position when he is able to establish the relationships in the church, which are usually maintained in a good family or among close friends. As Basil writes to the Neocaesareans on the death of their bishop, "Your boys have lost a father, your elders a brother, your nobles one first among them, your people a champion, your poor a supporter."[107] That expresses another conviction of St. Basil concerning the role of a bishop in the church. He is expected to create "a bond of peace" between his people and encourage their common desire to serve God that the church "may rest firm and unshaken."[108] When St. Basil shares his high opinion of Athanasius of Ancyra, he asserts that this bishop was "in truth a pillar and foundation of the Church."[109] "The limbs of the Church," he says, "knitted together by his superintendence as by a soul, and joined into a union of sympathy and true fellowship, are not only steadfastly preserved by the bond of peace for the spiritual communion, but will also be preserved for ever."[110] Therefore, the peace and unity in the church has eternal consequences, and the responsibility to facilitate and maintain this unity is placed on the bishop and other ministers. Following the example of Christ, with the help of the Holy Spirit, they are supposed to serve their people in order that the whole community should grow toward Christlikeness and enjoy peace and relationships of love.

---

106. Ibid.
107. *Letter* 28.2.
108. *Letter* 29 (Deferrari, 1:173).
109. Ibid.
110. Ibid.

The brotherly union of all bishops in the church

St. Basil's passionate longing for church unity made him write letters to many people from different geographical locations.[111] This correspondence is a great evidence of his strong commitment to the idea that the church should be restored to a previous condition when though the districts "were divided in position, yet in mind they were one, and were governed by one sentiment."[112] St. Basil is convinced that communication between bishops as heads of the local communities may help to find solutions to many problems and create "the union effected by love."[113] In the epistles, he often recalls the good old times and uses this as an example, which his contemporaries should follow. "Intercourse of the people was frequent," St. Basil says, "frequent the visits of the clergy; the pastors, too, had such mutual affection, that each used the other as teacher and guide in things pertaining to the Lord."[114] In St. Basil's view, this mutual love of bishops is one of the main principles that form the foundation for unity in the church.[115]

A very good example of this way of thinking can be found in his letter to the bishops of the sea coast of Pontus. Following the Bible, he reminds them of the words of Christ that people will know his disciples if they love each other.[116] Then he conveys the idea that peace is the farewell gift of the Lord to the believes. Therefore, St. Basil admits, "I cannot persuade myself that without love to others, and without, as far as rests with me, peaceableness towards all, I can be called a worthy servant of Jesus Christ."[117] St. Basil wants them to recognize that in order to be good ministers of God they are supposed to have the relationship of love with other Christians. He is trying to convince his readers to look at the fact that nothing except "deliberate estrangement" may separate these bishops from him because they have "one

---

111. St. Basil wrote the letters to different categories of people and on various occasions. Probably not all of his letters were preserved, but he mentions that he still communicates with "the multitude of bishops" and he names the locations: "Pisidians, Lycaonians, Isaurians, Phrygians of both provinces, Armenians your neighbors, Macedonians, Achaeans, Illyrians, Gauls, Spaniards, the whole of Italy, Sicilians, Africans, the healthy part of Egypt, whatever is left of Syria." See *Letter* 204.7.

112. *Letter* 204.7.

113. *Letter* 70. See the same notion in Vischer, *Basilius der Große*, 65.

114. *Letter* 204.7. See also *Letter* 191 and especially *Letter* 164.

115. As Rousseau noted, St. Basil was trying to apply "on a world scale the principle of collegiality that had inspired him in his relations with bishops in Cappadocia and Armenia." See Rousseau, *Basil of Caesarea*, 299.

116. *Letter* 203.1.

117. Ibid.

Lord, one faith, the same hope."[118] Even Gentiles, St. Basil continues his argument, "on account of the uncertainty of the future, make much of alliances with each other, and seek mutual intercourse as being advantageous to them."[119] All the more, peace and union in the church is an advantage for Christians in this world where the future events are unknown. According to St. Basil's thinking, this fellowship is necessary, because in the case of a war or persecution the separated community may be easily destroyed. Similar arguments can be found in his letter, which was written three years earlier to the bishop Atarbius. In this epistle, St. Basil begs him "to peace" with the brothers who are of one mind with him, and zeal and anxiety "for the continued safety of the Churches of the Lord."[120] St. Basil is very anxious about the situation in the church because he feels that someday the disunity may lead to complete destruction. He exhorts this bishop,

> Drive out of your mind the idea that you need communion with no one else. To cut one's self off from connexion with the brethren is not the mark of one who is walking by love, nor yet the fulfilling of the commandment of Christ. At the same time I do wish you, with all your good intentions, to take into account that the calamities of the war which are now all round about us may one day be at our own doors, and if we too, like all the rest, have our share of outrage, we shall not find any even to sympathize with us, because in the hour of our prosperity we refused to give our share of sympathy to the wronged.[121]

Although Basil takes as a matter of course that a bishop may have the freedom to rule the community entrusted to him by God using universal principles in the concrete situations, he does not agree that the community may maintain a healthy existence if it is separated from the rest of the body of Christ. For him the church does not consist of independent parts, but it lives only as a united organism whose members function in concordance with each other. St. Basil places strong emphasis on the idea that every bishop needs his brother bishops. Sharing his thoughts and experience with the Senate of Tyana, he admits, "I could never take upon myself so much as to think myself able to manage matters without support. I know perfectly well that I stand more in need of the succor of each of the brethren than one hand does of the other. Truly, from our own bodily constitution, the Lord

---

118. *Letter* 203.3.
119. Ibid.
120. *Letter* 65. For the historical details about the situation with Atarbius, see Ayres, *Nicaea and Its Legacy*, 224–25.
121. *Letter* 65.

has taught us the necessity of fellowship."[122] He stresses the idea that God perceives unity between Christians as one of conditions for their access to him. "Even prayer," St. Basil continues, "when it is not united prayer, loses its natural strength and the Lord has told us that He will be in the midst where two or three call on Him in concord."[123] In this sense, unity between believers is not the option, but the only way of life, which is provided and accepted by God.

St. Basil is concerned with the schisms and fights between the orthodox believers. He admits in his epistle to the Italians and Gauls that the saddest thing about it all is that "the sound part is divided against itself."[124] He compares the troubles they suffer with those, which once happened in Jerusalem when Vespasian was besieging it because the Jews of that time were at once consumed by the internal sedition of their own people. St. Basil explains with sorrow, "In our case, too, in addition to the open attack of the heretics, the Churches are reduced to utter helplessness by the war raging among those who are supposed to be orthodox."[125] St. Basil believes that one of the reasons for all these battles between the orthodox party is "jealousy of authority and the lust of individual mastery," which leads to separation and fights.[126] As he describes,

> We attack one another. We are overthrown by one another. If our enemy is not the first to strike us, we are wounded by the comrade at our side. If a foeman is stricken and falls, his fellow soldier tramples him down. There is at least this bond of union between us that we hate our common foes, but no sooner have the enemy gone by than we find enemies in one another.[127]

St. Basil is very much concerned about dissensions and disagreements in the church. He keeps reminding all Christians that these conflicts will

---

122. *Letter* 97.

123. Ibid. See the same idea in *Hom.* 29.2 (DelCogliano, 270).

124. *Letter* 92.3. See also *Letter* 164, "Our afflictions are heavy, martyrdom is nowhere to be seen, because those who evilly entreat us are called by the same name as ourselves." See the same idea in *Letter* 243: "the name of Christians is applied to the persecutors."

125. Ibid.

126. *HS* 30.76.

127. Ibid., 77. As Ayres very helpfully noted that two constant problems made St. Basil's attempts at "alliance-building" unsuccessful, "The antipathy of Valens and the imperial government to pro-Nicenes made it difficult to act openly against Homoians, and the constant unpredictability of personal antipathies and personal ambitions made it difficult for Basil to achieve alliances even where doctrinal agreement seemed close." Ayres, *Nicaea and Its Legacy*, 222.

not lead them to the heavenly kingdom and to communion with the Triune God. On the contrary, he asserts that those who are "divided and at variance with one another deserve to perish."[128] Therefore, bishops, as head leaders of communities, should really be aware of the eternal consequences and make every effort in order to bring peace in the church. Recalling the biblical verse about peacemakers and the reward, which is promised to them from God, St. Basil confirms that with every desire on his own part he "did enroll in the lists of communicants all who accepted that creed [Nicene Creed]."[129] On this ground, he communicates with other bishops from different geographical parts of the empire.

Repeatedly calling on the western bishops, St. Basil expresses his belief that their letters "contain evidence of sound faith" and proof of their "inviolable agreement and concord, showing thus that the shepherds are following in the footsteps of the Fathers and feeding the people of the Lord with knowledge."[130] He is excited to know that at least some parts of the church are in a healthy condition. This gives St. Basil "a certain amount of comfort," which creates "something like a smile" in his soul, because he hopes that the whole church may recover from the distressing state in which it is now placed.[131] He considers "mutual sympathy and unity" of western bishops as an important blessing to themselves. St. Basil recognizes that though they are separated by a great extent of country, which parts them from each other, they still belong to "the concord of one body," because they are "united in the fellowship of the Spirit."[132] He constantly appeals to them thinking that such a natural obstacle as the long distances cannot really interfere if there is a good will and a desire to help the struggling brethren.

The sound trinitarian teaching and concord at the West makes St. Basil believe that their joint actions may establish the dogmatic union in the eastern part of the church. He beseeches the bishops using all the arguments,

> If then there be any consolation of love, any fellowship of the Spirit, any bowels of mercy, be stirred to help us. Be zealous for true religion, and rescue us from this storm . . . through your prayers and co-operation the Lord may grant to us that same

---

128. *The Morals* 60.1 (Clarke, 117).

129. *Letter* 204.6

130. *Letter* 90.1. See also *Letter* 92.3 where St. Basil says that the western bishops preach "the faith of the Fathers without any dissimulation."

131. Ibid.

132. Ibid.

boldness for the truth and glorying in the confession of the divine and saving Trinity which He has given you.[133]

Constantly using the bodily metaphor in his epistles, St. Basil insists that different parts of the body are obligated to provide support to each other. For instance, he persuades his "truly God-beloved and very dear" brethren, "fellow ministers of like mind," the bishops of Gaul and Italy, to help eastern Christians because the Lord Jesus Christ has decided "to style" the universal church of God, his body, in a way that they may live "in intimate association with one another, as befits the agreement of the members."[134] So in spite of distances, different languages, and cultures, St. Basil expects western bishops to feel the pain of the other part of this body. "Reckon then, as true disciples of the Lord," Basil appeals to them, "that our sufferings are yours."[135] He also reminds them of a reason why they should sympathize with eastern part of the church in their troubles:

> We are not being attacked for the sake of riches, or glory, or any temporal advantages. We stand in the arena to fight for our common heritage, for the treasure of the sound faith, derived from our Fathers. Grieve with us, all ye who love the brethren, at the shutting of the mouths of our men of true religion, and at the opening of the bold and blasphemous lips of all that utter unrighteousness against God.[136]

St. Basil does not have any doubts that this "common heritage," which is the faith in the Trinity, should be kept at any expense. Without a helping hand from the western part, the churches in the East will "suffer complete shipwreck of the faith."[137] His belief that the church is one in spite of geographical, cultural, and political obstacles, makes him appeal to all its members who hold on to the proper doctrine. He shares his thoughts in one of the epistles to the Italians and Gauls and expresses the idea of ecclesial synod, which should be held in order to restore peace and unity in the eastern part of the church.[138] St. Basil perceives such assemblies of bishops as a means by which the Christians may discern the truth and collectively decide what direction to follow. However, he regards any assemblies as au-

133. *Letter* 90.1.
134. *Letter* 243.1.
135. Ibid., 4.
136. Ibid.
137. Ibid.
138. *Letter* 92.3. This epistle was signed by thirty-two bishops. Therefore, St. Basil already united some Eastern bishops against heretics, and he wanted the western part of the church to take part in the process of healing and restoration.

thoritative only if they bear witness to the sound faith in the Trinity.[139] In this sense, in many of his works he refers to the creed and canons which were issued at the council of Nicaea as the valid authority.

St. Basil strongly believes that only collective efforts may bring reconciliation and keep the orthodox faith in all parts of the church. Therefore, he promotes the idea of an ecumenical council where different communities may send their representatives. Using very humble language, he writes to western brethren, ". . . hasten to us, hasten to us now, true brothers, we implore you; on our knees we implore you, hold out a helping hand . . . do not let the light of the faith be put out in the place where it shone first."[140] Although St. Basil confirms in this epistle that western bishops do not have any need to learn from him how to act, and that the Holy Spirit himself will direct them, he still shares some ideas about the future synod. He makes it clear that "considerable number of brethren" are expected from the West in order that the leaders who confess the orthodox faith outnumber those who do not. The presence of a majority of bishops who support the Nicene Creed is essential, because they must "have weight in effecting a reform, not merely from the dignity of those whose emissaries they are, but also from their own number."[141] St. Basil is trying to secure the number of orthodox bishops, which may take part in the future synod, because the decisions become authoritative if they are approved by the majority of leaders present there. Then St. Basil formulates the goal of this synod, according to his vision: through the collegial decision, "they will restore the creed drawn up by

---

139. St. Basil admits that nobody makes him to keep communion with the person if he "does not agree with the sound doctrine of the faith." See *Letter* 214 about Antiochian schism. For historical and theological background, see chapter 9 in Ayres, *Nicaea and Its Legacy*, 222–29. In his correspondence, St. Basil also mentions episcopal meetings where many problems were discussed, which could not be solved by means of letters and personal visits. In addition to that, there were held episcopal conferences at Caesarea on the occasions of festivity of the local martyrs. See *Letter* 100. Many episcopal synods were held to secure advice "on the matters in hand" and to discuss current issues of the local communities. *Letter* 201, *Letter* 98. See this idea in Fedwick, *The Church*, 123–24. The purpose of such local synods or "festal assemblies" is stated in his *Homily on Not Three Gods*. See *Hom.* 29.2 (DelCogliano, 270–71). "The present spectacle is but a remnant of the ancient love of the fathers. For its sake, they inaugurated the practice of holding these festal assemblies, so that the estrangement that develops over time could be dissipated through personal interaction at set intervals, and those who live far away, by gathering in this one place, could use the event to initiate relationships of friendship and love. This is a spiritual assembly that renews old relationships and provides a starting point for those to come."

140. *Letter* 92.3. St. Basil constantly writes letters to the western brethren asking for help. For example, *Letter* 20, *Letter* 92, *Letter* 243, *Letter* 263. In the years 371, 372, 376, 377 accordingly. See chronology in Fedwick, *The Church*, 133–53.

141. *Letter* 92.3.

our fathers at Nicaea, proscribe the heresy, and, by bringing into agreement all who are of one mind, speak peace to the Churches."[142] In St. Basil's thinking, all believers must follow the decisions made by the bishops present at the synod as legitimate delegates. He clearly explains what kind of results he expects from the council in his epistle to the western brethren.

> For the future all who confess the apostolic faith may put an end to the schisms which they have unhappily devised, and be reduced for the future to the authority of the Church; that so, once more, the body of Christ may be complete, restored to integrity with all its members.[143]

St. Basil perceives such ecumenical councils as the highest human authority, which is competent to solve the problems and to maintain ecclesiastical unity. They are important steps in the life of the church that help to keep peace and the right balance between diversity and unity within the church through affirmation of the proper doctrines and beliefs. These councils ensure that what the local communities receive from their bishops is faithful to the teaching of the past, which goes back to the Gospel of Jesus Christ. Therefore, convocation of the council and consequent submission to all decisions serves as the collective affirmation of God's will, which is revealed to all the participants and through them to all the members of the church.

CONCLUSION TO CHAPTER 6

In St. Basil's understanding, all local congregations and all Christians separated by long distances still constitute one universal church of God, body of Christ, which is united by his Spirit. Consequently, all the schisms and battles in the church are perceived by him as disobedience to God himself and as a sinful behavior. St. Basil strongly believes that in order to fulfill God's plan for them the believers have to communicate in love and concord. At the same time, the trinitarian confession, as the "saving confession," should become a foundation for their unity.

Although St. Basil is completely convinced that the Triune God is the real Creator and the head of the church who also maintains its existence, he pays a lot of attention to the role of bishops and clergy in the local communities. They are the ones who are given the authority from God in order to bring peace and unity among believers. St. Basil emphasizes the importance

142. Ibid.
143. Ibid.

of personal example of each leader in the church. Serving God as the faithful stewards, they are supposed to take care of all the believers entrusted to them teaching the proper doctrine of God the Trinity and helping their people to grow toward Christlikeness.

In St. Basil's opinion, love and mutual communications among these leaders should be the essential part of the life in the church. This may create the desirable union and bring reconciliation between the divided groups. Writing to the western and eastern brethren, St. Basil expresses his belief that the ecumenical councils should help to achieve agreement about common beliefs and to sustain the communication between all communities worldwide. In this sense, such conciliar gatherings become the means of restoration and maintenance of fellowship of love among the believers.

CHAPTER 7

Trinitarian Philanthropy as a Basis for Ministry of the Church

BUILDING ON MATERIAL OF previous chapters, this chapter links St. Basil's understanding of God with the practical actions of believers in the church and in the world around them. We have learned from the second chapter that St. Basil perceives God as the Triune Creator, the Father, Son and Holy Spirit, who created humanity and leads it to salvation, to eschatological union with himself. In chapter three, we came to a conclusion that in St. Basil's thought philanthropy of all trinitarian Persons forms a foundation for the relationships in the church. St. Basil's battle for the proper trinitarian confession and its use in the liturgical life of the church from chapters five and six informs our understanding that every time he uses the word God he implies trinitarian *koinonia* and conjoined actions of all Persons of God. This chapter will develop these ideas further and help us to understand how St. Basil's perception of the Triune God and his vision of the created world shapes his attitude toward people both in the church and in the world and his ideas of the church's ministry.

In St. Basil's thought, the ministry of mercy originates from the fulfillment of the commandment of God to love one's neighbor. It is based on the imitation of his φιλανθρωπία or the love of the Father, and of the Savior, and of the Spirit toward all humanity. In this sense, St. Basil's perception of compassion is rooted in his theological presuppositions concerning the relationship of the Triune Creator to human beings. Hence, his ministry to the poor and the needy is the application of this teaching in his life and the life of the church. Many theological principles can be seen behind his actions and practical achievements done by the church, but four major interrelated ideas can be formulated as: a) respect for human life and recognition of the worth of all human persons in the eyes of the Triune God; b) the role of human beings as stewards of God in a world created by him; c) evaluation of all human actions in the light of eschatological consequences and the life in the heavenly *ekklesia* in the presence of all Persons of the Trinity; d) a theocentric philanthropy as a basis for ministry of every member of the church. In this chapter, we will discuss these directions of St. Basil's thought, which serve as a foundation for his actions and which reveal to us his understanding of ministry of the Christian community.

HUMANS, GREAT AND SMALL, IN THE EYES OF THEIR TRIUNE CREATOR

One of the great theological presuppositions, which forms the foundation for St. Basil's social activity and the works of mercy performed by the church, is his belief that all people deserve compassion and they are equal in the presence of their Triune Creator.[1] In his treatise *On the Holy Spirit*, St. Basil asserts, "Even though one man be called master and another servant, nevertheless, both in view of our mutual equality of rank and as chattels of our Creator, we are all fellow slaves."[2] The same idea he shares in his conversation with a prefect Modestus. St. Basil reminds him that so he is a prefect and an illustrious one, but he still is the creature of God as any other of St. Basil's subjects.[3]

In St. Basil's theology, what constitutes human value and dignity is God's love toward all his children. Every person is precious because God created all humans, Christ died for them, and the Holy Spirit works with all believers until their death. For each person God the Trinity has a plan on how to deliver him or her from death and to bring each to the heavenly dimension of the church. God uses various approaches in the lives of different

---

1. See *Homily delivered in Lakizois: Hom.* 26.2 (DelCogliano, 197–98). "These differences that exist among the brothers are obvious to you: one is poor, another rich, one is a stranger, another a family member . . . They have one and the same nature: they both—this one and that one— are human beings . . . He [God] wants you to be the comforter of those in need."

2. See *HS* 20.51.

3. See *Oration* 43.63.

people, but through the presence of the Holy Spirit he guides all of them, whether rich or poor, to the same destination where they will become equal indeed.

The perspective from which St. Basil looks at people's social position, status in society, and origin is built on the recognition that all humans have a common nature, and everything on the earth is provided by their Creator for their common possession.[4] Throughout his homilies on social issues, he constantly emphasizes that nobody really owns anything in this world. He is convinced that people cannot claim something as their own "by right of preemption"[5] and seize common goods before others have the opportunity.

Defending his point of view, St. Basil address his listeners with the following questions: "Tell me, what is your own? What did you bring into this life? From what did you receive it?"[6] He tries to make his audience realize that the world is created by the Triune God in order to be shared. St. Basil continues, "For if we all took only what was necessary to satisfy our own needs, giving the rest to those who lack, no one would be rich, no one would be poor, and no one would be in need."[7] In this sense, the wealth does not belong to anyone in the world, and "one person alone cannot enjoy what is offered for the benefit of all in common."[8] Using his rhetorical skills, St. Basil persuades his listeners,

> O mortal, recognize your Benefactor! Consider yourself, who you are, what resources have been entrusted to you, from whom you received them, and why you received more than others. You have been made a minister of God's goodness, a steward of your fellow servants. Do not suppose that all this was furnished for your own gullet! Resolve to treat the things in your possessions as belonging to others.[9]

According to St. Basil's understanding, God distributes things that are necessary for life unequally among people, but there is a purpose in it. They have to recognize their Triune Creator and acknowledge that all their possessions were given to them by him. Therefore, those who are wealthy may become the good and wise stewards of what they received and share their possessions with those who are in need. Then at the end, the rich "might receive the reward of benevolence and good stewardship, while the poor are

4. *Hom.* 6.1 (Schroeder, 60). See *Hom.* 26.2 (DelCogliano, 197–98).
5. *Hom.* 6.7 (Schroeder, 69).
6. Ibid.
7. Ibid.
8. Ibid. See the same idea in *Hom.* 7.3 (Schroeder, 46–47).
9. *Hom.* 6.2 (Schroeder, 61).

honored for patient endurance in their struggles."[10] In this sense, the lack of wealth is beneficial to the poor, because they have the better opportunity to conform to the requirements and commandments of the Lord through obedience and patience in the time of troubles. At same time, the rich have a chance to demonstrate their ability to manage their possessions well in order to relieve the sufferings of those who are tormented by hunger. In this way, they may be healed from their selfishness through the expression of love to the needy and through manifestation of the compassion of Christ. As a result, both groups of people will benefit from the acts of compassion and will learn how not to be attached to the earthly treasures.

In his homilies on the words "Give heed to thyself,"[11] St. Basil reminds his listeners that all people look equal after death: "Look down into their graves and see if you are able to discern which is the slave and which the master; which the pauper, which the rich man. Distinguish, if you can, the captive from the king, the strong man from the week, the comely from ill-favored."[12] Both the rich and the poor have to remember their nature that they are mortal and "be mindful of themselves." If the wealthy "give heed to themselves," then they will not "yield to vanity," because their earthly glory or status will not be taken into account in the heavenly *ekklesia* in the presence of the Trinity. St. Basil believes that the wealth or the grandeur are only "instruments for practicing virtue to those who use them well."[13] In the case of the poor, there is always a "good hope" because the present state is not the end. For the faithful, there are always the blessings granted by Creator, and for those people they are "reserved by promise for the future."[14] Therefore, the rich should not boast of their wealth or be proud of their lineage, and the poor should not despair because of their pitiful conditions. All of them have to think about their future life after death where God the Trinity chooses different criteria for their evaluation. Finishing his discourse, St. Basil provides at least two answers about what constitutes human value and why God participates in the lives of everyone both the wealthy and the poor.

> First of all, you are a man, the only one of all living beings to have been formed by God. Is not this enough to call forth the most ecstatic joy in a man who reasons intelligently—that you have been formed by the very Hands of God who created all things? Secondly, having been made according to the image of

---

10. *Hom.* 6.7 (Schroeder, 69).
11. *Hom.* 3. The words are from Deut 15:9.
12. Ibid. (Wagner, 441).
13. *Hom.* 11 (Wagner, 471).
14. *Hom.* 3 (Wagner, 441).

the Creator, you are able to arrive at a dignity equal to that of the angels by leading a good life.[15]

Describing the dignity of an individual person, St. Basil also says that in every one of us, as in "a miniature replica of cosmic order," it is possible to "contemplate the great wisdom of the Creator."[16] In this sense, every human being contains in himself or herself a great value compatible with the information about the universe. St. Basil is convinced that every person has the opportunity to reach this dignity, which the Triune God originally expected from humans. The condition now is "a good life" here on earth, which implies the fulfillment of some responsibilities in this world. Although St. Basil constantly repeats the idea that human life on the earth is temporary and it is only a time of preparation for the life to come, he wants his listeners to be actively involved in this life and to do what their Creator prepared for them as a part of their earthly assignment. In some sense, Christians in the church are supposed to become God's co-workers in this world where they have to live until the last day, which is appointed for them by the Lord. "Leading a good life," in St. Basil's thinking, implies obedience to God's commandments and fulfillment of his plans for humanity. In order to accomplish everything that God prepared for them, Christians have Christ as their example, the Holy Spirit as their guide who illuminates them and leads them in their work, and the Father who is the source of everything including life and love.

According to St. Basil, the grace is granted to the believers by the Holy Spirit during their baptism that "we may fulfill our duties by faith through charity, and, thus, the satisfaction of the divine love in Christ may be perfectly accomplished in us."[17]

One of the most important commandments of God, which St. Basil describes as "the mother of the commandments,"[18] is the requirement to love and care of your neighbor as yourself. Therefore, if the Christians call the Lord their teacher, they have to "carry out the duties of the disciples,"[19] which implies the simplification of their own needs for the satisfaction of the needs of others. St. Basil explains this principle of applied love with following words:

> Care for the needy requires the expenditure of wealth: when all share alike, distributing their possessions among themselves,

---

15. Ibid.
16. Ibid. (Wagner, 444). PG 31:216A. The Greek: μικρῷ τινι διακόσμῳ.
17. *CBap* 1 (Wagner, 360).
18. *Hom.* 8.7 (Schroeder, 85).
19. *Hom.* 7.1 (Schroeder, 42).

they each receive a small portion for their individual needs. Thus, those who love their neighbor as themselves possess nothing more than their neighbor.[20]

This idea of equality among Christians is clearly reflected in St. Basil's ideal vision of the church. He promotes the relationships, which existed in the community of the first Christians, as the best example that the believers have to follow. St. Basil persuades his listeners, "Let us zealously imitate the early Christian community, where everything was held in common—life, soul, concord, a common table, indivisible kinship—while unfeigned love constituted many bodies as one and joined many souls into a single harmonious whole."[21] He introduces them to the church, which is able to fulfill its purpose intended by God. This gathering of believers based on love presents a new social reality where the needs of people are met and God the Trinity is worshiped and glorified. Christians enjoy equal rights in this community in order to serve the hungry, the thirsty, the unclothed, or the imprisoned.

St. Basil reminds his audience that God himself was "filled with sympathy and compassion for the hungry."[22] As faithful followers of Christ, believers are expected to live according to the model, which he provided for them while teaching here on earth. For this reason, some of them "have received wealth as a stewardship, and not for their own enjoyment."[23] Therefore, through showing mercy, giving, and sharing, they may imitate the loving attitude of the Triune God from whom "comes everything beneficial."[24] By such acts, believers become his true stewards in this world and fulfill the obligations imposed on them by their Creator. If they manage common resources properly, then everybody may benefit in this world.[25]

Another reason why every person deserves respect and an attitude of compassion is because "those who believe" have the potential to be "made sons of God through faith" and "are worthy of being called gods themselves."[26] Therefore, to turn back on your fellow believer is to dishonor Creator and his loving plans toward humanity. This leads us to an idea that

---

20. Ibid., 43. See this idea also in *The Morals* 48 (Clarke, 113–14).

21. *Hom.* 8.8 (Schroeder, 87). St. Basil implies the words from Acts 2:41–46; 4:32. He also uses the same idea that believers had "all things common" in *LR* (Clarke, 166).

22. *Hom.* 8.7 (Schroeder, 85).

23. *Hom.* 7.3 (Schroeder, 46). See the same idea in *Hom.* 11 (Wagner, 472).

24. *Hom.* 6.1 (Schroeder, 60). See also *Hom.* 7.8 (Schroeder, 57–58). St. Basil believes that the instances of God's providence is the evidence of his "fatherly care which he often demonstrates towards humanity." See *Hom.* 8.6 (Schroeder, 83).

25. See this idea in *Hom.* 11 (Wagner, 473).

26. *Ps.* 7 (Way, 171). PG29:238B, believers will be called gods—Θεοί.

although the rich and the poor have different starting points, they should strive to reach the same goal—godliness, and use the opportunities, which are provided in their lives by the Triune God from the beginning. From some of them it is expected that they become faithful servants or stewards. The others have to go through hardships of life with patience hoping that they will receive from the abundant wealth of those who were entrusted by Creator with his recourses.

As far as the common property and resources are concerned, St. Basil believes that everything that is created by the Triune God is interconnected and constitutes a single and whole entity including people. In connection with this, he expresses the conviction that the actions of people toward each other may influence the created order both in a positive and in a negative way. This view is employed by St. Basil in one of his homilies, which was preached in the time of drought and famine.[27] In this homily, he points out that even the fields and nature suffer because of human unwillingness to share with others what they received from God. In his opinion, the greediness and the lack of love toward the neighbor became a cause of the disorder. St. Basil is convinced that when in society people neglect the needy and become "grudging and unsociable toward the poor," then the Lord threatens them with righteous judgment and uses for this natural forces.[28] Therefore, unsocial behavior of those who have enough food for everyone leads to "the multitude of sins," which causes changes in the character of the seasons, the alternation of natural order, and fruitlessness of the earth.[29] St. Basil blames such selfish people openly,

> It is on your account that this catastrophe was decreed, because you have but do not give, because you neglect the hungry, because you pay no heed to the plight of the miserable, because you show no mercy to those who prostrate themselves before you. Evil things come upon the people for the sake of a few; for one person's depravity the people are punished.[30]

---

27. *Hom.* 8 (Schroeder, 73–88).

28. *Hom.* 8.2 (Schroeder, 76). See the similar idea that "disorder of cities and nations, drought in the air and barrenness of the earth, the harsh calamities in the life of each, cut short the growth of evil" in his *Homily* 9. St. Basil is convinced that these kinds of evil comes into being to stop true evil, which implies injustice in society. Harrison, *On the Human Condition*, 70–71.

29. Ibid., 75. St. Basil repeats this idea one more time in this homily: "Let us truly account this catastrophe as having occurred primarily because of our own sins." *Hom.* 8.5 (Schroeder, 80).

30. *Hom.* 8.4 (Schroeder, 79).

Using the example of Nineveh, St. Basil shows "the appropriate mindset for wise servants," which implies the repentance of those people "who are entangled in sins."[31] In order to restore balance in nature and bring an end to the drought, human beings have to reverse their activity and to recompense their evil deeds with the good ones. St. Basil appeals to people, "Tear up the unjust contract, so that sin might also be loosed. Wipe away the debt that bears high rates of interest, so that the earth may bear its usual fruits."[32] He suggests that the provisions, which everybody needs in the country, "might now be measured back" by the Triune Creator if they start to care for the strangers, to support the orphans, and to minister to the widows.

Stressing the idea that gracious acts of mercy toward the hungry may change the existing circumstances, St. Basil comes to an interesting theological insight in this homily about "the primal sin."[33] Once again, St. Basil returns to the story of creation and to the moment in the history of humanity when the relationships with their Triune Created were broken. He suggests that with sharing the food people may "undo," in some sense, the original sin of first humans. As St. Basil explains it, "Just as Adam transmitted sin by eating wrongly, so we wipe away the treacherous food when we remedy the need and hunger of our brothers and sisters."[34] Therefore, acts of mercy help to improve not only material condition of the existing world but the spiritual as well. St. Basil tries to convey the idea that fulfillment of God's commandments, which includes compassion toward the neighbor, makes people more sociable and better humans. On the contrary, greedy people show themselves "to be more savage than the unreasoning animals" that are able to use in common the plants, which grow from the earth.[35] Through images of nature, he illustrates his point that selfishness is not a normal condition of the creation. Therefore, when people keep to themselves what belongs to many others, they indicate that they have lost their original humanness and that their nature was corrupted. In St. Basil's opinion, the only reason why their Triune Creator continues to provide the rich people with recourses is his patience and his hope to convert them and to change their attitude. As "the lover of humankind,"[36] God did not immediately judge them. St. Basil believes that the divine goal is to help them understand the purpose of their existence, to lead them out of misanthropy to philanthropy,

---

31. Ibid., 78.
32. *Hom.* 8.4 (Schroeder, 78).
33. *Hom.* 8.7 (Schroeder, 86).
34. Ibid.
35. Ibid. In *Hom.* 7.3. St. Basil calls such behavior "inhuman" (Schroeder, 45).
36. *Hom.* 6.1 (Schroeder, 60).

and to make them share with his other children and relieve their sufferings. Through these actions, both the rich and the poor will be able to reach the perfection in their lives. In connection to this, St. Basil addresses the believers in the church with the following words, "Let us now examine our lives, both individually and corporately."[37] This implies that after examining their conditions, people may realize that they need less material things for their earthly life, but they need more spiritual ones, which are necessary for the life eternal. At the same time, this corporate examination may reveal the hardships in the lives of others due to the lack of food and clothes. Therefore, the church may become the place where people are able to compensate the needs of each other. Those who experience a spiritual destitution may enrich themselves through giving to others who lack the material goods for physical survival. The poor and the needy can share with the rich what they learned from their circumstances about God's mercy and faithfulness. As a result, all of them will be able to improve their human dignity, to move forward to Christlikeness, and to enter together the heavenly *ekklesia* praising God the Trinity for his mercy and wisdom.

UNION WITH GOD THE TRINITY AS THE ULTIMATE GOAL OF CHRISTIANS AND A MINISTRY OF COMPASSION

As we have seen earlier, St. Basil perceives the church as a social event, which all believers begin to experience here on earth, and which continues in the heavenly realities.[38] Life in a Christian community leads the people to union with the Father, Son and Holy Spirit into the age to come when all their relations will be maintained according to God's law of love. In this sense, the church is the sphere where believers should be united to their Triune Creator and to each other by the same law in this present life. In St. Basil's opinion, this should be demonstrated as "faith working through love"[39] that includes feeding the hungry, offering hospitality to the stranger, and helping the sick and the needy. Describing dangerous and destructive consequences of sin for the community in his prologue to ascetic rules, *De judicio Dei*, St. Basil ends his discourse with an interesting conclusion concerning compassion and acts of mercy in the church:

---

37. *Hom.* 8.5 (Schroeder, 80).

38. See, for example, the discussion of the idea of the church as a new social reality in chapter 4 of this book.

39. *The Morals* 80.22. See also *De Jud.* (Clarke, 89).

> For it is written: "The Lord is faithful in all his words"—whether forbidding anything, or commanding, or promising, or threatening, whether He refers to the doing of what is forbidden, or to the leaving undone what is commanded. For that leaving of good works undone is punished equally with perpetrating evil works.[40]

He develops this idea further and explains in more detail the relation of eternal punishment to the undone actions of mercy. St. Basil believes that at the day of last judgment God will say to some people "Depart from me, you cursed, into everlasting fire . . ." not because they committed murder or fornication, but because they "neglected good works."[41] In St. Basil's thinking, omitting acts that are commanded is disobedience to God, and therefore, it deserves an equal punishment as any other form of disobedience. The only way to "escape the wrath that comes upon the sons of disobedience" and be able to participate in "the future age of immortality" is to live the life pleasing to their Triune Creator through not only avoiding what is forbidden, but earnestly observing "what is approved."[42] St. Basil is convinced that a person can be found worthy of obtaining eternal life in the heavenly kingdom only if he or she keeps God's covenant and is "mindful of his commandments to do them."[43]

A similar idea about the eternal punishment for neglecting good works here on earth is repeated one more time in *The Morals* when he recalls the words from Matt 3:10 that "every tree that does not bear good fruit is cut down and thrown into the fire." Therefore, St. Basil affirms, "After departure from this life there is no opportunity for good deeds, since God in his forbearance has provided the present life for doing those things that please Him."[44] Our present life on earth is temporary, and in order to gain the life eternal, people have to follow the commandments given in the Gospel not only by words but also by deeds. It is expected of every true believer to live her/his life in balance thinking not only of their own needs but the needs of others and producing works of mercy.

---

40. *De Jud.* (Clarke, 87–88). See the same idea of punishment for "the lack of good works" in *The Longer Rules* (Clarke, 146).

41. Ibid., 88. See the same idea in *Homily 6*. St. Basil repeats the word from Matt 25:41–43 and adds, "Moreover, those who under accusation in this passage are not those who have stolen anything; these are rather leveled against those who have not shared with others" (Schroeder, 70).

42. Ibid., 89.

43. *De Jud.* (Wagner, 54). See this idea also in *LR* 3.R.2 (Clarke, 157–58).

44. *The Morals* (Wagner, 73).

St. Basil keeps reminding his listeners and readers in his homilies that their lives in this world stretch before them like a long road, and the periods of life look as stages in a journey. "This road," St. Basil goes on, "however, draws those who travel it by main force toward the end which has been appointed by the Lord," and at this end everybody has to arrive.[45] He wants the believers to remember that they must prepare themselves daily for departure from this world and keep their eyes fixed upon Christ. They have to understand that "none of the pleasures of this life" can be truly possessed by them.[46] Even if they keep them while they are alive and these material things do not pass into the hands of others, they will be lost to these people at their death, because the nature of things is not such that they could accompany them at their departure.[47] In this sense, nothing from the material world can belong to humans forever. Gold or acres of land, horses or herds of animals may be enjoyed in this life only briefly.

What really belongs to us as people, in St. Basil's opinion, is only "a soul, a light and spiritual being," and "a body, which was provided for the soul by the Creator as a vehicle for carrying on life."[48] He believes that every human being as "a mind united with a fitting and serviceable body" at the end "will receive the recompense for the deeds performed during this life."[49] The only things that do not abandon us on our way toward the next world are our virtues if they become our possessions through practice while we labor on earth. St. Basil is convinced that only this kind of possessors will be placed "in the ranks of angels and will shine for all eternity"[50] in the presence of their Triune Creator.

Answering the question about the way of life that can help gain such virtues, St. Basil uses a metaphor of a storm on the sea. He leads his listeners to the conclusion that as sailors reduce the load of their cargo in order to save their lives so believers have to place their "burden" and riches in "safer ships."[51] He assures them that if they use "the stomachs of the poor" as such ships, then their money is not lost. On the contrary, all the riches invested in the lives of the needy are preserved and help them to reach "the

---

45. *Hom. 21* (Wagner, 490).

46. Ibid., 491. See also *Hom.* 26.5 (DelCogliano, 201).

47. *Hom. 21* (Wagner, 491). See similar idea in *Homily 7* when St. Basil affirms, "Even if your belongings could follow you to the future life, they would not be particularly desirable there, since they would be overshadowed by truly precious things" (Schroeder, 47).

48. *Hom. 21* (Wagner, 494).

49. Ibid.

50. Ibid.

51. Ibid., 496–97.

harbor in advance" and enter into glory.[52] In St. Basil's view, distribution of possessions among poor leads to salvation and helps to escape "the fire of hell" to those who are the owners.[53] He himself calls it "a paradox," but at the same time, he is convinced that it is entirely true:

> When wealth is scattered in the manner, which our Lord directed, it naturally returns, but when it is gathered, it naturally disperses. If you try to keep it, you will not have it; if you scatter it, you will not lose it. "They have distributed freely, they have given to the poor; their righteousness endures forever."[54]

St. Basil believes that heavenly *ekklesia* or "the Kingdom of Heaven does not receive such people" who resist laying aside their property, but who "gladly undertake other tasks" in order to enter it. As he affirms, "I know many who fast, pray, sigh, and demonstrate every manner of piety, so long as it cost them nothing, yet would not part with a penny to help those in distress."[55] Therefore, he implies that salvation depends not only on spiritual exercises or mystical experiences and contemplation, but also on people's willingness to serve God and the neighbors with all their strength and private possessions. In this sense, the acts of compassion are the condition for entering the heavenly dimension of the church and have union with the Triune God. St. Basil's harsh words sound as a serious warning: "You showed no mercy; it will not be shown to you. You opened not your house; you will be expelled from the Kingdom. You gave not your bread; you will not receive eternal life."[56]

The logic and method of persuasion behind St. Basil's words are simple. He shows the attractiveness of life eternal in the presence of their loving Triune Creator and then reminds his audience of the negative consequences in a case of disobedience to God's commandments.[57] In order to convince them, St. Basil tells about "fearful things" that await them when "the wrath of God" will be revealed from heaven, about "the resurrection of condemna-

---

52. Ibid., 497. St. Basil repeats exactly the same idea in another homily, "If you want storehouses, you have them in the stomachs of the poor. Lay up for yourself treasure in heaven." *Hom.* 6 (Schroeder, 68).

53. *Hom.* 21 (Wagner, 497).

54. *Hom.* 7 (Schroeder, 44). Basil uses the same verse from Ps 112:9 in *Hom.* 6 (Schroeder, 63).

55. Ibid. (Schroeder, 46).

56. Ibid. See also *Hom.* 6 (Schroeder, 61). St. Basil keeps reminding that "a strict accounting" will be demanded from the rich people who did not share the possessions with the needy.

57. *Hom.* 6 (Schroeder, 70).

tion" for those who have done evil, about "the everlasting shame," which will be a portion of sinners, and about "a fury of fire that will consume the adversaries."[58] He admits that he uses all these things and examples to make them sad, to move them, to make them desire the kingdom, and fear hell. He appeals both to their conscience and to their awareness of eternal punishment.[59] St. Basil wants the rich people to realize that in the eyes of God the Trinity a person who has not shared with others is guilty as much as a robber and a thief.

> The bread you are holding back is for the hungry, the clothes you keep put away are for the naked, the shoes that are rotting away with disuse are for those who have none, the silver you keep buried in the earth is for needy. You are thus guilty of injustice toward as many as you might have aided, and did not.[60]

Talking of salvation, St. Basil uses an interesting language. Although he strongly believes that all humans are called by the Triune God into his kingdom and they can get there only by his grace, he still says that somebody's "riches may become a ransom" for him.[61] In the other sermon, he explains that people have "the opportunity to exchange corruptible things for the kingdom of heaven."[62] He believes that people's labor here on earth is "their provision for the future life," and their "good works will treasure up for *them* glory and honor according to the just requital of the Judge."[63]

In St. Basil's thought, the wish to obtain salvation *per se* and the unseen rewards of God's kingdom should determine believer's behavior. Therefore, he persuades the listeners of his sermons to achieve such rewards through

---

58. *Hom.* 7 (Schroeder, 52). See also *Hom.* 8.7 (Schroeder, 85). Basil affirms, "The person who is good and gives generously will enter into eternal life before the rest. But the unsociable and stingy will be the first to be given over to the eternal fire."

59. St. Basil appeals with eagerness to rich and greedy people, "Will you never regain consciousness? . . . Will you not bring before your eyes the Judgment Seat of Christ?" *Hom.* 7 (Schroeder, 51–52).

60. *Hom.* 6 (Schroeder, 70). In some cases, when people were really starving to death St. Basil accused the rich to be the murderers. In his homily "*In Time of Famine and Drought*," he says, "For whoever has the ability to remedy the sufferings of others, but chooses rather to withhold aid out of selfish motives, may properly be judged the equivalent of a murderer." *Hom.* 8 (Schroeder, 85).

61. Ibid. (Schroeder, 71). St. Basil is using masculine language. Therefore, it is used in this example.

62. *Hom.* 7.3 (Schroeder, 47). Similar thinking can be found in *The Longer Rules* where St. Basil affirms that the heavenly kingdom can be attained only if people sacrifice all their possessions and whatever is commonly cherished. See Clarke, 168.

63. *Hom.* 13 (Way, 194).

donations and help to starving and dying people.⁶⁴ If we look closely at St. Basil's arguments, we notice that his purpose is not only to help those who suffer, to make the rich share their wealth, and to bring peace to his community. One of the main goals of his discourses is to save the souls of everyone who is under his spiritual guidance: both the poor and the rich. He wants all of them to enter the heavenly *ekklesia* and enjoy fellowship with the Triune God as his children whom he loves. Obviously, he believes that the rich people deserve salvation as much as the poor ones, but it requires them to make an extra effort in order to follow God's commandments. In St. Basil's opinion, the more people are attached to their possessions the more they "lack in love."⁶⁵

According to St. Basil's thinking, the Triune God as "the Great Physician of souls and bodies," seeing their deficiency in this vital area wishes to make them whole.⁶⁶ Both the rich and the poor are led by the "loving Spirit"⁶⁷ through hardships and difficult situations in order that their hearts might be changed and healed from selfishness and greed. St. Basil believes that Christ, as the good counselor, shows the best example. He "became poor for us so that He might make us rich through His poverty, and 'gave Himself a ransom for all.'"⁶⁸ Therefore, Christians have to follow what they have been commanded in order "to become heirs of eternal life in Christ Himself."⁶⁹ In this sense, the willingness of believers to share their possessions, to take part in lives of other people, and to care for their needs helps them to obtain the Christlikeness and salvation, which implies life in the heavenly dimension of the church with all the Persons of the Trinity.

FAITH INTO ACTION: TRANSFORMATION OF LIVES THROUGH A THEOCENTRIC PHILANTHROPY

Throughout his life, St. Basil not only preached in the church about the pressing needs of his time sharing his theological ideas and concerns with

---

64. See, for example, *Hom.* 11, *Concerning Envy* (Wagner, 473–74). St. Basil affirms, "In this way, you will win salvation for yourself and, the greater your good deeds, the greater will be the glory manifested in you."

65. *Hom.* 7 (Schroeder, 43).

66. Ibid.

67. *Ps.* 33.5, PG 29:361D.

68. *Hom.* 7 (Schroeder, 57).

69. Ibid., 58. In *The Morals* St. Basil also reminds believers that the goal of every Christian is to be conformed to the pattern, which they behold in Christ. See *The Morals* (Wagner 196).

others, but he actively applied his teaching in the lives of people around him. He believed in education through liturgical practice. He promoted the idea that Christians have to gain "the knowledge of God." He fought for the correct theological terms and formulations. At the same time, St. Basil truly believed that one of the best ways to let people know about love of the Triune God is to minister to them as to God's children.[70] For him this work of ministry and compassion was the way to follow Christ, to fulfill His commandments, and to attain the kingdom of heaven. In connection with this, in St. Basil's thought the church, as the community of faithful, had to fulfill both functions: to save the souls of people through teaching the trinitarian faith and to minister to their bodies through the improvement of their social conditions.

St. Basil demonstrated his faithfulness to the words of the Gospel about compassion by literally following Jesus's advice to the rich young man. Soon after his baptism, he sold his possessions, which he inherited from his, and distributed among the poor. Later in his life, he spent the remaining portion of his family property feeding the hungry during the drought and famine in the region of Cappadocia.[71] When he served as an ecclesiastic leader, St. Basil devoted all his time and energy to the ministry of others living in simplicity. From the conversation with the prefect Modestus we learn that, as a bishop, he had only "his tattered rags and the few books."[72]

The highest expression of St. Basil's attempts to realize what he taught in practice was the building of a great philanthropic center, later came to be known as the Basileias,[73] which developed under his leadership into a complex of buildings for different purposes. According to St. Basil's witness, there were "hospices for strangers, for those who visit us while on a journey, for those who require some care because of sickness," with "the necessary comforts, such as nurses, physicians, beasts for travelling, and attendants."[74] They organized also a place where food and donated goods were distributed. There was a hospital for sick, especially for the victims of leprosy that were marginalized by the society.[75] A very eloquent description of this cen-

---

70. As we have seen earlier in chapter 4 of this book, St. Basil believes that all people are children of God and he is their real Father.

71.. *Oration* 43.43. A great number of poor people died of starvation between 368 and 375 because of the climatic conditions that prevailed in this region. For background information, see chapter 2 in Holman, *The Hungry are Dying*, 64–98.

72. Ibid., 49.

73. Sozomen, *HE* 6.34.9.

74. *Letter* 94.

75. *Oration* 43.63. See also Theodoret, *HE* 4.16. See eight facts about Basileias in Patitsas, "St. Basil's Philanthropic Program and Modern Microlending Strategies for

ter can be found in Gregory of Nazianzus's funeral oration for St. Basil.[76] In many aspects of social life, such as education, health, and welfare, this philanthropic organization became influential and produced great results: people were saved there in both senses physically and spiritually.[77] Every positive thing that was accomplished in Basileias served as the affirmation of the trinitarian faith and Christian lifestyle.[78]

Through works of mercy, St. Basil exercised what was presented in his homilies and sermons as his beliefs. These philanthropic endeavors were "the consequence of his philosophy."[79] His life as a Christian became a living testimony to the whole country and beyond so that the leaders of society engaged in competition with one another in their philanthropy and magnanimity.[80]

St. Basil not only provided an example of a proper treatment, which all human beings deserve, but at the same time, as the bishop, he showed the attitude of the church toward the needy, the poor, and the sick in the society and, in this way, he witnessed to view of God the Trinity on this issue. St. Basil emphasized in his writings that the love of God should be visible in the lives of Christians. Following the biblical text from Matt 5:16, he affirmed that the actions of mercy might serve as the confession of their faith, and at the end, God will be glorified due to "the light," which "shines before men."[81]

St. Basil admitted that he did not discover something completely new, because even among "the pagan Greeks" a law of philanthropy was exercised.[82] He also mentioned that it is possible to find numerous examples of such love for others in both the Old and the New Testaments. Therefore, the idea of philanthropy was not foreign to his audience, but building on this foundation, St. Basil repeatedly reminded his listeners of the Source of all goodness and of the reasons why this should become an everyday practice

---

Econimic Self-actualization," 269–68.

76. Ibid. See also *Letter 94*. See the ideas of how this "new city" functioned in Crislip, *From Monastery to Hospital*, 103–20.

77. Even earlier, before this community was founded, Gregory testifies that during the famine St. Basil "attended to the bodies and souls to those who needed it, combining personal respect with supply of their necessity, and so giving them a double relief." See *Oration* 43.35.

78. See more details on this issue in the next chapter.

79. *Oration* 43.63.

80. Ibid.

81. *LR* (Clarke, 166).

82. *Hom.* 8.8 (Schroeder, 86). See a very good overview of Hellenistic background of philanthropy and how this idea was developed and applied by the Fathers in the Church in Constantelos, "The Hellenistic Background and Nature of Patristic Philanthropy in the Early Byzantine Era," 187–208.

of the Christian community. He stressed the idea that Christian God, who is the Father, the Son and the Holy Spirit, is the "true Philanthropist,"[83] and "He is our Benefactor."[84] Consequently, the believers as his followers should be "persuaded" by Christ and "give to Him in return."[85] This implies that what was done by Christ must be done by the church. In St. Basil's thought, imitation of Christ through participation in the sufferings of other humans makes the church his real body, which serves here on earth and continues her ministry to this world.[86]

St. Basil's understanding that the lives of all people and the land itself are interdependent led him to the social interactions, which he thought might help restore the balance in the province that was previously broken.[87] He was ready to intercede in person before the imperial court in order to defend the interests of the city.[88] Therefore, in this way, he expressed his conviction that part of his ministry and the ministry of the church was an active involvement into the life of society. This implies the idea that Christian community has to become the agency, which may transform the situation and bring positive changes in the lives of many people.

St. Basil believed that, as the church leader, he had to assume the responsibilities connected even with the state decisions regarding the territory, because the lives of his people were influenced by the introduced innovations. In this sense, he acted as the mediator of people entrusted to him by the Triune God in order to defend their interests.[89] St. Basil demonstrated that he really cared of his country and its conditions. St. Basil was convinced that God ordained him and put him into this position that he could fulfill his plan and to support those who were in need of his assistance.[90] Therefore, he conveyed the idea that his duty—as a Christian and

83. *Ps.* 14 (Schroeder, 98).

84. *Hom.* 7.9 (Schroeder, 58).

85. Ibid. (Schroeder, 57–58).

86. St. Basil explains that Christians should serve using both words and deeds. *CBap* 1 (Wagner, 363).

87. See the examples of interactions with his fellow Cappadocians who held the influential positions in Van Dam, *Emperor, Bishops, and Friends in Late Antique Cappadocia*, 55–56. See also Karayannopoulos, *St. Basil's Social Activity: Principal and Praxis*, 377–78.

88. See *Letter* 76.

89. See *Letter* 74. In the year 371 the political division of Cappadocia happened.

90. See St. Basil's conversation with the prefect Modestus. *Oration* 43.63. See also *Letter* 96 to another powerful man, Sophronius the Master, where St. Basil affirmed that he wrote on behalf of all his people: "I am speaking here not for myself alone, but for the whole community." See also *Letter* 104 written in the same year to prefect Modestus, where Basil emphasizes that he addressed him because of his great distress

as the head of his community—was to become a protector and a caretaker of his people. This offered a distinctive perspective on life and actions of the church leaders, which formed the attitude of many toward their fellow Christians. In the time of crisis, they are supposed to act as the representatives of all believers in the region in orders to defend their rights or to save their lives.

Living in the situation where climatic conditions and cultural traditions generated poverty, St. Basil was able to reconcile his theological views and his practical actions with existing social concerns. He used his considerable rhetorical and organizational talents in the church to improve the living conditions of the poorest and the discriminated members of society. With the assistance of different people, including state officials, St. Basil was able to put into action the principles, which he believed were taught by the Lord and were exercised by the New Testament church. He showed that this ideal model of philanthropic relationships, which reflects an initial plan of the Triune God and his love toward humanity, might work in reality, and therefore, it could be followed by others.

CONCLUSION TO CHAPTER 7

St. Basil's teaching about the ministry of the church is based on the view that the Triune God as the loving Creator and "true Philanthropist" provides everything in this world for common use so that people may have enough material things to satisfy their immediate needs. Therefore, inequality, which exists in the society, is the consequence of human selfishness and greed. St. Basil believes that through sharing and giving it is possible to bring the world to the conditions that were intended by their Triune Creator when he distributed the wealth and property among different people. In St. Basil's opinion, the role, which the church and the believers play in God's plans, is clearly revealed in the Scripture and the teaching of the Lord. This suggests that the merciful attitude of Christ should be imitated by everyone in the world, and this will lead to positive changes in the lives of many people and to the renewal of existing circumstances. The church under the guidance of the Holy Spirit should take the initiative in society and become the community, which brings relief and redemption.

The understanding that all people are equally precious in God's eyes should determine the social actions of believers in the church. Their faith must be demonstrated not only through spiritual disciplines and words, but also through their practical achievements. In this sense, the church, as a

---

at the condition of his whole country.

community of brothers and sisters, is the best place for a Christian to exercise his or her philanthropy knowing that because of these good deeds God the Trinity will be praised and glorified.

St. Basil is convinced that, as the faithful Master, God prepared the reward for all his servants who are obedient to his commandments. Both the poor and the rich in this life go through the test whether they are able or not to manage properly the common recourses, which were entrusted to all, and to fulfill the role appointed to them by the Triune God. The poor Christians should not envy the rich ones, but be patient and trust God in their struggle against poverty and injustice. The wealthy people in the church must remember their responsibilities and the judgment of the Lord, which awaits them in the future after death. St. Basil constantly emphasizes in his homilies that the doors of the heavenly *ekklesia* will be opened only to those who are able to show love of the Triune Creator toward the needy and the oppressed in this life.

Under prevailing circumstances, St. Basil was able to create an alternative "new city" and to show how the church was to operate in this world according to God's plan for humanity and to fulfill its social ministry in order to reverse all negative consequences of human disobedience to God's will. Thus, he introduced the practical way in which the Christian community may become the redeeming social force. As successful ecclesiastical administrator, he left an example, which for centuries determined the attitude of Christians toward the social issues. His strategies and approaches were used by many other believers and leaders of the church both in the East and in the West.

CHAPTER 8

Monastic Communities as Practical Realization of an Ideal Community

In St. Basil's ecclesiology, all the themes that were previously discussed come to their practical realization in the life of the monastic communities. Building communities where Christians were able to live and serve together, St. Basil followed the ideas, which reflected his understanding of the proper life of the church, of the Triune God, and his way of dealing with this world. This kind of community of shared life and resources became for him a place where he tried to embody his ideal of the church, which should not be limited only to a monastic context, but should become a model to be imitated by all. In this sense, monastic community, as a miniature "mirror," reflects the features of the whole church and her connections with the Triune God in St. Basil's thought.

KOINONIA OF LOVE

In the middle of the fourth century, various modes of ascetic life existed in Asia Minor beginning with extreme forms of separation and rejection of social communications to the communal type of asceticism represented by the family monasteries and the double monastic communities.[1] The

---

1. For the background, see Elm, *Virgins of God*; See also Silvas, *The Asketikon of*

Monastic Communities as Practical Realization of an Ideal Community 167

characteristic features of this movement among believers were renunciation of the traditional expectation of society, celibacy, refusal of any extra possessions except necessities of life, and withdrawal from the world in order to spend more time on meditation and prayer. The main goal of these Christians was to reach union with God using spiritual disciplines as the means of perfection. There was not any single cause of the monastic activity, but it was a complex and diffused movement.[2]

St. Basil accepted the ascetic ideas and joined the monastic community, which was organized mostly by his sister Macrina, after he finished his education and returned home.[3] Thereby, he was not so much the innovator of the communal type of monasticism as the reformer who wanted to transform different patterns of ascetic life into a system, which could be perfectly integrated into the life of the church in general. As St. Gregory of Nazianzus in his *Panegyric* explains, St. Basil "reconciled most excellently ... the solitary and the community life."[4] He brought together ascetics and hermits and united them "in order that the contemplative spirit might not be cut from society, nor the active life be uninfluenced by the contemplative, but that, like sea and land, by an interchange of their several gifts, they might unite in promoting the one object, the glory of God."[5] In this sense, St. Basil tried to combine the strongest sides of the many Christian groups and individuals who practiced asceticism. In order to learn more about the existing ascetic methods and life styles, St. Basil visited many places.[6] The experiences of the first Christian monks in the desert both positive and negative brought him to an idea to produce the guiding rules for this unorganized movement.[7] The knowledge about the challenges related to monasticism that could in-

---

St. Basil the Great; and "Introduction" in Crislip, *From Monastery to Hospital*, 1–8. See Appendixes B and C in Fedwick, *The Church*, 156–65.

2. See Crislip, *From Monastery to Hospital*, 143n3. See also Clarke, *St. Basil the Great: a Study in Monasticism*, 13–14.

3. See *Life of Macrina* (Clarke, 28). The role of Macrina in the development of the monastic communities is so important that Silvas uses a title for her—"The Mother of Greek Monasticism." See Silvas, *Asketikon*, 148. See also Rousseau, *Basil of Caesarea*, 61–92. Many scholars agree on the issue that both Macrina and Basil were influenced by their family friend Eustathius of Sebaste. For the details of their complicated relationships, see Rousseau, *Basil of Caesarea*, 232–69. See also an article by Frazee, "Anatolian Asceticism in the Fourth Century," 16–33.

4. *Oration* 43.62.

5. Ibid.

6. *Letter* 204.6.

7. In her book Silvas argues that the *Asketikon* was not written at once, but this work was augmented and rearranged over years, usually by way of response to living situations and particular occasions. Silvas, *The Asketikon*, 2.

fluence the life of the church in a negative way made St. Basil discuss many things in detail.[8] At the same time, his rules describe not so much the life of existing communities, but rather an ideal for which all Christians should strive.

In St. Basil's thinking, the idea of common life (*koinonikos bios*) is related to the idea of *koinonia* of the Trinity[9] and to the initial plan of God for humanity as the life in community.[10] Accordingly, this implies an agreement between all members, the life of service to others, and the fulfillment of God's commandments.[11] In addition, there is an understanding that all relations and actions should be based on love, which brings unity.

In the writings where St. Basil introduces his thinking about the ascetic life, he recognizes the dangers involved in an isolated search for personal holiness and purity. He emphasizes the idea that the mutual interactions with other believers are needed in order to obtain Christian virtues.[12] Especially the ones, which are impossible to practice in solitude: obedience, love or servant's attitude. They imply the presence of other humans whom the person should love, serve, and obey. St. Basil believes that one of the advantages of life in community is the opportunity to be corrected in love by other believers, because an isolated man "will not even recognize his defects readily, not having anyone to reprove him and to set him right with kindness and compassion."[13] This implies a very significant ecclesiological idea that a person may develop as a Christian only in relation to others when his attitude and behavior depends on the opinions and actions of his fellow believers. Therefore, in St. Basil's understanding, the being of the church consists in the relationships, which people have with each other.[14] In some

---

8. According to Meyendorff, when St. Basil speaks of community in the *Asketikon*, "he does not mean a monastery, but the Church itself." Meyendorff, *The Byzantine*, 201. The negative experiences and abuses on the part of mid-fourth-century ascetics were discussed and some of them were condemned by the church at Council of Gangra. See Sterk, *Renouncing the World Yet leading the Church*, 28. A selection of canons of this Council can be found in *Creeds, Councils and Controversies*, ed. J. Stevenson. See also Appendix 7 in Silvas, *Asketikon*, 488–94. According to Ayres, "we cannot date this council with certainty: dates proposed vary between 340 and 370." See Ayres, *Nicaea and its Legacy*, 225n9.

9. See HS 18.46–47 for the concept of *koinonia* inside the Trinity. See *De Fide* (Clarke, 96). See *De Jud.* (Clarke, 81).

10. See the discussion in chapter 2 of this book.

11. St. Basil even calls the Christians from monastic communities "the athletes of the commandments of Christ." LR 17 (Clarke, 181).

12. LR (Clarke, 157–58, 163–65).

13. Ibid., 163.

14. The same idea can be found in Gunton, "The Church on Earth: the Roots of

sense, this again reminds us of St. Basil's idea that the being of the Triune God consists of Persons in relation whose concordance of will should be modelled by all Christians in community.[15]

THE ESCHATOLOGICAL GOAL OF COMMUNITY—UNION WITH THE TRIUNE GOD

Within the monastic community St. Basil tried to create the social environment, which could help different people not only fulfill a set of rules imposed on them, but to go through spiritual formation in order that every person in the end would be able to enter the future heavenly kingdom and experience a union with their Triune God. Therefore, their relationships in this new society must reflect, in some sense, the eschatological union of redeemed children of God. Consequently, even the perception of such categories as gender or social class becomes the subject of transformation. In St. Basil's thinking, "there is no male and female in the resurrection, but there is one certain life and it is of one kind, since those dwelling in the country of the living are pleasing to their Lord."[16] This idea finds its realization in the construction of community. It was a double monastery where both male and female ascetics lived together as equals and served to the common good.[17] In addition, children of both genders lived with them in the community in regulated separate houses for boys and girls.[18] These "common children of brotherhood" were equally expected to live the same life of godliness in similar conditions. The community also included people from different social classes who had to follow prescribed norms of monastic life and to share the same space, the same food, and common tasks in this new social reality. Actually, for people from "the highest ranks of society" St. Basil suggests a test where they are supposed to accomplish "some task which is distasteful to worldlings."[19] During such examination, the person should be watched "whether with full conviction he presents himself to God as a workman" or

---

Community," 71.

15. See *HS* 16.38; *De Jud.* (Clarke, 81).

16. *Ps.* 114 (Way, 357). See also *SR* 309 (Clarke, 350). For more on the issue of gender in St. Basil, see Harrison, "Male and Female in Cappadocian Theology," 441–71.

17. This means that they were equal as humans, but their physical appearance was very much distinguishable as feminine and masculine. Actually, the wearing of opposite sex clothing and behaving as opposite sex was condemned by the Council of Gangra. See Silvas, *Asketikon*, 19.

18. *LR* 15 (Clarke, 175).

19. *LR* 10 (Clarke, 172).

not.[20] In this way, the believers were able to prove their complete devotion to the life in the Christian community according to its principle of equality. St. Basil is convinced that the hard and unpleasant manual work helps the believers to acquire the true Christian character if they "aspire to humility after the likeness of our Lord Jesus Christ."[21] This implies that the real status of humans in the church does not depend on their belonging to a particular family, or on their occupations and the work, which they perform, or on their possessions. The only thing, which matters in this new society, is their likeness to Christ. On entering the community, people receive a new social identity, which corresponds to their faith and their spiritual perfection, but not to the previous status in the world. From now on, they are supposed to acquire a new way of thinking as it were the migration to "another world" in their "habit of mind."[22] With the guidance of the Holy Spirit their "fleshly relations," the patterns of communication, and the perception of things or people should be changed according to their new "citizenship," which is "in heaven."[23]

Discussing the rules for monastic communities, St. Basil thinks this group of Christians is an example for the rest of believers in the church. He sees the potential and the strength of life in organized community where everybody's actions are known and, in some sense, even controlled by the other Christians. Meyendorff is convinced that St. Basil "was promoting monasticism not as a separate order, not even as a particular category of Christians, but as an ideal for 'complete' or 'perfect' Christians (*teleioi cristianoi*) constituting the community of the church."[24] In St. Basil's opinion, these monastic communities remind the primitive church in Jerusalem, which he perceives as the best model for the life of the church.[25] The common life and the common possessions allow the Christians not to be distracted by material things, but to strive for spiritual perfection through the prayers and

---

20. Ibid.
21. *LR* 10 (Clarke, 172).
22. *LR* 5 (Clarke, 159).
23. Ibid.

24. Meyendorff, *The Byzantine Legacy*, 201. Silvas provides the arguments for this statement. She asserts that there are some marks in St. Basil's discourse, which show that monastic communities are considered as part of the church: 1) in his ascetic writings there is a "sense of the 'Church of God' and the necessity of inclusion in it"; 2) in his language he avoids "a specialized terminology for Christian ascetics," such as monk or nun. See Silvas, *Asketikon*, 20.

25. *LR* (Clarke, 166). The central, evocative text with which St. Basil connects his ideal is Acts 2:44: "And all who believed were together and had all things in common." See Meredith, *The Cappadocians*, 25.

the actions of love toward their neighbors.[26] Together, as the community of the faithful, believers have the opportunity to develop into the "complete" or full humans personally and corporately in order to experience a union with their Triune Creator.

MINISTRY TO OTHER PEOPLE AS A TESTIMONY OF LOVE OF GOD THE TRINITY

The practical achievements of the community in Basileias, which was organized by St. Basil near Caesarea, reflect his ideas connected with the ministry of the church in the world. This is an attempt to build a community, where people are able to get an education and the proper skills for everyday life, which demonstrates St. Basil's intention to bring changes into the lives of people.[27] Through service to the poor, the sick, strangers, and the needy, he introduces his view that the church is supposed to influence the life around her and to transform it in a positive way according to God's plan of salvation for the whole humanity. Through sharing and giving, the principle of "faith working through love"[28] is realized in practice by the Christians of this "new city." The social ministry of this monastic community served as a great testimony of love of God the Trinity in time of troubles and distress.

For St. Basil self-denial is not a virtue in itself, but only the means, which may strengthen the believer's faith and release God's love through giving extra possessions to others. In this sense, withdrawal from the society should be not so much physical, which implies the break of all contacts with the outside world, but spiritual.[29] This thinking leads to a different attitude toward other people in this world: not thoroughly negative, but life giving and transforming. In St. Basil's opinion, this demonstrates an attitude of the

26. See "Preface" to *The Shorter Rules*, where St. Basil asserts that God has brought them together so that "they have much freedom from external distractions" and may meditate on God's law day and night (Clarke, 229).

27. The pressing needs of community suggest that monastics were expected to practice carpentry, masonry, agriculture or blacksmithing. See *LR* 38 (Clarke, 210). We also have to mention that St. Basil did not want to bring the radical changes into existed society. According to his rules, slavery was allowed and usually the slaves were not accepted by the monastic communities. See *LR* 11 (Clarke, 172–73).

28. *The Morals* 80.22 (Clarke, 129).

29. *Letter* 2.2. This was one of the reasons St. Basil founded the monastic communities in the cities and not in the desert. See also his *Letter* 295 (to monks): "For you know that unless illumined by faith in God, strictness of life availeth nothing; nor will a right confession of faith, if void of good works, be able to present you before the Lord. Faith and works must be joined: so shall the man of God be perfect, and his life not halt through any imperfection."

Triune Creator toward humanity and his plan for people. Therefore, believers in the monastic communities are supposed to work for the benefit of the whole community and "to those in want"—the elderly and the sick. As he explains, "For such a mode of life is useful to us not only because of the body-buffeting it entails, but because of love to our neighbour, in order that God by our means may bring sufficiency to the weak among the brethren, after the example given us in Acts by the apostle."[30] St. Basil himself set a great example when during the years of drought and famine, he worked with his own hands serving food to the victims of starvation: "men and women, infants, old men, every age which was in distress."[31] According to Gregory, St. Basil attended to the bodies and souls of those who needed it "imitating the ministry of Christ, Who, girded with a towel, did not disdain to wash the disciples' feet."[32] Thus, he confirmed that the spiritual perfection of ascetic is due not only to spiritual disciplines but to manual labor, which is performed in love for the good of other people. The goal of the work is not only to satisfy one's own needs, but also to create an atmosphere in the community, where people feel that they are responsible for each other's life. In this context, their work becomes the manifestation of love toward the neighbor through ministry to people. The service to others and the distribution of goods show their inner disposition when the believers demonstrate solidarity with other humans. Responding to the pressing needs of the society, Christians, at the same time, learn the new life style. This new model of relationships of mutual love, respect, and interdependence in the Christian community reflects the plan of the Triune God for humanity and serves as a testimony of His love.

THE LIFE OF COMMUNITY AND OBEDIENCE TO THE LEADERS APPOINTED BY GOD

Throughout his writings, St. Basil stresses the importance of obedience, which facilitates unity in a particular community and in the church in general. Unfortunately, one of the weaknesses of the earlier ascetic movements was their unwillingness to obey the church authorities. Some of the ascetics and communities even deliberately set themselves apart from the structure of the church. They lived according to their own standards avoiding the normal ecclesiastical assemblies of other Christians. They were not

---

30. *LR* 37; 42 (Clarke, 205, 214–15).
31. *Oration* 43.35.
32. Ibid.

interested in "public worship or instructions from the bishop."[33] Often there were only lay people in these communities. Therefore, they did not participate in the "mysteries" of the church and especially in Eucharist, which, according to St. Basil, is a source of nutrition for their spiritual life. At the Council of Gangra bishops criticized these ascetics especially for not being "of a common mind" and for maintaining their own laws.[34] As Meredith noticed, "They did not owe their existence to the inspiration of bishops, and they certainly did not consider themselves as owing them any allegiance. It is no small measure of Basil's sagacity that he saw the enormous power for good locked up in a movement that had been condemned for its antisocial behavior."[35] Such an attitude of these ascetics and the existence of these groups of believers undermined the unity of the church and its functioning as the one body of Christ.[36] The necessity to protect the ecclesiastical unity brought St. Basil to the idea of introducing the norms of discipline in the monastic communities, which might help to develop an attitude of obedience and respect toward the authorities of the church among ascetics.[37]

Opposing those who considered the power of the bishops and superiors as only of human origin, St. Basil asserts in his writings that the hierarchy and obedience in community corresponds to the authority of the Triune God. In his letters, he explains that the ordination of bishops is done according to God's will.[38] In the same way, St. Basil in his ascetic rules defends the role of superiors in communities. Using the words of Jesus from Luke 10:16, St. Basil openly declares that the authority of the superior as the Christian leader is derived from the Lord himself. Therefore, the one who receives a command and refuses to obey should be recognized as an evil man that actually rejects the Lord's commandment.[39] In his *Shorter Rules* St.

33. Fedwick, *The Church*, 156.

34. See Ballan, "Basil of Caesarea on the Ascetic Craft," 2. See also Silvas, *Asketikon*, 488–94.

35. Meredith, *The Cappadocians*, 25.

36. At that time, there were heretical movements among ascetics known as "Messalianism" the followers of which rejected the sacramental life of the church. They received their name from Syrian *msallyana*, meaning "one who prays" (translates into Greek as *euchites*). They hoped that constant prayer would lead them to possession by the Holy Spirit. Due to their denial of the sacraments, the Messalianism was almost entirely a lay movement. See for details Meyendorff, "St. Basil, Messalianism, and Byzantine Christianity," 219–34.

37. As Fedwick noted, "Basil's full support and further elaboration of the communal type of asceticism was aimed at healing the church wounds caused by internal divisions." Fedwick, *The Church*, 5.

38. *Letter* 227; 197.

39. *SR* 38 (Clarke, 243).

Basil reminds the believers that the Lord himself for our sake was obedient to the Father unto death.[40] He implies that following Christ's example they must obey God and submit to the leaders, which he appoints.[41]

It is important to recognize that the prime purpose of such power delegated to the leaders is the spiritual growth and perfection of the believers. According to St. Basil, the superiors should make themselves "an accurate model" by observing the standards, which were handed down from the Lord Jesus Christ. "For if this is the standard of Christianity," St. Basil asserts, "the imitation of Christ according to the measure of His Incarnation as is appropriate to the calling of each, those who are entrusted with the guidance of the many ought by their own mediation to lead on the weaker to the imitation of Christ."[42] It is expected from the Christian leaders that they must practice humility in the love of Christ so much that even when they are silent their "deeds may stand out more strongly than any word as a means of teaching."[43] For this reason, each superior was chosen by the superiors from the other brotherhoods after careful inspection of his past life in order to find "sufficient proof of possessing the requisite character."[44] The logic behind this is simple and clear. In order to represent Christ in their communities, the leaders in the church should copy and imitate him. Then all the people trusted to them by God will be able to follow their example and to strive for Christlikeness in their turn watching these leaders. With the guidance of the Holy Spirit, they will obey their leaders modeling their behavior. Therefore, the whole church, which consists of different members, both communities and people, may be brought in unity to its eschatological purpose—the union with God the Trinity in the heavenly kingdom.

CONCLUSION TO CHAPTER 8

The efforts of St. Basil to develop further and to reform an existing monastic movement are based on the ideas, which reflect his understanding of the common life (*koinonikos bios*) in a Christian community. As a monk and a bishop, he tried to reconcile the life styles, which some believers perceived as opposing to each other—ascetic and non-ascetic. Applying the idea of

---

40. *SR* 199 (Clarke, 303).

41. As Silvas noted, "This order of priority is most important: the Lord first, and in the Lord, one's superiors. Silvas, *Asketikon*, 25. See also the description of "office-bearers," which she provides in the same paragraph.

42. *LR* 43 (Clarke, 216).

43. Ibid.

44. Ibid., 216–17.

koinonia and "the law of love," which according to his beliefs reflect God's will for humans, St. Basil showed in practice how the whole body of the Church may benefit from the close cooperation of her different members.

St. Basil's organization of community, which consists of people of both genders and different ages, conveys the idea of the future eschatological union with the Triune Creator when all the faithful will be able to live and praise God together. He is strongly convinced that the main goal of every believer, Christlikeness, may be realized only through participation in the life of the community. Solitary life and rejection of their fellow Christians does not facilitate spiritual perfection, but, on the contrary, leads to a violation of God's commandment to love your own neighbor. In St. Basil's thought, monks, like any other followers of Christ, are servants and ministers, but not elite. Although the lives of ascetics are considered, in some sense, to be an example for other believers in the church, they are supposed to serve denying their own will and obeying the leaders of the church who were appointed by the Triune God. St. Basil believes that only this ministry to others for the good of the whole community may serve as a means of perfection of the Christian character. Accordingly, everybody in a Christian community is supposed to follow the same rules including the leaders who should work even harder in order to provide a good example for their brothers and sisters in the church. On the one hand, these leaders, like all other believers, need to go through the process of restoration and transformation that they may become "complete" Christians themselves. On the other hand, they deserve respect from the rest of believers, because, as chosen by the Triune God, they are allowed to exercise the power entrusted to them by God in order to correct the behavior of people in the community. Consequently, actions of all members of the church will be confirmed by one great commandment to love God and to love a neighbor so that at the end they may live and enjoy life in the presence of the Triune God and their neighbors.

Final Conclusions

USING MOSTLY AN ANALYTICAL approach, this book presents St. Basil's understanding of the church and the interrelation of his ecclesiology and trinitarian theology. The research shows that in St. Basil's thought the existence of the church is due to the work of the Persons of the Trinity, and that the ultimate goal is the re-establishment of fellowship with the Triune God. Accordingly, in the heart of St. Basil's doctrine of the church is the eschatological perspective from which he perceives the divine actions and a destiny of humanity that is Christlikeness and life eternal into the heavenly realm with the Father, Son and Holy Spirit, which is a part of the divine plan from the beginning of the world.

Although in St. Basil's thinking the ideas of the church and his theology of the Triune God were interwoven together, we do not find in St. Basil too simplistic a correspondence between the trinitarian communion and a human community because he believed that God's Triune nature forever remains a mystery. For this reason, he used necessarily limited language about God.[1] However, St. Basil perceives the church in a consistently trinitarian fashion when all *hypostaseis* of God are involved in the life of this special community. In this regard, chapter 2 highlights St. Basil's idea that after the first humans failed the opportunity to live in communion with God, according to His initial plan, the main goal of the work of the Trinity in salvation history became the creation of a new eschatological community and the restoration of the human depraved nature. In this sense, the divine economy includes the redevelopment of the image of God in people and their incorporation into *ekklesia* of the Triune God. The church in St. Basil's writings is portrayed as a special *koinonia*, which provides the way and the means

---

1. As we have seen in Introduction, St. Basil preferred the term *hypostasis* in order to guard the proper meaning of words *person* and *communion* when used to reference to the doctrine of the Trinity.

for believers to restore the original type of relationships between God and humans and among all people as his children. That culminates in their living together in heavenly community being reconciled to their Triune God.

Following St. Basil's non-systematic and mystical way of thinking, this book shows in chapter 3 his perception of the church as a two-dimensional reality. This enables us to unfold St. Basil's idea that the church is something bigger than the collection of the congregations scattered geographically. The book emphasizes that in St. Basil's thought, the heavenly part is not an inaccessible ideal, but this is the part of the church, which is actively involved in the lives of all believers here and now. This worldwide fellowship of Christians includes the saints who already have overcome evil and those on earth who are still struggling against it. Therefore, in St. Basil's opinion, the church is the assembly of Christlike saints who are guided be the Spirit, but some of them are still in the process of transformation. All of them together strive for the final term of human history and the glorious transfiguration of the world. In some sense, the church consists of representatives of future humanity: those who after the final consummation will live in communion with the Triune God according to the requirements of the Gospel. Interestingly enough, in St. Basil's opinion, all of humanity from the beginning of creation until the judgment day has a chance to participate in this special fellowship in God's kingdom. The eternal life of this community is built on love and mutual support of its members, which is based on God's philanthropy.

Through the exploration of different metaphors, which St. Basil uses in his writings, chapter 4 analyses the relationships of the church with her Triune Creator. One of the significant characteristics of the church is the presence of the Triune God with her or among his people. The church is the house or the courtyard of the Lord as long as he rules the community and the believers, as the true worshipers, follow him in obedience. Presenting the church as the daughter of the King, the mother of believers, the bride of Christ, and his body, St. Basil conveys the idea that there is only one church, which is indivisible however extended it might be geographically. All faithful believers are gathered by God the Trinity to comprise one single body or family, where people acquire their new identity.

Chapter 5 of this book explores St. Basil's ideas about the inward life of this mystical body. The areas of consideration are liturgical services where trinitarian confession is recited, baptism as the universally accepted rite of admission to the church, Eucharist as the most important mystery for maintaining the life of Christians, and the penitential discipline that is exercised in order to restore the sinners to life eternal. The research shows how important for St. Basil is the idea that there is no salvation apart from the church where the "sound and unperverted" doctrine is taught and the valid mysteries are provided with the invocation of Triune names. He believes that the proper teaching about God the Trinity during liturgical services provides the knowledge that helps to secure the eternal life of the Christians.

Chapter 6 investigates St. Basil's perception of the church's unity in times of troubles and disagreements through the discussion of the criterion for this unity. In St. Basil's thinking, this unity is based on the trinitarian confession and the mutual love of the Christians, and especially bishops as head leaders of communities. The book proceeds with the analysis of the role of the Christian leaders and the councils that were supposed to maintain ecclesiastical unity. Although St. Basil supports the idea of hierarchy and highly esteems the role of the bishops and ministers, he expects them to be the examples of Christlike ministry for their people. As appointed by the Triune God, they are supposed to become the eyes and the heads of the local congregations, but they should have the attitude of servants who with all their strength care for people whom God put under their supervision. The bishops and ministers also have to teach their people the proper beliefs and preserve the faith, which was delivered to them from the time of the apostles and the fathers. In order to be faithful to the right doctrine, they should submit to all decisions of the ecumenical councils as the highest human authority. That should help to keep the right balance between diversity and unity within the church.

The social life of the church and the proper attitude of the Christians toward their fellow believers and the rest of society are examined in the next chapter of the book. Beginning with the theological ideas, such as trinitarian philanthropy and human worthiness in the eyes of the Triune God, the book reveals St. Basil's thoughts about the role of the church as an agent of justice, mercy, and love. He strongly believes that through the acts of Christians and the church, God the Trinity deals with this world in order to save, to transform, and to bring into heavenly kingdom as many people as possible, both rich and poor.

The last chapter of the book is concerned with monastic communities in general and the life of "new city" Basileias in particular. It helps to draw the book to its conclusion by showing to what extend St. Basil motivated by his beliefs was able to apply his ideas about the church in practice, and how his ideal of the church was realized in order to change and transform the world. The life of the community reflects the ideas, which were previously discussed, about the involvement of the Triune God in the life of the church: fulfillment of God's commandments, *koinonia* in love, the eschatological union, ministry to others, and the leadership under guidance of God. In some sense, this was an attempt to build the community, which gives the people a foretaste of what is coming. The research shows that St. Basil was faithful to his teaching and used all his strength and power to make the reality of what he believed in a particular socio-historical context.

Bibliography

PRIMARY SOURCES

Editions and Translations of St Basil's Works

For each text reference to the editions and translations is provided. Translations, which provide substantial commentary, are also listed among the secondary sources.

Basil of Caesarea. *Ad adulescentes.* In PG 31:563–90. *Saint Basile, Aux jeunes gens surla maniére de tirer profit des lettress helléniques.* Edited and translated by Fernand Boulenger. 2nd ed. Paris: Les Belles Lettres, 2002. *Saint Basil on the Value of Greek Literature.* Edited by N. G. Wilson. London: Duckworth, 1975. English translation: *Address to Young Men on Reading Greek Literature.* In *Saint Basil, The Letters,* translated by Roy J. Deferrari, 4:379–435. Loeb Classical Library. London: Heinemann, 1934.
———. *Ascetica.* Long Rules=Regulae fusius tractatae. In PG 31:889–1052. Short Rules=Regulae brevius tractatae. In PG 31:1080–1305B. English translations: *The Ascetic Works of Saint Basil.* Translated by William Kemp Lowther Clarke. Translations of Christian Literature I. Greek Texts. London: SPCN, 1925. *Saint Basil, Ascetical Works.* Translated by M. Monica Wagner. Fathers of the Church 9. New York: Catholic University of America Press, 1950. *The Asketikon of St Basil the Great.* Translated by Anna M. Silvas. Oxford Early Christian Studies. Oxford: Oxford University Press, 2005.
———. *Contra Eunomium.* In PG 29:497–670. *Basile de Césarée, Contre Eunome, suivi de Eunome, Apologie.* Edited and translated by Bernard Sesboüé, et al. 2 vols. Sources chrétiennes 299, 305. Paris: Cerf, 1982–83. English translation: *Against Eunomius* (books 1–3). Translated by Mark DelCogliano and Andrew Radde-Gallwitz. Fathers of the Church 122. Washington, DC: Catholic University of America Press, 2011.

———. *De baptismo libri duo.* In PG 31:1514–29. *Il battesimo.* Edited by Umberto Neri. Testi e ricerche di scenze religiose 12. Brescia: Paideia Editrice, 1976. English translation: *Concerning Baptism* (2 books). In *Saint Basil, Ascetical Works,* translated by M. Monica Wagner, 339–430. Fathers of the Church 9. New York: Catholic University of America Press, 1950.

———. *De fide.* In PG 31:676–92. English translations: *On the Faith.* In *Saint Basil, Ascetical Works,* translated by M. Monica Wagner, 57–69. Fathers of the Church 9. New York: Catholic University of America Press, 1950. *Concerning Faith.* In *The Ascetic Works of Saint Basil,* translated by William Kemp Lowther Clarke, 90–99. Translations of Christian Literature I. Greek Texts, London: SPCN, 1925.

———. *De judicio Dei.* In PG 31:653–78. English translations: *On the Judgment of God.* In *Saint Basil, Ascetical Works,* translated by M. Monica Wagner, 37–56. Fathers of the Church 9. New York: Catholic University of America Press, 1950. *On the Judgment of God.* In *The Ascetic Works of Saint Basil.* Translated by William Kemp Lowther Clarke, 77–89. Translations of Christian Literature I. Greek Texts, London: SPCN, 1925.

———. *De spiritu sancto.* In PG 32:67–218. *Basile de Césarée, Sur le Saint-Esprit.* Edited and translated by Benoit Pruche. 2nd ed. Sources chrétiennes 17 bis. Paris: Cerf, 1968. English translations: *Saint Basil the Great. On the Holy Spirit.* Translated by George Lewis. London: Religious Tract Society, 1888. *The Treatise De Spiritu Sancto.* In *Basil: Letters and Selected Works,* vol. 8 of NPNF, series 2, edited by Philip Schaff and translated by Blomfield Jackson, 1–50. 1895. Reprint, Grand Rapids: Eerdmans, 1968. *St. Basil the Great on the Holy Spirit.* Translated by Blomfield Jackson, revised by David Anderson. Crestwood, NY: St. Vladimir's Seminary Press, 1980. *On the Holy Spirit.* Translated by Stephen M. Hildebrand. Yonkers, NY: St. Vladimir's Seminary Press, 2011.

———. *Epistulae* in PG 32:219–1112. *Saint Basile, Lettres.* Edited by Yves Courtonne. 3 vols. Collection Guillaume Budé. Paris: Les Belles Lettres, 1957, 1961, 1966. English translations: *Letters.* In *Basil: Letters and Selected Works,* vol. 8 of NPNF, series 2, edited by Philip Schaff and translated by Blomfield Jackson, 109–328. 1895. Reprint, Grand Rapids: Eerdmans, 1968. *Saint Basil, The Letters.* Translated by Roy J. Deferrari. 4 vols. Loeb Classical Library. London: Heinemann, 1926, 1928, 1930, 1934. *Saint Basil, Letters.* Translated by Sister Agnes Clare Way. 2 vols. Fathers of the Church 13, 28. New York: Fathers of the Church, 1951, 1955.

———. *Hexaemeron Homiliae 1–9.* In PG 29:4–208. *Basile de Césarée, Homélies sur l'Hexaéméron.* Translated and edited by Stanislas Giet. 2nd ed. Sources Chrétiennes 26 bis. Paris: Cerf, 1968. English translations: *Hexaemeron.* In *Basil: Letters and Selected Works,* vol. 8 of NPNF, series 2, edited by Philip Schaff and translated by Blomfield Jackson, 51–108. 1895. Reprint, Grand Rapids: Eerdmans, 1968. *Homilies on the Hexaemeron 1–9.* In *Saint Basil: Exegetic Homilies,* translated by Sister Agnes Clare Way, 3–150. Fathers of the Church 46. Washington, DC: Catholic University of America Press, 1963.

———. *Homiliae variae.* In PG 31:163–481, 489–617, 1437–76, 1488–96. English translations: Homilies 3, 10, 11, 20, 21 in *Saint Basil, Ascetical Works.* Translated by M. Monica Wagner. Fathers of the Church 9. New York: Catholic University of America Press, 1950. Homilies 3, 9, 10 in *On the Human Condition: St Basil the Great.* Translated by Nonna Verna Harrison. Popular Patristics 30. Crestwood, NY: St. Vladimir's Seminary Press, 2005. Homilies 6, 7, 8 in *St Basil the Great: On*

Social Justice. Translated by C. Paul Schroeder. Popular Patristics 38. Crestwood, NY: St. Vladimir's Seminary Press, 2009. Homilies 11, 12, 15, 16, 20, 21, 24, 26, 29 in *St Basil the Great: On Christian Doctrine and Practice.* Translated by Mark DelCogliano. Crestwood, NY: St. Vladimir's Seminary Press, 2012. Homilies 18, 19 in *Let Us Die That We May Live: Homilies on Christian Martyrs from Asia Minor, Palestine and Syria (c. AD 350–AD 450),* 56–76. Translated by Pauline Allen. London and New York: Routledge, 2003. Homily 13 (*Exhortation to Holy Baptism*) in *Baptism: Ancient Liturgies and Patristic Texts,* translated by Thomas P. Halton, edited by Andre Hamman, 75–87. Staten Island: Alba House, 1967.

———. *Homiliae in psalmos.* In PG 29:307–494; 30:104–16. English translations: On Psalms 1, 7, 14.2, 28, 29, 32, 33, 44, 45, 48, 59, 61, 114 in *Saint Basil: Exegetic Homilies,* translated by Sister Agnes Clare Way, 151–360. Fathers of the Church 46. Washington, DC: Catholic University of America Press, 1963. On Psalm 14.1 in *St Basil the Great: On Social Justice,* translated by C. Paul Schroeder, 89–99. Popular Patristics 38. Crestwood, NY: St. Vladimir's Seminary Press, 2009.

———. *Liturgiae S. Basilii.* In PG 31:1630–77. 1st critical edition by M. I. Orlov, Литургия Святого Василия Великого. С. Петербург: Синодальная Типография, 1909. (*Liturgiya Svyatogo Vasiliya Velikogo,* St Petersburg: Sinodalnaya Tipographiya). English translation: *The Orthodox Liturgy Being the Divine Liturgy of S. John Chrysostom and S. Basil the Great.* London: SPCK, 1939.

———. *Regulae morales.* In PG 31:700–869. English translations: *The Morals.* In *The Ascetic Works of Saint Basil,* translated by William Kemp Lowther Clarke, 101–31. Translations of Christian Literature I. Greek Texts, London: SPCN, 1925. In *Saint Basil, Ascetical Works,* translated by M. Monica Wagner, 71–206. Fathers of the Church 9. New York: Catholic University of America Press, 1950.

Other primary sources

An Ancient Christian Sermon Commonly Known as Second Clement. In *Early Christian Fathers,* edited by Cyril C. Richardson, 184–89. Library of Christian Classics 1. New York: Collier, 1970.

Cyprian. *On the Lord's Prayer.* In *Fathers of the Third Century: Hippolytus, Cyprian, Caius, Novatian, etc.,* vol. 5 of ANF, edited by A. Roberts and J. Donaldson and translated by Ernest Wallis, 448–57. 1885. Reprint, Grand Rapids: Eerdmans, 1971.

———. *On the Unity of the Church.* In *Fathers of the Third Century: Hippolytus, Cyprian, Caius, Novatian,* vol. 5 of ANF, edited by A. Roberts and J. Donaldson and translated by Ernest Wallis, 421–29. 1885. Reprint, Grand Rapids: Eerdmans, 1971.

Eusebius of Caesarea. *Ecclesiastical History.* Greek text and English translation in *Eusebius, Ecclesiastical History.* 2 vols. Translated by Kirsopp Lake and J. E. L. Oulton. Edited by H.J. Lawlor. Loeb Classical Library. 7th ed. Cambridge, MA: Harvard University Press, 1980.

Gregory of Nazianzus. *Epistulae.* In PG 37:21–387. *Gregor von Nazianz. Briefe.* Edited by Paul Gallay. Die griechischen christlichen Schriftsteller der ersten Jahrhunderte 53. Berlin: Akademie, 1969. English translation: *Letters.* In *Cyril of Jerusalem, Gregory of Nazianzen,* vol. 7 of NPNF, series 2, edited by Philip Schaff and Henry

Wace, translated by Charles Gordon Browne and James Edward Swallow, 435–82. 1893. Reprint, Peabody, MA: Hendrickson, 1994.

———. *Oratio XLIII*. In PG 36:493–605. *Grégoire de Nazianze: Discours 42–43*. Translated and edited by Jean Bernardi. Sources Chrétiennes 384. Paris: Cerf, 1992. English translation: *Oration XLIII*. In *Cyril of Jerusalem, Gregory of Nazianzen*, vol. 7 of NPNF, series 2, edited by Philip Schaff and Henry Wace, translated by Charles Gordon Browne and James Edward Swallow, 396–422. 1893. Reprint, Peabody, MA: Hendrickson, 1994.

Gregory of Nyssa. *De Vita Sanctae Macrinae*. In PG 46:960A–1000B. *Grégoire de Nysse, Vie de sainte Macrine*. Translated and edited by Pierre Maraval. Sources chrétiennes 178. Paris: Cerf, 1971. English translation: *Life of Macrina*. Translated by W. K. L. Clarke. Early Church Classics. London: SPCK, 1916.

———. *Epistulae*. In *Gregorii Nysseni opera*. Edited by Werner Jaeger et al. 8:1. Leiden: Brill, 1963. English translation: *Letters*. In *Gregory of Nyssa: Dogmatic Treatises, etc.*, vol. 5 of NPNF, series 2, edited by Philip Schaff and Henry Wace, translated by William Moor and Henry A. Wilson, 521–43. 1892. Reprint, Grand Rapids: Eerdmans, 1972.

Ignatius of Antioch. *To the Ephesians*. In *The Apostolic Fathers, Justin Martyr, Irenaeus*, vol. 1 of ANF, edited by Alexander Roberts and James Donaldson, 49–58. 1885. Reprint, Grand Rapids: Eerdmans, 1981.

———. *To the Magnesians*. In *The Apostolic Fathers, Justin Martyr, Irenaeus*, vol. 1 of ANF, edited by Alexander Roberts and James Donaldson, 59–65. 1885. Reprint, Grand Rapids: Eerdmans, 1981.

———. *To the Philadelphians*. In *The Apostolic Fathers, Justin Martyr, Irenaeus*, vol. 1 of ANF, edited by Alexander Roberts and James Donaldson, 79–85. 1885. Reprint, Grand Rapids: Eerdmans, 1981.

Irenaeus. *Against Heresies*. In PG 7:437–1224. *Irénée de Lyon: Contres les heresies*, Livres 3, 4, 5. Edited and translated by A. Rousseau et al. 6 vols. Sources chrétiennes 210, 211, 100.1, 100.2, 152, 153. Paris: Cerf, 1974, 1965, 1969. English translation: *Against Heresies*. In *The Apostolic Fathers, Justin Martyr, Irenaeus*, vol. 1 of ANF, edited by Alexander Roberts and James Donaldson, 316–567. 1885. Reprint, Grand Rapids: Eerdmans, 1981.

The Letter of the Romans to Corinthians Commonly Known as First Clement. In *Early Christian Fathers*, edited by Cyril C. Richardson, 33–39. Library of Christian Classics 1. New York: Collier, 1970.

Socrates. *Historia ecclesiastica*. In PG 67:9–842. English translation: *Socrates, The Ecclesiastical History*. Translated by Valesius. London: Bohn, 1853.

Sozomen. *Historia ecclesiastica*. In *Sozomenus, Kirchengeschichte*. Edited by Joseph Bidez. Die griechischen christlichen Schriftsteller der ersten Jahrhunderte 50. Berlin: Akademie, 1960. English translation: *Ecclesiastical History*. In *Socrates, Sozomenus: Ecclesiastical Histories*, vol. 2 of NPNF, series 2, edited by Philip Schaff and Henry Wace, translated by Chester D. Hartranft, 179–420. 1890. Reprint, Peabody, MA: Hendrickson, 1995.

Tertullian, *On the Modesty*. In *Fathers of the Third Century: Tertullian, Minucius Felix, Commodian, Origen*, vol. 4 of ANF, edited by A. Roberts and J. Donaldson, translated by S. Thelwall, 74–75. 1885. Reprint, Grand Rapids: Eerdmans, 1972.

Theodoret, *Historia Ecclesiastica*. *Thedoret, Kirchengeschichte*. Edited by Léon Parmentier, with 2nd ed., edited by Flix Scheidweiler. Die griechischen christlichen Schriftsteller der ersten Jahrhunderte 44. Berlin: Akademie, 1954. English translation: *The Ecclesiastical History of Theodoret.* In *Theodoret, Jerome, Gennadius, Rufinus: Historical Writings,* vol. 3 of NPNF, series 2, edited by Philip Schaff and Henry Wace, translated by Blomfield Jackson, 33–159. 1893. Reprint, Peabody, MA: Hendrickson, 1994.

SECONDARY SOURCES

Afonsky, Gregory. *Christ and the Church.* Crestwood, NY: St. Vladimir's Seminary Press, 2001.

Aghiorgoussis, Maximos. "Application of the Theme 'eikon theou' (image of God) according to Saint Basil the Great." *Greek Orthodox Theological Review* 21, no. 3 (1976) 265–88.

———. "Image as 'Sign' (*semeion*) of God: Knowledge of God through the Image according to Saint Basil." *Greek Orthodox Theological Review* 21 (1976) 19–54.

Allen, Diogenes, and Eric O. Springsted. *Philosophy for Understanding Theology.* 2nd ed. London: Westminster John Knox, 2007.

Awad, Najeeb G. "Between Subordination and *Kiononia*: Toward a New Reading of the Cappadocian Theology." *Modern Theology* 23, no. 2 (2007) 181–204.

Ayres, Lewis. *Nicaea and its Legacy: An Approach to Fourth Century Trinitarian Theology.* Oxford: Oxford University Press, 2004.

Baghos, Mario. "St Basil's Eschatological Vision: Aspects of the Recapitulation of History and the 'Eighth Day.'" *Phronema* 25 (2010) 85–103.

Ballan, Joseph. "Basil of Caesarea on the Ascetic Craft: The Invention of Ascetic Community and the Spiritualization of work in the *Asketikon.*" *Heythrop* 48 (2010) 1–10.

Batiffol, P. "L'ecclésiologie de s. Basile." *Échos d'Orient* 21 (1922) 9–30.

Bebis, George S. "Introduction to the Liturgical Theology of St Basil the Great." *Greek Orthodox Theological Review* 42 (1997) 273–85.

Beeley, Christopher A. "The Holy Spirit in the Cappadocians: Past and Present." *Modern Theology* 26, no. 1 (2010) 90–119.

Behr, John. *The Nicene Faith: One of the Holy Trinity.* Crestwood, NY: St. Vladimir's Seminary Press, 2004.

Bettenson, Henry. *The Later Christian Fathers.* 8th ed. Oxford: Oxford University Press, 1987.

Bobrinskoy, Boris. *The Mystery of the Trinity.* Crestwood, NY: St. Vladimir's Seminary Press, 1999.

Болотов В. В. «Заметки по поводу текста литургии св. Василия Великого». *Христианское чтение* 3 (1914) 281–98.

Bonis, Constantine G. "Problem concerning Faith and Knowledge, or Reason and Revelation, as Expounded in Letters of St Basil the Great to Amphilochius of Iconium." *Greek Orthodox Theological Review* 5 (1959) 27–44.

Борисовский, Н. «Св. Василий Великий как пастырь церкви». *Вера и Разум* (1901) 23–41, 82–106.

Bright, William. *The Canons of the First Four General Councils of Nicaea, Constantinople, Ephesus, and Chalcedon.* Oxford: Clarendon, 1892.

Chadwick, Henry. *East and West: The Making of a Rift in the Church. From Apostolic Time until the Council of Florence*. Oxford: Oxford University Press, 2003.

Clarke, William Kemp Lowther. *The Ascetic Works of Saint Basil*. Translations of Christian Literature I. London: SPCN, 1925.

———. *St Basil the Great: a Study in Monasticism*. Cambridge: Cambridge University Press, 1913.

Collins, Paul M. *Trinitarian Theology West and East: Karl Barth, the Cappadocian Fathers, and John Zizioulas*. Oxford: Oxford University Press, 2001.

Constantelos, Demetreios J. "The Hellenistic Background and Nature of Patristic Philanthropy in the Early Byzantine Era." In *Wealth and Poverty in Early Church and Society*, edited by Susan R. Holman, 187–208. Grand Rapids: Baker Academic, 2008.

———. "Basil the Great's Social Thought and Involvement." *Greek Orthodox Theological Review* 26 (1981) 81–86.

Costache, Doru. "Christian Worldview: Understanding from St. Basil the Great." *Phronema* 25 (2010) 21–56.

Crislip, Andrew T. *From Monastery to Hospital: Christian Monasticism and the Transformation of Health Care in Late Antiquity*. Ann Arbor: University of Michigan Press, 2005.

Daley, Brian E. "Building a New City: The Cappadocian Fathers and the Rhetoric of Philanthropy." *Journal of Early Christian Studies* 7, no. 3 (1999) 431–61.

De Mendieta, Emmanuel Amand. "The Pair ΚΗΡΥΓΜΑ and ΔΟΓΜΑ in the Theological Thought of St. Basil of Caesarea." *Journal of Theological Studies* 16 (1965) 129–42.

———. *The "Unwritten" and "Secret" Apostolic Traditions in the Theological Thought of St. Basil of Caesarea*. London: Oliver and Boyd, 1965.

Deferrari, Roy Joseph. "The Classic and the Greek Writers of the Early Church: Saint Basil." *Classical Journal* 13, no. 8 (1918) 579–91.

DelCogliano, Mark. "Basil of Caesarea on Proverbs 8:22 and the Sources of Pro-Nicene Theology." *Journal of Theological Studies* 59 (2008) 183–90.

———. "Basil of Caesarea, Didymus the Blind, and the Anti-Pneumatomachian Exegesis of Amos 4:13 and John 1:3." *Journal of Theological Studies* 61 (2010) 644–58.

———. *Basil of Caesarea's Anti-Eunomian Theory of Names: Christian Theology and Late-Antique Philosophy in the Fourth Century Trinitarian Controversy*. Leiden: Brill, 2010.

———. "The Influence of Athanasius and the Homoiousians on Basil of Caesarea's Decentralization of 'Unbegotten.'" *Journal of Early Christian Studies* 19, no. 2 (2011) 197–223.

———. *On Christian Doctrine and Practice*. Popular Patristics 47. Crestwood, NY: St. Vladimir's Seminary Press, 2012.

———. "Tradition and Polemic in Basil of Caesarea's Homily on the Theophany." *Vigiliae Christianae* 66 (2012) 30–55.

Dinan, Andrew. "Manual Labour in the Life and Thought of St Basil the Great." *Logos* 12 (2009) 134–57.

Ditmars, Ron. "Gregory the Theologian's Panegyric on Saint Basil: A Literary Analysis of Chapters 65–67." *Greek Orthodox Theological Review* 39 (1994) 199–210.

Drecoll, Volker Henning. *Die Entwicklung der Trinitätslehre des Basilius von Cäsarea: Sain Weg vom Homöusianer yum Neonizäner.* Göttingen: Vandenhoeck & Ruprecht, 1996.

Dunzl, Franz. *A Brief History of the Doctrine of the Trinity in the Early Church.* Translated by John Bowden. New York: T. & T. Clark, 2007.

Elm, Susanna. *Virgins of God: the Making of Asceticism in Late Antiquity.* New York: Clarendon, 1996.

Ericson John H. "Reception of Non-Orthodox into the Orthodox Church." *Diakonia* 9 (1984-85) 68-86.

Farrar, Frederic W. *Lives of the Fathers.* London: Adam and Charles Black, 1907.

Fedwick, Paul Jonathan, ed. *Basil of Caesarea: Christian, Humanist, Ascetic. A Sixteen-Hundredth Anniversary Symposium.* 2 vols. Toronto: Pontifical Institute of Mediaeval Studies, 1981.

―――. *The Church and the Charisma of Leadership in Basil of Caesarea.* Toronto: Pontifical Institute of Medieval Studies, 1979.

Fisher, J. D. C. "Baptism: 1. Patristic." In *A New Dictionary of Liturgy and Worship*, edited by J. G. Davis, 55-56. 5th ed. London: Butler & Tanner, 1996.

Флоровский, Георгий. *Восточные Отцы IV века.* Минск, Белоруссия: Жатва, 2006.

Florovsky, George. "St Basil and 'Unwritten Tradition.'" In *The Collected Works of Georges Florovsky*, 1:85-89. Belmont, MA: Nordland, 1972.

―――. "The Patristic Age and Eschatology: Introduction." In *The Collected Works of Georges Florovsky*, 4:63-78. Belmont, MA: Nordland, 1975.

Forell, George Wolfgang. *History of Christian Ethics: From the New Testament to Augustine.* Minneapolis: Augsburg, 1979.

Fortin, Ernest L. "Hellenism and Early Christian Thought in Basil the Great's Address Ad Adolescences." In *Neoplatonism and Early Christian Thought : Essays in Honour of A. H. Armstrong*, edited by H. J. Blumenthal and Robert A. Markus, 189-203. London: Variorum, 1981.

Fortman, Edmund J. *The Triune God: A Historical Study of the Doctrine of Trinity.* 2nd ed. Grand Rapids: Backer, 1982.

Fouyas, Methodios G. *St. Basil the Great and the Roman See.* Oxford: Fourth International Congress on Patristic Studies, 1963.

Frazee, Charles A. "Anatolian Asceticism in the Fourth Century: Eustathios of Sebastea and Basil of Caesarea." *Catholic Historical Review* 66, no. 1 (1980) 16-33.

Garnett, Sherman. "The Christian Young and the Secular World: St Basil's Letter on Pagan Literature." *Greek Orthodox Theological Review* 26, no. 3 (1981) 211-23.

Geanakoplos, Deno John. "St Basil, 'Christian Humanist' of the 'Three Hierarchs' and Patron Saint of Greek Letters." *Greek Orthodox Theological Review* 25 (1980) 94-102.

Георгиевский, В. «Василий Великий как пастырь и учитель церкви.» *Странник* (1896) 1:3-21; 2:185-208.

Giles, Kevin. *What on Earth Is the Church?* London: SPCK, 1995.

Grenz, Stanley J. *Theology for the Community of God.* 2nd ed. Grand Rapids: Eerdmans, 2000.

Griffith, Howard. "The Churchly Theology of Basil's *De Spiritu Sancto.*" *Presbyterion* 25 (1999) 91-108.

Gribomont, J. "Basil of Caesarea in Cappadocia." In *Encyclopedia of the Early Church*, edited by A. D. Berardina and translated by Adrian Walford, 1:114–15. Cambridge: Clarke, 1992.

Gross, Jules. *The Divinization of the Christian according to the Greek Fathers*. Anaheim, CA: A & C, 2002.

Guitton, Jean. *Great Heresies & Church Councils*. London: Harvill, 1965.

Gunton, Colin E. "The Church on Earth: The Roots of Community." In *On Being the Church: Essays on the Christian Community*, edited by Colin E Gunton and Daniel W. Hardy, 48–80. Edinburgh: T. & T. Clark, 1989.

———. *The Promise of Trinitarian Theology*. Edinburgh: T. & T. Clark, 1991.

Haight, Roger. *Christian Community in History: Ecclesial Existence*. 3 vols. 2nd ed. Bloomsbury: London, 2014.

Hallburton, R. J. "The Patristic Theology of the Eucharist." In *The Study of Liturgy*, edited by Cheslyn Johns et al., 245–51. 2nd ed. London: SPCK, 1992.

Hamell, Patrick J. *Introduction to Patrology*. Cork, Ireland: Mercier, 1968.

Hamman, Adalbert. *How to Read the Church Fathers*. 2nd ed. London: SCM, 1993.

Hamman, Andre. *Baptism: Ancient Liturgies and Patristic Texts*. Translated by Thomas P. Halton. Staten Island: Alba House, 1967.

Hanson, Richard P. C. "Basil's Doctrine of Tradition in Relation to the Holy Spirit." *Vigiliae Christianae* 22 (1968) 241–55.

———. *The Search for the Christian Doctrine of God: The Arian Controversy, 318–381 A.D.* London: T. & T. Clark, 1988.

Harrison, Nonna Verna. "Male and Female in Cappadocian Theology." *Journal of Theological Studies* 41 (1990) 441–71.

———. *On the Human Condition: St Basil the Great*. Popular Patristics 30. Crestwood, NY: St. Vladimir's Seminary Press, 2005.

Haykin, Michael A. G. "And Who Is the Spirit? Basil of Caesarea's Letters to the Church at Tarsus." *Vigiliae Christianae* 41 (1987) 377–85.

———. "'In the Cloud and in the Sea': Basil of Caesarea and the Exegesis of 1Cor 10:2." *Vigiliae Christianae* 40 (1986) 135–44.

Hildebrand, Stephen M. "A Reconsideration of the Development of Basil's Trinitarian Theology: The Dating of Ep.9 and Contra Eunomium." *Vigiliae Christianae* 58 (2004) 393–406.

———. *St Basil the Great: On the Holy Spirit*. Popular Patristics 42. Yonkers, NY: St. Vladimir's Seminary Press, 2011.

———. *The Trinitarian Theology of Basil of Caesarea: A Synthesis of Greek Thought and Biblical Truth*. Washington, DC: Catholic University Press, 2007.

Holder, Arthur G. "Saint Basil the Great on Secular Education and Christian Virtue." *Religious Education* 87 (1992) 395–415.

Holman, Susan R. "The Hungry Body: Famine, Poverty, and Identity in Basil's Hom.8." *Journal of Early Christian Studies* 7, no. 3 (1999) 337–63.

———. *The Hungry Are Dying: Beggars and Bishops in Roman Cappadocia*. New York: Oxford University Press, 2001.

———. "Rich City Burning: Social Welfare and Ecclesial Insecurity in Basil's Mission to Armenia." *Journal of Early Christian Studies* 12, no. 2 (2004) 195–215.

Hunt, Anne. "The Trinity and the Church: Explorations in Ecclesiology from a Trinitarian Perspective." *Irish Theological Quarterly* 70 (2005) 215–35.

Hutcheon, Cyprian Robert. "'A Sacrifice of Praise': A Theological Analysis of the Pre-Sanctus of the Byzantine Anaphora of St Basil." *St Vladimir's Theological Quarterly* 45 (2001) 3–23.
Ihssen, Brenda Lewellyn. "Basil's and Gregory's Sermon on Usury: Credit Where Credit is Due." *Journal of Early Christian Studies* 16 (2008) 403–30.
Jacobs, Nathan. "On 'Not Three Gods'—Again: Can a Primary-Secondary Substance Reading of *Ousia* and *Hypostasis* Avoid Tritheism?" *Modern Theology* 24, no. 3 (2008) 331–58.
Jackson, Blomfield. "Prolegomena. Sketch of the Life and Works of Saint Basil." In *Basil: Letters and Selected Works*, vol. 8 of NPNF, series 2, edited by Philip Schaff and translated by Blomfield Jackson, xiii–lxxvii. Reprint, Grand Rapids: Eerdmans, 1968.
Jeremias, Joachim. *Infant Baptism in the First Four Centuries*. 2nd ed. London: SCM, 1964.
Jevtich, Atanasij. "Between the 'Niceaens' and the 'Easterners': 'Catholic' Confession of Saint Basil." *St Vladimir's Theological Quarterly* 24 (1980) 235–52.
Jewett, Paul King. *Infant Baptism & the Covenant of Grace*. Grand Rapids: Eerdmans, 1978.
Jungmann, Josef A. *The Early Liturgy: To the Time of Gregory the Great*. London: Darton, Longman & Todd, 1959.
Karavites, Peter. "Saint Basil and Hymnology." *Greek Orthodox Theological Review* 37 (1992) 203–14.
Karayannopoulos, Ioannes. "St Basil's Social Activity: Principles and Praxis." In *Basil of Caesarea: Christian, Humanist, Ascetic*, edited by Paul J. Fedwick, 375–91. Toronto: Pontifical Institute of Mediaeval Studies, 1981.
Kariatlis, Philip. "St Basil's Contribution to the Trinitarian Doctrine: a Synthesis of Greek *Paideia* and the Scriptural Worldview." *Phronema* 25 (2010) 57–83.
Kärkkäinen, Veli-Matti. "Ecclesiology." In *Global Dictionary of Theology*, edited by William A. Dyrness and Veli-Matti Kärkkäinen, 251–62. Nottingham, UK: InterVarsity, 2008.
———. *An Inrtoduction to Ecclesiology*. Downers Grove, IL: InterVarsity, 2002.
Kelly, J. N. D. *Early Christian Doctrines*. 5th ed. London: Continuum, 2006.
Khodr, Georges (Metropolitan). "Basil the Great: Bishop and Pastor." *St Vladimir's Theological Quarterly* 29 (1985) 5–27.
Хрептак, В. *Отношение Св. Василия Великого к Церкви*. Ленинград, Россия: Библиотека Духовной Академии, 1967.
Kopecek, Thomas A. "The Cappadocian Fathers and Civic Patriotism." *Church History* 43, no. 3 (1974) 293–303.
——— *A History of New-Arianism*. 2 vols. Patristic Monograph 8. Cambridge, MA: Philadelphia Patristic Foundation, 1979.
———. "The Social Class of the Cappadocian Fathers." *Church History* 42 (1973) 453–66.
Koschorke, Klaus. *Spuren der Alten Liebe: Studien zum Kirchenbergriff des Basilius von Caesarea*. Freiburg, Schweiz: Universitätsverlag Freiburg Schweiz, 1991.
Кривошеин, Василий (Krivoshein). «Экклезиология Святого Василия Великого.» http://mystudies.narod.ru/library/k/krivoshein/basil.html.
Lampe, Geoffrey William Hugo, ed. *A Patristic Greek Lexicon*. 4th ed. Oxford: Clarendon, 1976.

L'Huillier, Peter. *The Church of the Ancient Councils: The Disciplinary Work of First Four Ecumenical Councils.* Crestwood, NY: St. Vladimir's Seminary Press, 1996.

Lienhard, Joseph T. "Basil of Caesarea, Marcellus of Ancyra, and 'Sabellius.'" *Church History* 58, no. 2 (1989) 157–67.

———. "*Ousia* and *Hypostasis*: The Cappadocian Settlement and the Theology of 'One Hypostasis.'" In *The Trinity*, edited by Stephen T. Davis et al., 99–121. Oxford: Oxfors University Press, 1999.

Lietzmann, Hans. *The Era of the Church Fathers.* A History of the Early Church 4. 5th ed. London: Lutterworth, 1960.

Lim, Richard. "The Politics of Interpretation in Basil of Caesarea's Hexaemeron." *Vigiline Christianae* 44 (1990) 351–70.

Limberis, Vasiliki. "The Eyes Infected by Evil: Basil of Caesarea's Homily, On Envy." *Harvard Theological Review* 84 (1991) 163–84.

Lloyd-Moffett, Stephen R. "The 'Anchorite within': Basil of Caesarea's Erotapokrisis 7 and the Ascetic Challenge to Christian Identity." *Religion & Theology* 17 (2010) 268–88.

Lossky, Vladimir. *The Mystical Theology of the Eastern Church.* London: Clarke, 1957.

———. "The Orthodox Church." In *The Christian Church: Introduction to the Major Traditions*, edited by Paul Avis, 1–17. London: SPCK, 2002.

———. *Orthodox Theology: Introduction.* Crestwood, NY: St. Vladimir's Seminary Press, 1989.

Louth, Andrew. "The Cappadocians." In *Cambridge History of Early Christian Literature*, edited by Frances Young and Lewis Ayres, 289–301. Cambridge: Cambridge University Press, 2004.

Ludlow, Morwenna. "Demons, Evil, and Liminality in Cappadocian Theology." *Journal of Early Christian Studies* 20, no. 2 (2012) 179–211.

Mayer, Annemarie C. "Ecclesial Communion: The Letters of St Basil the Great Revisited." *International Journal for the Study of the Christian Church* 5 (2005) 226–41.

Matz, Brian J. et al. "De Beneficentia: A Homily On Social Action attributed to Basil of Caesarea." *Vigiliae Christianae* 66, no. 5 (2012) 457–81.

———. "The Principle of Detachment from Private Property in Basil of Caesarea's Homily 6 and its Context." Pages 173–98. https://lirias.kuleuven.be/bitstream/123456789/254799/2/Article_PrivProp_BasilHom6.pdf.

McGrath, Alister E. *Christian Theology.* 5th ed. West Sussex, UK: Wiley-Blackwell, 2011.

McGuckin, John A. *The SCM Press A-Z of Patristic Theology.* 2nd ed. Suffolk: SCM, 2005.

Meredith, Anthony. "Asceticism—Christian and Greek." *Journal of Theological Studies* 27 (1976) 313–32.

———. *The Cappadocians.* London: Chapman, 1995.

Meyendorff, John. *The Byzantine Legacy in the Orthodox Church.* Crestwood, NY: St. Vladimir's Seminary Press, 2000.

———. "St Basil, Messalianism, and Byzantine Christianity." *St Vladimir's Theological Quarterly* 24 (1980) 219–34.

Moltmann, Jürgen. *The Church in the Power of the Spirit.* 3rd ed. Suffolk, UK: SCM, 1981.

Monge, Rico Gabriel. "Submission to One Head: Basil of Caesarea on Order and Authority in the Church." *St Vladimir's Theological Quarterly* 54, no. 2 (2010) 219–43.

Morison, E. F. *St. Basil and His Rule: A Study in Early Monasticism.* Oxford: Oxford University Press, 1912.

Noble, Thomas A. "The Deity of the Holy Spirit according to Gregory of Nazianzus." PhD diss. University of Edinburgh, 1989.

———. *Holy Trinity: Holy People. The Theology of Christian Perfecting.* Didsbury Lecture. Eugene, OR: Cascade, 2013.

Olson, Roger E. *The Story of Christian Theology.* Leicester: Apollos, 1999.

Orphanos, M.A. *Creation and Salvation according to St Basil of Caesarea.* Athens, 1975.

Quasten, Johannes. *Patrology.* 2nd ed. Utrecht: Spectrum, 1975.

Paget, James Carleton. "The Vision of the Church in the Apostolic Fathers." In *A Vision for the Church: Studies in Early Christian Ecclesiology,* edited by M. Bockmuehl and M. Thomson, 193–206. Edinburgh: T. & T. Clark, 1997.

Patitsas, Timothy. "St Basil's Philanthropic Program and Modern Microlending Strategies for Econimic Self-actualization." In *Wealth and Poverty in Early Church and Society,* edited by Susan R. Holman, 267–86. Grand Rapids: Baker Academic, 2008.

Pelican, Jaroslav. *The Emergence of The Catholic Tradition (100–600).* Chicago: University of Chicago Press, 1971.

Phan, Peter. *Social Thought: Message of the Fathers of the Church.* Wilmington, DE: Glazier, 1984.

Pomazansky, Michael. *Orthodox Dogmatic Theology.* Saint Herman of Alaska Brotherhood, 1997.

Prestige, George Leonard. *God in Patristic Thought.* 3rd ed. London: SPCK, 1969.

———. *St. Basil the Great and Apollinaris of Laodicea.* London: SPCK, 1956.

Radde-Gallwitz, Andrew. *Basil of Caesarea: A Guide to His Life and Doctrine.* Eugene, OR: Cascade, 2012.

———. *Basil of Caesarea, Gregory of Nyssa, and the Transformation of Divine Simplicity.* Oxford: Oxford University Press, 2009.

Rainey, David. "The Argument for Deity of the Holy Spirit, according to St Basil the Great, Bishop of Caesarea." MTh thesis. Vancouver School of Theology, 1991.

Robertson, David G. "Stoic and Aristotelian Notions of Substance in Basil of Caesarea." *Vigiliae Christianae* 52, no. 4 (1998) 393–417.

Rousseau, Philip. *Basil of Caesarea.* Berkeley: University of California Press, 1994.

———. "Human Nature and its Material Setting in Basil of Caesarea's Sermons on the Creation." *Heythrop Journal* 49 (2008) 222–39.

———. "The Pious Household and the Virgin Chorus: Reflections on Gregory of Nyssa's Life of Macrina." *Journal of Early Christian Studies* 13, no. 2 (2005) 165–66.

Routley, Erik. *The Wisdom of the Fathers.* London: SCM, 1957.

Rudberg, Stig Y. "Manuscripts and Editions of the Works of Basil of Caesarea." In *Basil of Caesarea: Christian, Humanist, Ascetic,* edited by Paul J. Fedwick, 49–65. Toronto: Pontifical Institute of Mediaeval Studies, 1981.

Rusch, William G. "Basil the Great views of the unity of the Church." *Mid-Stream* 35 (1996) 283–89.

Sandwell, Isabella. "How to Teach Genesis 1:1–19: John Chrysostom and Basil of Caesarea on the Creation of the World." *Journal of Early Christian Studies* 19 (2011) 539–64.

Schroeder, C. Paul. *On Social Justice: St Basil the Great.* Popular Patristics 38. Crestwood, NY: St. Vladimir's Seminary Press, 2009.

Schlager, Bernard. "Saints Basil and John Chrysostom on the Education of Christian Children." *Greek Orthodox Theological Review* 36, no. 1 (1991) 37–55.

Siepierski, Paulo. "Poverty and Spirituality: Saint Basil and Liberation Theology." *Greek Orthodox Theological Review* 33(1988) 313–25.

Silvas, Anna M. *The Asketikon of St Basil the Great.* Oxford Early Christian Studies. Oxford: Oxford University Press, 2005.

———. "Interpreting the Motives of Basil's social Doctrine." *Journal of the Australian Early Medieval Association* 5 (2009) 165–75.

———. *Macrina the Younger, Philosopher of God.* Brepols: Turnhout, 2008.

Smith, Richard Traver. *St Basil the Great.* London: Wyman and Sons, 1879.

Staniloae, Dumitru. *Theology and the Church.* Crestwood, NY: St. Vladimir's Seminary Press, 1980.

Stead, Christopher. *Philosophy in Christian Antiquity.* 3rd ed. Cambridge: Cambridge University Press, 1996.

Sterk, Andrea. *Renouncing the World Yet Leading the Church: The Monk-Bishop in Late Antiquity.* Cambridge, MA: Harvard University Press, 2004.

Stevenson. J. *Creeds, Councils and Controversies: Documents Illustrating the History of the Church, AD 337–461.* SPCK Church History. 9th ed. Cambridge: Cambridge University Press, 1995.

Stramara, Daniel F., Jr. "Double Monasticism in the Greek East, Fourth through Eighth Centuries." *Journal of Early Christian Studies* 6 (1998) 269–312.

Sunberg, Carla Dawn. *The Cappadocian Mothers: Deification Exemplified in the Writings of Basil, Gregory and Gregory.* PhD diss. Manchester University. 2012.

Timiadis, Emilianos. "The Trinitarian Structure of the Church and Its Authority." In *Theological Dialogue between Orthodox & Reformed Churches*, edited by Thomas F. Torrance, 121–58. Edinburgh: Scottish Academic, 1985.

Torchia, N. Joseph. "Sympatheia in Basil of Caesarea's Hexameron: A Plotinian Hypothesis." *Journal of Early Christian Studies* 4, no. 3 (1996) 359–78.

Torrance, Thomas F. *Theology in Reconstruction.* London: SCM, 1965.

———. *The Trinitarian Faith.* 3rd ed. Edinburgh: T. & T. Clark, 1997.

Turcescu, Lucian. "Prosōpon and Hypostasis in Basil of Caesarea's 'Against Eunomius' and the Epistles." *Vigiliae Christianae* 51, no. 4 (1997) 374–95.

Turner, C. H. "Introduction to 'La Tradition Manuscrite de la Correspondance de Saint Basile.'" *Journal of Theological Studies* (1919) 1–9.

Van Dam, Raymond. *Becoming Christian: The Conversion of Roman Cappadocia.* Philadelphia: University of Pennsylvania Press, 2003.

———. "Emperor, Bishop and Friends in Late Antique Cappadocia." *Journal of Theological Studies* 37 (1986) 53–76.

———. *Families and Friends in Late Roman Cappadocia.* Philadelphia: University of Pennsylvania Press, 2003.

———. *Kingdom of Snow: Roman Rule and Greek Culture in Cappadocia.* Philadelphia: University of Pennsylvania Press, 2002.

Vischer, Lukas. *Basilius der Große: Untersuchungen zu einem Kirchenvater des vierten Jahrhunderts*. Basel: Buchdruckerei Friedrich Reinhardt AG, 1953

Volf, Miroslav. *After His Likeness: The Church as the Image of the Trinity*. Grand Rapids: Eerdmans, 1998.

Waddell, James Alan. "Identifying Authorities and Pastoral Practice in the Early Church. Two Case Studies: Basil of Caesarea and Ephrem of Syria." *Concordia Journal* 1 (2005) 48–59.

Wall, William. *The History of Infant Baptism*. London: Griffith, Farran, Browne, 1889.

Wagner, M. Monica. *Saint Basil, Ascetical Works*. Fathers of the Church 9. New York: Catholic University of America Press, 1950.

Ware, Timothy. *The Orthodox Church*. 3rd ed. London: Clays, 1991.

Way, Agnes Clare. *Saint Basil: Exegetical Homilies*. Fathers of the Church 46. 2nd ed. New York: Catholic University of America Press, 1981.

———. *Saint Basil: Letters*. Vol. 1. Fathers of the Church 13. New York: Fathers of the Church, 1951.

———. *Saint Basil: Letters*. Vol. 2. Fathers of the Church 28. New York: Fathers of the Church, 1955.

Wilken, Robert Louis. *The First Thousand Years: A Global History of Christianity*. London: Yale University Press, 2012.

———. "The Spirit of Holiness: Basil of Caesarea and early Christian Spirituality." *Worship* 42 (1968) 77–87.

Winn, Robert E. "Revisiting the Date of Authorship of Basil of Caesarea's Ad Adolescents." *Greek Orthodox Theological Review* 44 (1999) 291–307.

Wright, David F. *What Has Infant Baptism Done to Baptism?* Milton Keynes, UK: Paternoster, 2005.

Zizioulas, John D. *Being as Communion: Studies in Personhood and the Church*. Crestwood, NY: St. Vladimir's Seminary Press, 1985.

———. *Eucharist, Bishop, Church: The Unity of the Church in the Divine Eucharist and the Bishop during the First Three Centuries*. Brookline, MA: Holy Cross Orthodox, 2001.

———. *Lectures in Christian Dogmatics*. London: T. & T. Clark, 2008.

———. "On Being a Person: Towards an Ontology of Personhood." In *Persons Divine and Human*, edited by Christoph Schwöbel and Colin E. Gunton, 33–46. 2nd ed. Edinburgh: T. & T. Clark, 1999.

Yamamura, Kei. "Development of the Doctrine of the Holy Spirit in Patristic Philosophy: St Basil and St Gregory of Nyssa." *St Vladimir's Theological Quarterly* 18 (1974) 3–21.

Young, Frances. "The 'Penultimate' Nature of the Church—the Eschaton Is Not Yet!" In *Orthodox and Wesleyan Ecclesiology*, edited by S. T. Kimbrough Jr., 199–211. Crestwood, NY: St. Vladimir's Seminary Press, 2007.

———. "Cappadocians." In *From Nicaea to Chalcedon: A Guide to the Literature and Its Background*, edited by F. M. Young and Andrew Teal, 135–72. 2nd ed. London: SCM, 2010.

Index of Names

A

Athanasius of Alexandria, 13–14, 22, 131, 138
Aghiorgoussis, Maximos, 20, 22, 51
Ayres, Lewis, 3, 26, 34, 121, 140, 141, 144, 168

B

Baghos, Mario, 16
Ballan, Joseph, 173
Batiffol, Pierre, 3
Bebis, George S., 83, 108
Behr, John, 3, 8, 84, 131
Bettenson, Henry, 41, 68, 69, 97, 100
Bobrinskoy, Boris, 13, 28, 34
Bonis, Constantine G., 86
Bright, William, 98

C

Clarke, William Kemp Lowther, 8, 10, 167
Constantelos, Demetroios J., 162
Crislip, Andrew T., 162, 167
Cyprian, 11, 12, 61, 68, 99, 105

D

Daley, S. J., 50
De Mendieta, Emmanuel Amand, 84, 88, 93
Deferrari, Roy Joseph, 134
Drecoll, Volker Henning, 3
Dunzl, Franz, 14

E

Elm, Susanna, 166
Ericson, John H., 98
Eusebius of Caesarea (*EH*), 61
Eusebius of Samosata, 124

F

Fedwick, Paul Jonathan, 2, 8, 10, 21, 54, 56, 57, 74, 105, 107, 132, 144, 167, 173,
Fisher, J. D. C., 93, 106
Florovsky, George, 7, 33, 84, 88
Fouyas, Methodios G, 131
Frazee, Charles A., 167

G

Giles, Kevin, 11
Gregory of Nazianzus, 10, 12, 161, 162, 167, 172
Gregory of Nyssa, 8, 12, 18
Gregory Thaumaturgos, 112
Grenz, Stanley J., 22
Gross, Jules, 43
Guitton, Jean, 97
Gunton, Colin E, 11, 53, 168

H

Haight, Roger. 4
Hallburton, R. J., 110
Hamman, Adalbert, 10
Hamman, Andre, 99, 105
Hanson, Richard P. C., 84

Harrison, Nonna Verna, 72, 153, 169
Hildebrand, Stephen M., 3, 13, 14, 34
Holder, Arthur G., 48
Holman, Susan R., 161
Hutcheon, Cyprian Robert, 83, 84, 110

I
Ignatius of Antioch, 12
Irenaeus, 22, 61, 68

J
Jackson, Blomfield, 109
Jevtich, Atanasij, 13, 121
Jewett, Paul King, 104
Jungmann, Josef A., 84, 94, 106

K
Karavites, Peter, 88
Karayannopoulos, Ioannes, 163
Kärkkäinen, Veli-Matti, 4, 29
Kelly, J. N. D., 11, 65, 109, 118
Kopecek, Thomas A., 7
Koschorke, Klaus, 2, 50, 65
Кривошеин, Василий (Krivoshein), 3, 131

L
Lampe, Geoffrey William Hugo, 39
Lienhard, Joseph T., 14
Lietzmann, Hans, 121
Lossky, Vladimir, 13, 22, 29, 31, 32, 44, 101
Louth, Andrew, 7

M
Macrina, 8, 9, 10, 167
Mayer, Annemarie C., 96
McGrath, Alister E., 4
Meredith, Anthony, 10, 170, 173
Meyendorff, John, 9, 12, 56, 168, 170, 173

N
Noble, Thomas A., xi, 14

O
Olson, Roger E., 13, 34
Origen, 10, 13, 14, 78
Orphanos, M. A., 18, 22, 24, 30, 60

Q
Quasten, Johannes, 10, 82, 112

P
Paget, James Carleton, 11
Patitsas, Timothy, 161
Pomazansky, Michael, 59, 92, 101, 110, 116
Prestige, George Leonard, 13

R
Radde-Gallwitz, Andrew, 7, 123
Rainey, David, ix
Rousseau, Philip, 7, 10, 26, 121, 139, 167
Rusch, William G., 130

S
Silvas, Anna M., 166, 167, 168, 169, 170, 173, 174
Smith, Richard Traver, 65, 66, 74
Stead, Christopher, 13, 15
Sterk, Andrea, 168
Stevenson. J., 168

T
Tertullian, 12, 105
Theodoret, 161
Timiadis, Emilianos, 78
Torrance, Thomas F., 11, 38, 39
Turcescu, Lucian, 14

V
Van Dam, Raymond, 121, 163
Vischer, Lukas, 1, 2, 131, 139

W
Waddell, James Alan, 88
Wall, William, 104, 105
Ware, Timothy, 110
Wright, David F., 105

Z

Zizioulas, John D., 13, 14, 18, 33, 62

Y

Young, Frances, 7, 50

Index of Citations to Basil's Works

Ad adulescentes
    48

Ascetica

Regulae fusius tractatae (LR)
    19, 21, 22, 23, 25, 31, 32, 33, 37, 46, 47, 49, 50, 51, 52, 53, 57, 64, 68, 69, 76, 90, 137, 138, 162, 168, 169, 170, 172, 174

Regulae brevius tractatae (SR)
    27, 50, 108, 114, 171, 173, 174

Contra Eunomium
    60, 75

De baptismo libri duo
    93, 100, 108, 151

De fide
    13, 40, 41, 50, 52, 100, 101

De judicio Dei
    8, 26, 33, 48, 55, 56, 67, 68, 71, 125, 126, 130, 156

De spiritu sancto
  1   22, 51, 102
  5   67
  8   31, 33, 50
  9   24, 25, 35, 37, 39, 43, 71
  10   92, 93, 106, 108
  11   35, 86
  12   92
  13   35
  14   30, 32, 49
  15   20, 22, 23, 24, 25, 38, 46, 48, 49, 52, 71, 94, 104
  16   17, 27, 28, 29, 34, 35, 36, 38, 40, 48, 49, 101, 102, 103, 132, 169
  17   28
  18   28, 39, 86, 168
  19   34, 35, 38
  20   148
  26   35, 36, 70, 71, 73, 86
  27   84, 90, 91, 93, 94, 109
  30   54, 124, 125, 127, 128, 141

Epistulae
  2   21, 39, 90, 171
  5   46
  9   51
  22   65, 68
  23   56
  28   137, 138
  29   138

Epistulae (continued)

30	124
46	75
49	44
50	86, 131
51	137
53	116
54	134
62	133
65	140
70	50, 64, 65, 69, 131, 139
74	163
76	163
90	38, 127, 142, 143
92	141, 143, 144, 145
93	107, 108, 109
94	161
97	21, 25, 131, 141
113	123, 128, 129
114	129
125	126, 128
128	127, 128, 129, 133
133	123, 126
141	122
144	11
150	90
155	44, 45
156	65, 123
159	100
160	112
161	74, 133, 135, 136
164	65, 123, 125
172	129
188	57, 97, 98, 99, 100, 126
191	129, 130
197	44, 45
199	57, 97, 101
203	139, 140
204	9, 112, 139, 142, 167
207	89
210	27, 75
214	28, 60
217	57, 113, 116, 117, 118, 119
221	90
222	65, 67, 69, 132
223	9, 74
227	62, 132, 173
233	20, 23
234	86
235	86
236	27, 28, 29,
240	77
243	69, 122, 124, 143
251	63, 126
257	74
261	32, 74
287	116
288	115, 117, 118

Hexaemeron Homiliae 1–9

1	17, 18, 21, 24, 53
2	17, 18
3	87
4	85
5	17, 49, 52, 64, 127
7	18
9	32

Homiliae variae

3	20, 30, 52, 79, 80, 150, 151
4	32, 78
5	19, 44
6	48, 149, 150, 152, 154, 158, 159
7	151, 158, 159, 160, 163
8	70, 104, 117, 151, 152, 153, 154, 155, 162
9	22, 72
11	150, 152, 160
13	23, 47, 62, 63, 91, 92, 93, 94, 95, 96, 103, 104, 105, 115, 159
20	34
19	44, 45, 46, 63, 64, 75, 79
21	60, 61, 64, 90, 157, 158
26	60, 148

Homiliae in psalmos

1	19, 39, 88, 89
7	152
11	37
14	20, 47, 163
15	30
28	48, 77, 78, 87, 92, 135, 136
29	71, 78
32	37, 38, 53, 54, 71, 72, 114
33	30, 32, 35, 40, 50, 51, 160

44	33, 38, 54, 61, 62, 63, 64, 65, 66, 69, 70, 72, 76	*Liturgiae S. Basilii*
45	24, 29, 33, 43, 45, 46, 47, 69, 72, 75, 123	82, 85, 109, 111
48	20, 22, 24, 30, 31, 32, 35, 36, 45, 48, 53, 54, 72, 74	*Regulae morales* 48, 50, 54, 56, 64, 65, 66, 68, 74, 76, 77, 79, 102, 103, 106, 107,
59	38, 39	110, 111, 114, 116, 117, 132, 133,
61	73, 79	134, 135, 136, 137, 142, 155, 156,
114	45, 169	171

www.ingramcontent.com/pod-product-compliance
Lightning Source LLC
Chambersburg PA
CBHW070313240426
43663CB00038BA/2227